India's Economic Future

Some Books from Social Science Press

Reflections on Cambridge (HB)
Alan Macfarlane

'Good Women do not Inherit Land': Politics of Land and Gender in India (HB)
Nitya Rao

New Mansions for Music: Performance, Pedagogy and Criticism (HB)
Lakshmi Subramanian

Writing History in the Soviet Union: Making the Past Work (HB)
Arup Banerji

Political Theologies: Public Religions in a Post-secular World (HB)
Edited by Hent de Vries and Lawrence E. Sullivan
(With Orient Longman for South Asia)

Regulation, Institutions and the Law (HB)
Edited by Jaivir Singh

Globalization and the Millennium Development Goals: Negotiating the Challenge (HB)
Edited by Manmohan Agarwal and Amit Shovon Ray

Cultural History of Medieval India (PB)
Edited by Meenakshi Khanna

Religious Division and Social Conflict: The Emergence of Hindu Nationalism in Rural India (HB)
Peggy Froerer

The Enigma of the Kerala Woman: A Failed Promise of Literacy (HB)
Edited by Swapna Mukhopadhyay

Cultural History of Modern India (PB)
Edited by Dilip M. Menon

Delhi: Ancient History (PB)
Edited by Upinder Singh

Unbecoming Modern: Colonialism, Modernity and Colonial Modernities (HB)
Edited by Saurabh Dube and Ishita Banerjee-Dube

After the Iraq War: The Future of the UN and International Law (HB)
Edited by Bernhard Vogel, Rudolf dolzer and Matthias Herdegen

Social and Economic Profile of India (HB)
(In full colour)
Peeyush Bajpai, Laveesh Bhandari and Aali Sinha

India and China in the Colonial World (HB)
Edited by Madhavi Thampi

Everyday Politics of Labour: Working Lives in India's Informal Economy (HB)
Geert De Neve

Viramma: Life of a Dalit (PB)
Viramma, Josiane Racine and Jean-Luc Racine

Lived Islam in South Asia: Adaptation, Accommodation and Conflict (HB)
Edited by Imtiaz Ahmad and Helmut Reifeld

Reforming India's Social Sector: Poverty, Nutrition, Health and Education (HB)
Edited by K. Seeta Prabhu and R. Sudarshan

Human Security in South Asia: Energy, Gender, Migration, and Globalisation (HB)
Edited by P.R. Chari and Sonika Gupta

Middle Class Values in India and Western Europe (HB)
Edited by Imtiaz Ahmad and Helmut Reifeld

Religion and Personal Law in Secular India: A Call to Judgment (HB)
Edited by Gerald James Larson

WTO Agreement and Indian Agriculture (HB)
Edited by Anwarul Hoda

Trade, Finance and Investment in South Asia (HB)
Edited by T.N. Srinivasan

Forthcoming

The Sundarbans: Folk Deities, Monsters and Mortals
Sutapa Chatterjee Sarkar

Literature and Nationalist Ideology: Writing Histories of Modern Indian Languages
Edited by Hans Harder

Nature, Culture and Religions: People in the Himalayas
Edited by Marie Lecomte-Tilouine

State, Business and Labour in a Public Sector Company: Indian Telephone Industries (1948–2006)
Dilip Subramanian

'When the War Began One Heard of Many Kings': South Asian POWs in World War I, Germany
Edited by Ravi Ahuja, Heike Liebau, and Franziska Roy

India's Economic Future

Education, Technology, Energy and Environment

Edited by
Manmohan Agarwal

CIGI Addressing International Governance Challenges

SOCIAL SCIENCE PRESS

Published by
Esha Béteille
Social Science Press
69 Jor Bagh, New Delhi 110 003

Distributed by
Orient Blackswan Private Limited
Bangalore Bhopal Bhubaneshwar Chandigarh
Chennai Ernakulam Guwahati Hyderabad Jaipur
Kolkata Lucknow Mumbai New Delhi Patna
www.orientblackswan.com

ISBN 978-81-87358-17-6

Social Science Press thanks The Centre for International Governance Innovation (CIGI), for extending their help unhesitatingly and for providing a generous financial support for the publication of this book. CIGI is an independent, nonpartisan thinktank located in Waterloo, Canada.

Set in Plantin
Typeset by Eleven Arts, Delhi 110 035
Printed by De Unique, Delhi 110 018

Dedicated to my parents
Din Dayal and Sarla Agarwal

Contents

List of Tables and Figures

TABLES

Figures

Maps

Acknowledgements

This book has been undertaken as part of a broader research effort at the Centre for International Governance Innovation (CIGI) to analyse developments in Indian economics and politics and understand their implications for international governance.

I would like to thank Daniel Schwanen, Agata Antkiewicz and John Whalley for their strong support without which this project, which examines the sustainability of a high rate of growth of the Indian economy, could not have been completed. I would also like to acknowledge the help of Max Brem and Jessica Hanson of the publications team at CIGI for their assistance in the publication of the book.

The book could not have been completed without the whole hearted cooperation of the contributors in the completion of the text of the volume.

Finally I would like to thank Esha Béteille and her team, particularly Meenakshi Chawla, for their support, help and assistance in publishing this volume.

Any shortcomings are my sole responsibility.

Acknowledgements

List of Contributors

Manmohan Agarwal
Former Professor, Centre for International Trade and Development, School of International Studies, Jawaharlal Nehru University (JNU), New Delhi; Senior Visiting Fellow, Centre for International Governance Innovation (CIGI), Canada.

Yoginder K. Alagh
Chairman Institute of Rural Management (IRMA); Chancellor, Nagaland University and Vice Chairman, Sardar Patel Institute of Economic and Social Research, Ahmedabad.

Ramesh Chand
ICAR National Professor at National Centre for Agricultural Economics and Policy Research, New Delhi; Fellow, National Academy of Agricultural Sciences, India, New Delhi.

Muchkund Dubey
President, Council for Social Development; Vice Chairman, Planning Commission of Sikkim.

P.V. Indiresan
Former Director, Indian Institute of Technology (IIT), Madras.

Gurpreet Mahajan
Professor, Jawaharlal Nehru University (JNU), New Delhi.

Amit Shovon Ray
Professor, Centre for International Trade and Development, School of International Studies, JNU, New Delhi; Research Chair, Indian Council for Research on International Economic Relations (ICRIER), New Delhi.

Aparna Sawhney
Associate Professor, Jawaharlal Nehru University (JNU), New Delhi.

N.S. Siddharthan
Former Professor, Institute of Economic Growth, New Delhi; Hon. Professor, Madras School of Economics, Chennai; Hon. Director, Forum for Global Knowledge Sharing.

Introduction
The Sustainability of a High Economic Growth Rate in India

MANMOHAN AGARWAL

The Indian economy continues to grow rapidly, taking in its stride poor harvests and rising oil prices. Indeed, the rate of growth has been accelerating over the past quarter of a century. Even the growth rate of industrial output, which had tended to be relatively low, has increased to double-digit levels. Moreover, this acceleration of growth has been accompanied by rising levels of savings and investment. India's healthy export performance has resulted in increased amounts of foreign exchange reserves that provide an element of insurance against a large balance of payments (BOP) deficit in the future. Now, Indian firms are beginning to invest abroad in search of markets and other benefits. This outward foreign direct investment (FDI) suggests that Indian firms possess advantages that they are in a position to exploit. India's political front also seems to be favourable. Democracy is well entrenched—elections are held regularly and, with a more powerful Election Commission, more fairly; and changes of government occur peacefully.

Is there a fly in the ointment? Could the growth process slacken or can it be accelerated further? What are the constraints to maintaining a high rate of growth over the next decade or two? The papers in this book seek to answer these questions.

The current economic turmoil in the world has also affected India's economic performance. This book deals with the long-term prospects of the Indian economy. The current downturn is a part of the cyclical pattern that capitalist economies display, even though it is much more severe than a normal business cycle. In the immediate scenario, of course, policy makers have to act to reverse the downturn in economic activity and their attention may drift from actions needed to sustain long-term growth. But ultimately the world economy will turn around; there are already signs that a recovery is on the way. Since this is a book on long-term growth we do not deal with the exigencies of policy making in the immediate difficult situation. One could even argue that the stimulus needed to sustain growth in the current circumstances could be in areas that foster longer-term growth. As President Obama has argued, expenditures in the areas of energy, education and health are needed and have the virtue of stimulating the economy in the short run as well as laying a surer foundation for longer-term growth. Nor do we see the current circumstances permanently derailing growth in India.

In a standard growth model, growth depends on augmenting and enhancing the productivity of factors of production, usually taken as capital and labour.[1] However, since development is concerned with increasing per capita income, only increases in capital that raise the ratio of capital to labour are important in the augmentation of factors of production. Increases in the productivity of factors of production are usually conceived to be caused by technological innovation or by improvement in the educational levels of the labour force—referred to as the augmentation of human capital.

The papers in this volume adopt this broad framework to answer questions about the sustainability of Indian economic growth. In the Indian context, the sustainability of growth is not merely an economic issue. There has long been a strong strain of egalitarianism in Indian policy making, with the purpose of growth seen as reducing the extent and severity of poverty and reducing the inequalities in income distribution. India was one of the first countries to assess the effect of growth on poverty, with the Indian Government setting up a task force to examine this a mere ten years after the initiation of planning by the newly independent nation. This task force established the poverty line for India, which, updated for inflation, has continued

[1]Most studies find that technical progress accounts overwhelmingly for growth in developed countries. Its role in growth in developing countries, though still significant, is less so.

to be used as the benchmark for studies of the extent of poverty in the country. There is extensive debate about whether or not poverty has decreased and about the policies that should be adopted to reduce poverty rapidly. When the Bharatiya Janata Party (BJP) lost the 2004 election, many commentators opined that its economic policies had ignored the average citizen and had allowed most of the benefits of growth to be captured by the more prosperous.[2] A similar explanation had been offered for the defeat of the Congress government in the elections of the mid-1990s.

The papers in Section I, Macro Policy, Technology and Growth, examine the economic prospects for sustained growth. Manmohan Agarwal deals with the macroeconomic constraints. In the past, low levels of savings and investment were considered to be the major constraints to growth.[3] Even in the 1980s, when both savings and investment were in the 20 per cent range, many people argued that inadequate demand was a major problem in India, resulting in inadequate investment incentives and the need for the government to step in to raise demand and improve the environment for investment. This belief contributed, in part, to the high deficits in the government budgets of the 1980s, which, in turn, resulted in the BOP deficits that resulted in the 1991 exchange rate crisis.[4] Indeed, BOP crises had derailed the growth process on several occasions in the past, and although the drop in the growth rate was generally shortlived, the decline in investment was reversed only after a number of years.

One major reform since 1991 has been that the exchange rate has been made more flexible, meaning that an increase in the BOP deficit now results in a depreciation of the rupee which encourages

[2]Indeed, some suggested that the BJP's slogan, 'India Shining', merely rubbed salt into the wound.

[3]See Government of India (1952); also see Agarwal (1997). Early development economists such as Lewis (1954) and Rostow (1960) thought that raising the rate of savings from 5 per cent—the level they believed prevailed in developing countries—to 10 per cent was the key to achieving a sustainable rate of growth. A low level of investment was a particular problem, since income could not grow unless the rate of savings was raised. A low level of investment could be taken to represent inadequate demand or an imbalance in demand (see Rosenstein-Rodan 1943; Nurkse 1961).

[4]See Krugman (1979) for the analysis of a model with a fixed exchange rate where continuing budget deficits ultimately lead to an exchange rate crisis. See Agarwal (1997) for an analysis of how the government handled the deleterious effects of a budget deficit.

exports. This flexibility has contributed to the maintenance of a high rate of growth despite the continuation of high budget deficits.[5] Also, since the reforms, the extent of short-term borrowing has been considerably reduced and foreign exchange reserves have been built up. Consequently, the prospects of a disruption in growth because of a BOP crisis are slim. This does not necessarily mean that developments in the world economy will not affect the domestic economy,[6] but the reforms have led to a closer integration with the world economy as the ratio of trade to gross domestic product (GDP) has increased and capital flows in both directions are higher. Although full capital account convertibility does not exist in India, inflows are very free. Outflows by Indian companies are limited, however, outflows of large amounts by individuals are allowed. Savings and investment by the corporate sector have been rising, so that any problems in the capital markets have a limited effect. Also, reforms in the banking sector and in capital markets have been safely negotiated. The only continuing hitch is the high level of fiscal deficits.

Thus far, the Indian Government has successfully managed its fiscal position so as not to create too serious a constraint in the macroeconomic sense. Populist policies might be adopted just before the elections, but policy makers are sensitive even to high single-digit inflation rates and are likely to keep deficits under control. Of course, in an open economy such as India's, deficits might not raise the rate of inflation directly. Rather, their effect on inflation is indirect as excess demand spills into a BOP deficit. Therefore, domestic inflation is governed by international inflation and by any devaluation of the exchange rate because of the BOP deficit. All the signals seem to show that the Indian macro economy is in a sound position and should not be a constraint to growth.

India's budget deficits, however, have another implication with a significant influence on the rate of economic growth: their effect on the nature of expenditures. Deficits limit the government's ability to increase investment in infrastructure and health and education

[5]See Kenen (2000) for an analysis of the effects of a budget deficit in a regime of flexible exchange rates and significant capital flows. See also Agarwal (1997).

[6]The effect of the world economy on India's economy is evident in the current recession. However, the world economic recession is unlikely to be permanent. Furthermore, governments seem to have learnt from the experience of the Great Depression of the 1930s and from the research of Keynes, and are adopting expansionary monetary and fiscal policies.

facilities. The poor state of the country's roads, ports, airports and railways and the severe energy shortage are major handicaps for any entrepreneur. The problem is not so much the aggregate levels of savings and investment but the allocation of investment, since it is the government that is usually the major investor in infrastructure. In their desire to cut deficits, the Central and state governments have been cutting back on public investment. Although there has been talk of public–private partnerships, it is not clear whether many poor consumers can afford the price of infrastructure services that would offer the private providers a suitable rate of return.

Before the government's introduction of major economic reforms, there was hardly any increase in industrial productivity, and the situation has not improved in the post-reform period. Industry complains of a shortage of skilled persons, which, combined with a lack of interaction between industry and institutions of higher learning, is held responsible for the slow growth of productivity. Issues of governance are also important in determining industrial performance. Not only does FDI lead directly to higher productivity through the import of better technology, but also it indirectly raises productivity through higher technology levels as a result of diffusion, imitation and improved corporate governance. It is being seen that FDI is also changing the way industry operates—particularly with respect to research activity, as companies set up research centres in India.

N.S. Siddharthan's analysis of India's FDI is disquieting, particularly in the context of Mahajan's discussion of the country's economic and social inequalities. As FDI inflows are becoming more important, they might raise growth rates, but they might also exacerbate inequalities, with their attendant social and political costs. Siddharthan finds that FDI widens income inequalities in two ways. First, FDI flows to states with better infrastructure and a better socio-economic environment; also, FDI flows are highly concentrated, and the poorer states receive little of it. Second, firms with a small productivity gap relative to transnational corporations benefit from the spillover effects and are able to raise their own productivity, while no such benefits accrue to the more inefficient firms.

Amit Shovon Ray provides a more in-depth analysis of technical policies in India and their effect on productivity growth. He argues that there was a change in the government's policies when the economy became more open and market-oriented. Earlier—since at least the first technology policy was enunciated in 1958—policy had stressed the need for technological self-sufficiency and was designed so that specialized institutes, generally in the public sector, would develop technologies that enterprises would then be encouraged to adopt. With this in mind, the import of technology was restricted and controlled, resulting in very slow technological development. Enterprises neither developed their own technologies, nor developed mutually beneficial relations with universities or research institutes; they did not even adopt the technologies developed by the public sector institutes.[7] Subsequently, greater fiscal incentives were granted to enterprises to develop their own technologies, which resulted in greater effort by the private sector, although government enterprises still account for the majority of research expenditure. Industry, in general, has stressed on outputs such as patents, product development and import substitution, while the public sector institutes have stressed on consultancy services and publications. Productivity growth seems to have increased after 1982, although it is still limited to about 8 of the 29 sectors that Ray examines. His analysis confirms Siddharthan's finding that productivity growth is linked to learning, which, in some cases, is tied to new equipment and in others, to the firms' own research and development (R&D).

An area of increasing concern is the slowdown in productivity growth in agriculture, which Ramesh Chand finds is linked to increasing rural distress and a slowing down of the process of poverty reduction, given that about 70 per cent of India's population still lives in rural areas. The slowdown in agricultural productivity growth is also endangering the country's food security, as large imports of food grains result in higher international prices and BOP difficulties. Chand argues that changes in a number of policies are necessary to remove the constraints that have resulted in this slowdown. One urgent task is to upgrade agricultural technology and broaden its diffusion. This would require the strengthening of agricultural research institutions, which played a major role in the achievements of the Green Revolution, but have not produced any significant technical improvements in recent years. The agricultural extension service also needs to be strengthened to help spread good practices.

The issue of poverty in India is part of the broader debate about social justice, particularly in the context of the growth of human

[7]The institutes themselves argue that the technologies they have developed have been adopted by small and medium enterprises.

capital. In fact, India's remarkable economic growth has generated only limited new employment, bypassing many segments of the population. But citizens are now more aware of their rights and are willing to use their voting power to achieve them—voting percentages are much higher among the poor than among the middle and upper classes—while the armed protests that prevail in many parts of the country reflect the desire of the marginalized groups to assert themselves and establish their political identity.

To accelerate the spread of benefits of economic growth among backward communities, the government reserves places for members of such communities in government jobs and educational institutions. Indeed, reservations for scheduled castes (SCs)—that have been discriminated against for generations—and for scheduled tribes (STs) have existed almost since independence. About a decade and a half ago, reservations were extended to so-called other backward classes (OBCs) for government jobs and, more recently, for both admissions to and jobs in Central Government educational institutions such as Indian Institutes of Technology (IITs), Indian Institutes of Management (IIMs) and the Central Universities. So as not to reduce opportunities for the general categories, enrolment in these institutions is to increase by 54 per cent. These new reservations and the increase in enrolment will profoundly change India's educational system. Now, demands are being heard to extend reservations to jobs in the private sector and to admissions to non-government educational institutions.

However, demands that arise from identity-based politics can be divisive, and can lead to the wasteful use of public resources on redistribution rather than on investment. Reservations can also reduce efficiency as less-qualified people gain access to universities or find employment. On the other hand, reservations can draw in talent from a much larger part of the population, thus enriching the growth process. Papers in Section II, Education, examine issues regarding education at school and higher levels. The papers by P.V. Indiresan and Gurpreet Mahajan examine the consequences of reservations for India's educational sector and technological development, as well as the notion of social justice and its political consequences.

Indiresan deals with the consequences of reservations in the IITs on the competence of India's engineers, which could have a particularly strong effect on innovation and, consequently, on productivity growth as the Indian economy is opened up to increased foreign competition. Indiresan points out the difficulty of achieving the government's mandated increase in enrolment, given the already-severe shortage of faculty and facilities that are often not up to the level needed to maintain world-class teaching and research. Already, the IITs have slipped in the rankings of world institutions since little research is conducted in them; and the number of papers published by Indian academics in international journals is declining even as that by academics from many other developing countries increases.[8] He notes that the Indian Government's strategies differ considerably from those adopted by the Chinese, which illustrates the two ends of the debate on education and training, with India's policies stressing broader participation while China focuses on raising standards to world levels as it regards higher education as an elite endeavour. In recent years, China has made great strides in higher education, and is poised to play an important role internationally (Yao, Whalley, Zhang and Zhao, 2008).

Mahajan is more concerned about the long-term political and social challenges that the policy of reservations poses. She argues that policies with respect to the marginalized sections of society must not only respond to their concerns, but also be perceived to be just and fair. One consequence of unfair policies could be increasing demands from more and more sections of the population, leading to an overload on the polity.[9] Mahajan states that measures that make identity a permanent asset or an ever-renewable privilege open the doors for conflict that could weaken not only the educational system but also Indian democracy, with undesirable consequences for India's attempts to achieve social justice or become a global power.[10]

Muchkund Dubey deals with the other extreme of the educational spectrum: school education. He is concerned with both the effect of school education in raising the level of human capital and its role in developing a more egalitarian society. The state of school education in India is a matter of grave concern, with the extent of the system as well as its quality leaving much to be desired even 60 years after independence. Enrolment levels are very low in comparison with

[8]Furthermore, the benefits to the Indian economy have been limited as a very high proportion of the graduates from the IITs tend to emigrate.

[9]Already, there are demands from sections of the population to be treated as one of the OBCs or, as in the case of the Gujjars, as an ST (because of the perception that there is too much competition among the OBCs).

[10]The benefits from reservations seem to be concentrated among certain groups, who continue to enjoy them even after they no longer lag behind general society. This is likely to reduce support for reservations.

most other developing countries, with 30 to 50 per cent of Indian children still out of school, though there has been some improvement in recent years.[11] Drop out rates are also very high, averaging between 60 and 90 per cent in Classes I to X, leaving many unable to reach a sustainable level of functional literacy. The quality of school education is extremely poor because of its gross under-funding. The quality is also considerably uneven across the regions of the country, with the heavily populated states of Uttar Pradesh, Bihar and Madhya Pradesh having very low levels of achievement. The outlook for economic growth in these poorest of states is bleak, and large sections of their populations seem condemned to live without hope of any significant improvement in their living standards. Indeed, school education in India is characterized by the most widespread inequality as compared to anywhere else in the world. This inequality hinders the vast majority from benefiting from economic growth and increases demands for reservations and policies based on identity. At the same time, lack of education prevents these groups from taking advantage of the opportunities that reservations provide, and many reserved positions remain unfilled as sufficient numbers of qualified people are not available from the reserved categories. Primary education is now a right in India, but adequate resources are not being devoted to realize the objective of universal primary education. Dubey argues for the establishment of a common school system, which has been indispensable in enabling other countries to achieve universal education of a high quality. Without the reform of primary education, the provision of reservations in higher education can only be partially successful in achieving the goal of social justice, and might even aggravate identity-based politics. Since primary education is the first step in developing a skilled labour force and an innovation-minded community, besides helping to achieve other goals, such as lower fertility, failure on this front could have serious consequences for the sustainability of the current dynamism in the Indian economy.

Section III 'Sustainability, Energy and Environment' contains two papers by Yoginder Alagh and Aparna Sawhney. Infrastructure has been viewed for long as a critical constraint to achieving higher growth. While investment in roads and ports has been stepped up, the situation on the energy front is worsening. Yoginder Alagh looks at the various past attempts to improve the performance of the energy

[11]Unfortunately, enrolment figures are often rigged for political, administrative and other reasons.

sector, which has been plagued by inadequate investment, resulting in a lack of sufficient electricity generation capacity. Even the available capacity has not been used efficiently. The shortage of power and its erratic availability has forced companies to generate their own power from captive generation facilities, an expensive method of power production that raises the cost of production and affects the competitiveness of Indian companies. Furthermore, erratic power, with considerable fluctuations in voltage and cycles, takes its toll on equipment.

The policies adopted by the government have gone through various phases as it searches for institutional and financial arrangements that would raise investment in energy, particularly by the private sector. The government has also sought to improve the efficiency of energy production by raising the plant load factor. Immediately after it initiated sweeping economic reforms, the government sought to enter into contracts with large multinational companies to establish very large energy plants, but only one of the eight envisaged plants actually came on stream. Furthermore, in Maharashtra, the guarantees that were thought necessary to entice foreign investment resulted in costs to the state electricity board that contributed significantly to the bankruptcy of the state. Because of these failures, less energy capacity was created in the 1990s than in the 1980s; and the creation of new capacity has been even more dismal in the first decade of this century. So far, much improved plant load factors have partly compensated for the failure to install new capacity. But there is no slack in the system, and new investment is urgently needed.

Also important is the mix of sources of power generation. The use of poor-quality domestic coal is hindered by concerns about pollution and its contribution to climate change, while large imports of coal, natural gas, or oil for power generation might result in undesirable pressure on the BOP. It is, therefore, imperative to fully exploit all forms of renewable sources. Alagh concludes that this could necessitate the development of nuclear power based on domestic thorium in fast breeder reactors.[12]

Some progress has been made to improve plant-level efficiency, but the low levels of investment in the energy sector have meant that supply has not kept up with demand, despite the declining amount

[12]Alagh argues that the criticism of nuclear power as being too expensive is unfounded, although the issue of safety and disposal of spent fuel needs further analysis.

of energy used per unit of GDP. Public–private partnerships have not always worked, and further institutional and financial reforms are needed if the sector is to perform adequately. As it is, the system is plagued by the same problems that bedevil the public sector, leading to low rates and transmission losses (a euphemism for power theft). Attempts by the government to dissociate itself from micromanaging the energy sector have not been successful, as the public is only too aware that it is the government that ultimately sets policy, including power tariffs.

A key ingredient of the long-run sustainability of economic growth is the state of the environment, an issue which Alagh touches upon in his discussion of the deleterious consequences of burning India's poor-quality domestic coal. Environmental issues also come into play with respect to agricultural growth, particularly concerning the use of pesticides and fertilizers. Aparna Sawhney finds that, by and large, India's impressive economic growth of the past few years has been accompanied by ambiguous changes to the overall environmental situation, but clearly there has been large-scale deforestation, mining, depletion of groundwater, and degradation of air, water and soil quality. Meanwhile, environmental pollution from the services sector remains largely unaccounted for.

As the consumption of India's billion-plus population becomes more resource and energy intensive, albeit at a level far below that of the developed nations, policy changes might be necessary to ensure the sustainability of economic growth. Yet the direct and indirect demand for environmental resources and services far exceeds those available. Economic growth in India over the past 40 years has been running on an environmental deficit that has not been offset by enhanced physical and intellectual capital. Sawhney argues that high rates of growth cannot be sustained unless the quality of critical natural resources such as air and water is maintained and the resource cost of growth is reduced. She concludes that the empirical debate on the sustainability of the Indian growth path is still open. A leaning towards a positive outlook critically depends on increasing investment in human capital, the use of resource-saving technology, substitution with cleaner energy, and reinforcing the Indian culture of reuse, recycle and minimum wastage.

The overall conclusion of the contributions to this volume is that there are few macroeconomic constraints to the maintenance of a high rate of growth for the Indian economy. Savings and investment rates are high and are increasing, while exchange rate flexibility has largely insulated the economy from destabilizing BOP crises, although obviously a dynamic world economy helps India to achieve its high rate of growth. Problems continue to exist, however, in the maintenance of a high level of human capital formation and in infrastructure investment and management. Another area of concern is the environmental policy that supports a high rate of growth. These problem areas reflect the need for an enabling regime that gives individual households and enterprises the incentives and facilities to adopt patterns of behaviour conducive to maintaining a high rate of economic growth.

I would like to thank the Centre for International Governance Innovation (CIGI) for its strong support for the project so that it could be brought to fruition. I would also like to thank the contributors for their papers and the many discussions that have helped to develop a coherent analysis of India's achievements spanning almost a quarter of a century and also the current problems that might prevent the continuation of a high rate of economic growth.

References

Agarwal (1997), 'India', in P. Desai (ed.), *Going Global*, MIT Press, Cambridge, Mass.

Government of India (1952), *The First Five Year Plan*, Planning Commission, Government of India, New Delhi.

Kenen (2000), *The International Economy*, Cambridge University Press, Cambridge.

Krugman (1979), 'A Model of Balance of Payments Crises', *Journal of Money, Credit and Banking*, Vol. 11, No. 3, pp. 311–25.

Lewis (1954), 'Economic Development with Unlimited Supplies of Labour', *Manchester School*, Vol. 22 (May), pp. 139–91.

Nurkse (1961), *Problems of Capital Formation in Underdeveloped Countries*, Oxford University Press, New York.

Rosenstein-Rodan (1943), 'Problem of Industrialisation of South and South-Eastern Europe', *Economic Journal*, Vol. 53, No. 210/211, pp. 202–11.

Rostow (1960), *The Stages of Economic Growth: A Non-Communist Manifesto*, Cambridge University Press, Cambridge.

Yao Li, John Whalley, Shunming Zhang and Xiliang Zhao (2008), 'The Higher Education Transformation of China and its Global Implications', NBER Working Paper No. 13849, National Bureau of Economic Research, Cambridge, Mass.

PART I

Macro Policy, Technology and Growth

1

Maintenance of a High Rate of Growth
A Macroeconomic Perspective

MANMOHAN AGARWAL

Introduction

In this chapter we analyse the sustainability of a high rate of economic growth in India over the long term, from the macroeconomic point of view. To analyse this question of macroeconomic sustainability of growth, in the first section we discuss the conditions under which the growth process in India has been interrupted in the past. In the second section we analyse the nature of the current growth process in India before discussing in the third section whether interruptions such as those that have occurred in the past are likely to occur in the medium and long term.

Past Interruptions of the Growth Process

A sharp decline in agricultural output and a balance of payments (BOP) crisis, the two often being interconnected, have interrupted the growth of the Indian economy on a number of occasions: for example, 1957–58, 1965–67, 1973–74, 1980–81 and 1991–92. A poor harvest would necessitate large food imports leading to a large increase in the current account deficit; this created a BOP crisis when the deficit could not be financed.[1] The BOP crises could also be brought about by other supply shocks, usually an increase in the price of oil; crises caused by increased prices of oil have been more common in recent years. The exception to BOP crises caused by supply shocks was the 1957–58 crisis.[2] The supply shocks were usually accompanied by a higher rate of inflation, and governments in India have been very sensitive to the rate of inflation.[3] For instance, when the rate of inflation increased to over 20 per cent in 1974, the government adopted such strong contractionary monetary and fiscal policies that prices actually fell the next year. The crises were usually met by a combination of financing and adjustment, namely adoption of policy measures to tackle the demand–supply imbalance.

In each crisis new sources of financing the current account deficit were tapped. For instance, the 1957–58 crisis saw the Indian Government approach the World Bank (WB) and the establishment of the Aid India Consortium.[4] However, the WB was not a major aid giver during the Second and Third Five Year Plans. It contributed about 10 per cent of the aid during these Plans. Later, during the 1970s and early 1980s, it became a major aid giver—accounting for over 50 per cent of the aid given to India. The 1980–81 crisis saw the government borrow from the International Monetary Fund (IMF) in the short run, but turn to loans from commercial banks as well as deposits from non-resident Indians (NRIs) for the longer term.[5]

Adjustment policies to manage the supply–demand relation were of two kinds. Measures to raise the supply of some critical import

[1]Sometimes there was also a political aspect to the problem. The Indian Government, faced with food shortages in the 1950s and 1960s depended on food aid from the United States. The US sometimes tried to make the aid conditional on foreign policy stances of the Indian Government (Bowles 1971, Eldridge 1969, Lele and Agarwal 1991)

[2]This crisis was brought about by a surge in imports as private agents increased imports in anticipation of a BOP deficit and an exhaustion of the country's foreign exchange reserves.

[3]A high rate of inflation is socially unacceptable as it hurts the poor disproportionately. It is also politically unacceptable as the poor vote in larger proportions than the middle class or the rich. This sensitivity to inflation has increased in recent years, perhaps because of the financial liberalization.

[4]Recourse to newer sources of financing was also true for other crises.

[5]Borrowings in the form of deposits in banks held by NRIs had started after the 1973–74 crisis brought about by the higher oil and wheat prices. However, such deposits became much more important later, partly because of the large number of Indian workers in the Middle East.

were undertaken.[6] For instance, the 1965–67 crisis was caused by poor harvests necessitating large imports of wheat and rice. The response was the adoption of policies that later came to be known as the 'Green Revolution'. These successfully raised agricultural output and eliminated food imports. Similarly, the government responded to the 1973–74 crisis, caused by a sharp rise in the price of oil, by increasing investment in oil exploration and production which reduced oil imports in subsequent years. The level of demand was also reduced; usually an attempt was made to curtail consumption and investment. However, in practice, the cutback was mainly in public investment.[7] Since such investment was particularly import intensive its reduction helped reduce the BOP deficit.

Since there was a considerable lag before the supply measures became effective, the immediate burden fell on the investment rate. For instance, after gross fixed capital formation (GFCF) as a percentage of gross domestic product (GDP) reached a peak of 15.9 per cent in 1957–58, it fell and did not recover to the earlier rate till 1963–64 (RBI 2008). The fall in the GFCF rate after the 1965–67 crisis was particularly severe—from 20.4 per cent to 16.7 per cent—and it did not recover till 1977–78. Similarly, the GFCF rate fell from 24.4 per cent of GDP in 1990–91 and did not recover till 1994–95. The BOP deficit was also sought to be contained by tightening import controls. But by 1980 it was seen that such controls were not a solution and could aggravate the problem in the long run, and so further tightening of controls was avoided.[8]

While policies were adjusted in response to the various crises, the basic framework remained the same until the 1991 crisis. Policies were also adjusted in response to the changing constraints faced by the government (Agarwal 1997) This basic framework which relied

[6]A critical import would be an item that had a large share of total imports.

[7]This was particularly true after the public outcry against the large increase in taxes in 1963, though in this case the increase was caused by the increase in defence expenditures in the aftermath of the border war with China in 1962.

[8]In a two-sector model with full employment and production of both exports and import-competing goods, any increase in the production of import-competing goods can only be at the cost of lower production of exports. Such a conclusion would also hold if production of non-traded goods was included as supply of these must equal demand. Furthermore, a number of expert committees were set up to study the effects of the trade policy regime, particularly the role of licencing. These came to the conclusion that the regulatory framework had many adverse consequences and so was inadvisable.

extensively on controls to restrain imports and encourage the establishment of companies to produce substitutes for the restricted imports is usually called the import substitution industrialization (ISI) strategy.[9] One of the reasons for the maintenance of the development strategy was the resilience of the economy. The effect of the BOP crises on growth was usually short-lived, despite the slowdown in investment as noted above—a testimony to the resilience of the economy. The growth rate of GDP fell to –1.2 per cent in 1957–58 before it recovered to 7.6 per cent in the following year. Similarly, the growth rate declined from 4.7 per cent in 1973–74 to 1.3 per cent in 1974–75 before recovering to 9.1 per cent in 1975–76, and declined from 5.5 per cent in 1978–79 to –5 per cent in 1979–80 before increasing to 7.2 per cent in 1980–81.[10] The exception was the crisis during the years 1965–67 when the interruption in growth was much more substantial.

Differences in opinion between the Indian and US Governments regarding the appropriate policy framework resulted in cessation of aid from the US and a curtailment of aid from the WB.[11] Development Assistance pledged by the US and the WB at the Aid India Consortium declined precipitously from $545 million and $250 million, respectively for 1961–62 to $275 million and $73 million, respectively for 1967–68 and further to only $8.7 million and $15 million, respectively for 1968–69 (Bumb 1985).[12] Since the US provided half the aid during the last years of the Second Plan and for the Third Plan, the cessation of aid strongly affected the performance of the Indian economy. The growth rate of GDP which had accelerated from 3.6 per cent per year in the First Plan to 4 per cent per year during the Second Plan and further to 4.5 per cent per year during the first four years of the Third Plan plummeted in subsequent years and averaged a mere 2.6 per cent per year over the next ten years.[13]

[9]In the case of India, the government also sought to channelize private investments according to Plan priorities.

[10]The large variation in growth rates was due to the effects of the BOP position as well as fluctuations in agricultural output caused by variations in rainfall.

[11]About 60 per cent of external assistance during the Third Plan came from the US, with the EU contributing only 15 per cent (Lele and Agarwal 1991).

[12]Aid from the US has never been important since this episode. It was less than 3 per cent of total aid in the early 1980s. But the importance of aid from the WB, particularly its soft aid affiliate, IDA, became important in the 1970s and early 1980s.

[13]Many analysts have tended to calculate the growth rate for the entire period,

The adjustments that the Indian Government was forced to undertake, as far as macro policy was concerned, were similar to those that later came to be known as 'structural adjustment'.[14] Substantial efforts were made to raise the rate of savings. In the short run this had a deflationary effect and as a consequence, growth faltered. As the economy was recovering it was hit by the need to care of over 10 million refugees who came from Bangladesh, then East Pakistan, and the costs of the war against Pakistan that resulted in the creation of Bangladesh. Before it fully recovered from this shock the economy was buffeted by an increase in the prices of oil and many primary commodities in 1973–74.[15]

The restrictive import regime was maintained and a more export-oriented development strategy was not adopted as policy makers feared that the world market would not be able to absorb the exports that India would supply if its exports-to-GDP ratio reached the level in Korea.[16] Such fears were overcome only when the Chinese experience showed that it was possible for a large economy to sharply increase exports. Another factor that explains the reluctance to adopt a more open framework was the fear that the terms of trade would decline if growth of agricultural productivity lagged behind that in other countries, as argued by Lewis (1969)

The effect of this curtailment in aid and the subsequent events in the slowing down of the economy can be seen very clearly. The curtailment in aid had a particularly serious effect as the Indian development strategy was based on government investment for the

---

which tends to be low because of the prolonged slowdown and dubbed it the 'Hindu rate of growth'. We believe that this is misleading as the economy was on an accelerating path until the crisis.

[14]Major changes also occurred in the foreign trade policies. The rupee was devalued substantially, many of the subsidies and tariffs were either eliminated or consolidated so that the system was made simpler and the resource allocation incentives clearer. However, this liberalization was short-lived. One of the reasons for the reversal of the liberalization was the double tying of aid. The necessity to ensure that such tied aid was fully utilized resulted in licences being issued for each commodity from each country up to the amount of the aid.

[15]The effect of the increase in the price of wheat which had to be imported in large quantities because of the failure of the harvest had a larger effect on the BOP in the immediate short run than the increase in the price of oil.

[16]In the initial Plan years, there is no evidence of export pessimism. The Indian export basket was heavily dependent on a few primary commodities and policy makers believed that the manufacturing sector needed to be developed before exports could be increased.

production of capital goods which would be used for further investment.[17] The cutback in aid and the subsequent reduction in public investment meant that there was considerable excess capacity in the capital goods sector leading to inefficiency in the form of high capital–output ratios.[18] The incremental capital–output ratio increased from about 4 in the Second Plan to over 5 during the period 1961–62 to 1974–75. But growth resumed after the economy adjusted to the changed circumstances and, in fact, steadily accelerated as the drag of the excess capacity in the capital goods sector was progressively reduced. In the first phase of adjustment the rate of savings was increased—with a deflationary effect in the short run—to 17–18 per cent, the same as the rate of investment, so the need for aid was almost eliminated. Subsequent resumption of aid by the WB relaxed the foreign exchange constraint and enabled the government to liberalize the imports of intermediate goods which raised capacity utilization and laid the foundation for higher growth. This acceleration in growth has resulted in a lower incremental output ratio, and one that is comparable to that achieved by East Asian economies.[19] This raises some questions about whether the Indian policies were as inefficient as is often believed, and also which of the policies were really inefficient.[20]

[17]The Indian development strategy was in this respect very different from that followed by most other developing countries where import substitution was undertaken in consumer goods industries. This strategy was justified by the Mahalanobis growth model in which investment equals the output of the capital goods sector (Mahalanobis 1953, 1955). For an analysis of the model and its impact on Indian policies see Bhagwati and Chakravarty (1969). The cutback in aid forced the government to declare three years of Plan holidays and the implementation of the Plans was resumed only when the economy was deemed to have adjusted to the cutback in aid. But even then it was struck by a number of exogenous shocks.

[18]External aid financed about a quarter to a third of GFCF during the Second and Third Plans. But by the Sixth Plan it financed a mere 7.7 per cent. This massive savings effort resulted in many economists concluding that shortage of demand was the major constraint facing the Indian economy in that period (Chakravarty 1977).

[19]Since the mid-1970s, the incremental capital–output ratio has been relatively constant and about the same as in the rapidly growing economies of East Asia. There is a dispute on the contribution of productivity increase to growth in Korea and Taiwan (Krugman 1994); Young (1995); Bhanoji Rao (2001). The Indian experience is very much at variance with the experience in the rest of the world where capital–output ratios have doubled since the 1973–74 oil price rises (Agarwal 2008).

[20]The rate of growth of the economy did not accelerate immediately after the liberalization in 1991. Some economists then argued that the policy of liberalization was ineffective. Others argued that the higher rate of growth in the 1980s had been

Characteristics of Growth in India

The behaviour of the Indian economy has many similarities with that of other developing countries, particularly those in Asia. But there are also some significant differences. The progressive acceleration in the rate of growth of the Indian economy over the past 30 years has made the Indian economy one of the fastest growing economies in the world (Table 1.1).

Table 1.1: Rates of Growth in the Different Plans

(annual average)

Plans	*GDP*	*Agriculture*	*Manufacturing*	*Services*
Sixth (1980–84)	5.5	5.7	5.1	5.4
Seventh (1985–89)	6.0	2.8	6.0	6.1
Eighth (1992–96)	6.5	4.7	9.4	6.8
Ninth (1997–2001)	5.5	2.4	3.3	7.8
Tenth (2002–06)	9.6	2.7	11.0	12.0

Source: Reserve Bank of India (2008).

The rate of growth was about 4 per cent in the late 1970s; it increased to about 5 per cent in the early 1980s and was almost 6 per cent in the late 1980s. After liberalization was initiated in 1991, the rate of growth was over 6 per cent in the 1990s and in recent years it has been over 8 per cent, occasionally approaching even 10 per cent which is the target for the government. Even though the policy framework remained the same till 1991 the nature of the growth process had already changed. Output of both manufacturing and services grew at comparable rates except in the Ninth Plan when the manufacturing sector lagged behind services. However, growth of agricultural output has lagged, and substantially, since the mid-1990s.

With this high rate of growth, India has joined the club of fast growing Asian economies. The growth of the world economy and most of its regions has declined substantially since the oil price rise of 1973–74. The average annual rate of growth of per capita income in the world economy fell from 3.3 per cent before 1973–74 to 1.2

due to the liberalization then (Rodrik and Subramanium 2005; Panagariya 2008). It is difficult to separate the role of the trade reform from that of relaxation of domestic licencing in the acceleration during the 1980s.

per cent during the period 1974–2004. For much of the 1980s and 1990s, developing countries in Latin America and sub-Saharan Africa hardly grew. Between 1974 and 2004, per capita income in Latin America grew at about 1 per cent per year whereas in sub-Saharan Africa, per capita incomes remained almost constant. However, growth rates in Asia, both East and South, accelerated.

The Green Revolution resulted in a change in the sectoral composition of the government's investment; more of it went towards irrigation and other agriculture related investments and less was available for manufacturing and infrastructure, particularly power generation and transmission. The share of agriculture, including irrigation, in the Plan outlays of the government increased from 20.9 per cent in the Third Plan (1961–65) to 22.5 per cent in the Fourth Plan (1969–73), 22.2 per cent in the Fifth Plan (1974–78), 23.7 per cent in the Sixth Plan (1980–84) and 22 per cent in the Seventh Plan (1985–89).[21] The shift in investment allocation was accentuated by the increased investment in oil exploration and refining following the 1973–74 oil price rises.

These shifts in composition had important consequences for the economy. The importance of the private sector increased: agriculture was almost entirely in private hands; the lack of government resources for investment in manufacturing meant that here too the private sector began to play a greater role. Government investment in manufacturing and construction was 22.9 per cent in the Third Plan and 24.7 per cent in the interregnum, but fell to 19.7 per cent in the Fourth Plan, 15.5 per cent in the Sixth Plan, and 13.4 per cent in the Seventh Plan. Reliance on the private sector altered the structure of manufacturing.[22] Private investments took place mainly in the

[21]The relative small increase in the share of investment in the Fourth and subsequent Plans as compared to the Third Plan does not seem to justify the claim that is often made that the government rectified its neglect of agriculture in the Second and Third Plans. The government had been concerned about the slow growth of agriculture in the 1950s and early 1960s and had appointed a number of committees to analyse the problems of the sector. This analysis had clarified the choices the government faced as it sought to raise the rate of growth of agricultural output. But the government had been reluctant to make a choice because of the likely political consequences. The crisis forced the government to choose between the options and it chose the technological one, namely the introduction of new technology and the accompanying institutional innovations.

[22]This shift also resulted in changes in India's trade pattern and perhaps foreign policy imperatives. The importance of the Western countries which had the technology for consumer goods increased, and that of the erstwhile Soviet Union which had

consumer goods industries and much of the existing capacity in the public sector became redundant; thus creating the long-term need for restructuring of this sector.[23] Another consequence flowed from the lack of investment in the power sector: the economy has been plagued by power shortages. The State has not been able to supply the power needed by private manufacturers and as a result, they have had to set up their own captive power plants. This has led to increased costs of production.[24] However, the shift in investment allocations eased the BOP position. Food imports were eliminated and the value of imports of oil decreased in the 1980s (Lele and Agarwal 1991). This allowed the economy to achieve a very high rate of growth without immediately running into a BOP constraint despite the poor export performance.

Though the economy grew at an increasing rate during the 1980s, it suffered from certain weaknesses that brought about the 1991 crisis. Until the early 1980s, the government budget was in surplus on the revenue account.[25] Then the government started to run a deficit on the revenue account and this deficit grew during the 1980s.[26] The deficit added to the demand in the economy and so helped maintain a high rate of growth. But it also had other effects. As the economy had a fixed exchange rate and there were no market related capital flows, the increased deficit resulted in a higher interest rate domestically and a larger current account deficit (Kenen 2000). The deleterious effect of the higher interest rate on investment was sought to be countered by various incentives such as an accelerated depreciation allowance. Also financing of investments by bigger companies was shifted from loans from domestic finance companies to the stock market.[27] Thus more financing became available for medium sized enterprises which

---

been very helpful in the establishment of the basic industries decreased. Oil figured very prominently in India's imports from the Soviet Union in the 1980s.

[23]The large losses of the public sector are, in part, a reflection of this problem.

[24]Interruptions in the supply of power and variations in its voltage and cycles not only disrupt the production process but also damage equipment.

[25]The deficit in the overall budget had earlier been mostly due to the deficit in the budget for capital expenditures. There was a lively debate in the 1950s and 1960s about the safe limit for reliance on money creation to finance the deficit.

[26]See Joshi and Little (1994) for a detailed discussion on Indian fiscal policy.

[27]The Foreign Exchange Regulations Act of 1974 had forced many transnational companies to issue shares to the Indian public in order to bring the foreign shareholding down to 40 per cent so that they could benefit from being treated as Indian companies. These shares had appreciated considerably and whetted the appetite of the Indian middle class for investing in shares.

aided their rapid growth. The effect on the current account balance was sought to be countered by providing various export incentives including a faster rate of exchange rate depreciation in the second half of the 1980s. But this faster depreciation only resulted in maintaining a stable real effective exchange rate. As a consequence, while the government was successful in maintaining a high rate of investment it was less successful in increasing exports, and the current account deficit expanded substantially.

The large current account deficit and the manner of its financing made the economy vulnerable to any shock. Both the trade deficit and the current account deficit were increasing in this period. A progressively larger share of the current account deficit was being financed by variable interest rate short-term loans from commercial banks as well as deposits from NRIs which could be withdrawn in a crisis of confidence. The Gulf Crisis and War of 1990–91 that raised the price of oil and reduced the remittances from workers in the Middle East was the shock that substantially raised the current account deficit and made the situation unsustainable. India had accumulated a substantial short-term debt and creditors were apprehensive about the ability of the economy and the government to service the debt. Therefore, they refused further loans. The unstable political situation with three changes in government in about three years added to the jitteriness of foreign creditors. Furthermore, effective policy design and execution was hindered by some of these governments being in a minority or being a coalition. As it was the government had, the previous year, shifted a part of its gold holdings to London as collateral for a loan. Foreign exchange reserves had declined to about 14 days worth of imports. The Indian authorities approached the IMF for BOP support; otherwise the country might have had to default on its foreign obligations. The conditions attached to the IMF loan set in motion the reform process.

The Fund conditionalities called for policy changes. Anyway, by then, the substantial research that had accumulated and the experience of other countries had convinced policy makers in India of the need to change the development strategy based on ISI and the concomitant policies that relied on a dense network of quantitative restrictions (QRs).[28] Also, the relatively small liberalization that had

[28]The Chinese experience was particularly relevant, since a large economy benefited from following more open policies. Indian policy makers had not considered the benefits that small economies had derived from liberalization as being relevant

occurred in the mid-1980s—which had allowed private entrepreneurs some leeway in making production and investment decisions—had resulted in an acceleration of growth (Bhagwati 1993). This liberalization had allowed enterprises to expand modestly whereas earlier any expansion of capacity had required government permission. It also allowed entrepreneurs greater freedom in changing the relative composition of inputs used to produce a good.

The policy changes that have occurred since 1991 have meant a substantial opening of the economy as tariffs have been reduced, QRs on imports have been eliminated and inflow of capital has been made easier.[29] There have also been reforms in the domestic economy as the role of the market in resource allocation has increased and that of government directives has decreased. Domestic licencing for expansion has been eliminated, the private sector has been allowed into sectors that had earlier been almost reserved for the government, some public enterprises have been fully privatized, and more partially, and restrictions on foreign capital reduced. Another important change was that initially the exchange rate was devalued and a dual exchange rate was introduced. But soon the exchange rate was again unified at a devalued rate and made more flexible. By the mid-1990s the exchange rate was notified to the IMF as being convertible for the current account.

The government also made a commitment to the IMF to reduce the budget deficit. While initially the budget deficit was indeed reduced it soon increased and reached proportions approaching those before the crisis. But in the changed circumstances, mainly a flexible exchange rate and increased capital flows, the effect of the budget deficit was very different from what it had been when the exchange rate was fixed and there were no significant market related capital flows. Now the deficit on the current account resulted in a depreciation of the currency, as capital flows were still small, which resulted in an expansion of exports that gave a further fillip to growth. But as capital

for India. For a discussion of the effectiveness of ISI policies in general see Little, Scitovsky and Scott (1970), Bhagwati (1993) and Krueger (1978). The impact of such policies in India is discussed extensively in Bhagwati and Desai (1970) and Bhagwati and Srinivasan (1975).

[29]A substantial part of the liberalization was undertaken unilaterally by the Indian Government. There is a perception that policy makers had wanted to make such policy changes and the crisis provided them with an opportunity to do so. The elimination of the remaining QRs occurred when the US won its case for their rapid elimination at the WTO.

flows grew more important, the government had to intervene in the foreign exchange market to prevent an appreciation of the exchange rate. The effect of the resulting accumulation of foreign exchange reserves on the domestic money supply was neutralized by open market operations by the Reserve Bank of India (RBI). But the RBI ran out of securities in the early years of the new century and the currency started to appreciate. This forced the government to institute policies to sustain the profitability of exporting, and exports continued to grow strongly.

There was no considerable acceleration in the growth rate in the initial years after liberalization. However, the nature of growth changed, and, particularly, the chances of maintaining a high rate of growth improved. Perhaps the most important reason for this was that the increased flexibility of the exchange rate enabled the economy to cope better with the effect of the deficit on the current account.

Thirty years of rapid growth have seen a change in the structure of the economy. This change has, however, been gradual. There was very little structural change during the 1980s. The pace picked up in the 1990s and has been particularly fast in the last five years. The share of services has grown while that of agriculture has decreased (Table 1.2). The growth rate of value added in services has been over 8 per cent per year between 1991 and 2006. Consequently, the share of services in GDP has increased from 41 per cent to 60 per cent.[30]

Table 1.2: Changes in Structure of Output, 1980–2006

(per cent of GDP)

Plans	*Agriculture*	*Manufacturing*	*Services*
Sixth (1980–85)	41.0	14.6	37.1
Seventh (1986–90)	36.6	15.9	40.1
Eighth (1992–96)	32.3	17.1	43.1
Ninth (1997–2001)	27.5	17.1	47.9
Tenth (2002–06)	19.0	15.8	60.3

Source: Reserve Bank of India (2008).

[30]Despite the rapid growth of the services sector in India it does not seem to be disproportionately large, as the share of services in GDP for low income developing countries as a group is currently 54 per cent.

Value added in agriculture has grown at only about 2 per cent a year, and its share in GDP has decreased. The slow growth of the agricultural sector has many consequences. The poorest are in the rural sector and this slowdown has slowed the growth of employment in rural areas (Bhalla 2007) as well as the reduction of poverty. Slow growth of the rural economy, both agricultural and non-agricultural, can be an important factor in elections.[31] It has also meant that for the first time since the early 1970s India has imported food in recent years, and the high price of food in the international market has fuelled inflation. The growth rate of value added in manufacturing has been about 7 per cent per year during this period. The share of manufacturing increased till the mid-1990s. But in the Tenth Plan it has actually declined. The rate of growth of the manufacturing sector was particularly slow in the later years of the Ninth Plan and the initial years of the Tenth Plan so that its share in GDP declined. But later in the Tenth Plan it picked up. However, the share of manufacturing in GDP is still lower in India than in most other emerging economies.

On the demand side, the main changes have been the growing importance of investment and exports and the declining share of personal consumption (Table 1.3). The increase in the share of investment in GDP has been gradual and longstanding. The higher savings that have financed investment have implied a declining share for private consumption. The increase in the share of exports of

Table 1.3: Structure of Demand

(per cent of GDP)

Plans	*Personal Consumption*	*Government Consumption*	*Investment*	*Exports*
Sixth (1980–85)	76.9	10.5	19.8	6.2
Seventh (1986–90)	71.7	12.0	22.7	5.9
Eighth (1992–96)	65.4	11.0	24.3	10.2
Ninth (1997–2001)	65.0	12.3	24.3	12.1
Tenth (2002–06)	63.0	12.0	29.6	18.0

Source: Reserve Bank of India (2008).

[31]Analysts hold the unhappiness in rural areas due to the policies of the BJP-led coalition as a major case for their defeat in the 2004 elections. However, the Congress-led coalition that came to power subsequently seemed to follow similar policies.

goods and services has occurred only since the 1991 reforms. Exports of goods and services as a share of GDP declined in the 1980s including the late 1980s when the government followed an exchange rate policy that was more favourable to exports. Whereas in the early 1980s, the nominal effective exchange rate was kept constant so that in real terms it appreciated; since the mid-1980s, the real effective exchange rate was kept constant by allowing the nominal rate to depreciate. This decline in the share of exports in GDP was in contrast to the experience of many other developing countries. The East Asian and many Latin American countries had been following more export-oriented policies since at least the mid-1960s after their initial adoption of an ISI strategy. The share of exports of goods and services in GDP increased for Latin America as a whole from 9.5 per cent in the 1960s to 11.5 per cent in the 1970s and further to 14.8 per cent in the 1980s, while in East Asia it increased from 12.4 per cent to 18.9 per cent and subsequently to 23.5 per cent in the corresponding decades. Since the 1991 reforms, Indian exports of goods and services have been increasing rapidly, particularly in the Tenth Plan. Exports of goods and services as a share of GDP have almost tripled in the 15-year period from 1990–2005 from 7 per cent to 20 per cent (World Bank, 2007).[32] With this increase, India has joined the trend witnessed in other developing countries. However, despite this increase, the share of exports in GDP remains lower in India than in many other developing countries.

The share of merchandise exports in GDP has more than doubled to almost 12 per cent of GDP between 1990–2005. This increase in the importance of exports has also reversed a long trend of a decline in India's share of world exports. India's share of world exports of goods declined steadily from over 2 per cent at the time of independence to just 0.4 per cent in 1980. It stabilized at this rate in the 1980s. But since 1991, the share has been rising and it is now about 1 per cent of world exports. But the really dramatic change has been in the exports of services. Exports of services have increased so rapidly that the share of services in India's export earnings has increased from 20 per cent to 37 per cent between the early 1990s and the early 2000s.[33] With this performance the share of service

[32]This increase is comparable to that of China. In the first 15 years of China's reform the share of exports of goods and services increased from 6 per cent to 21 per cent, only slightly faster than the rate achieved by India.

[33]This increase has occurred, though India had opposed the inclusion of services in the agenda for the Uruguay Round of multilateral trade negotiations.

exports in GDP increased from a negligible percentage of GDP in 1990 to about 9 per cent of GDP in 2005. India's exports of services, as a share of world exports of services, increased from about 0.6 per cent prior to the reforms to 2.3 per cent by 2005. India's success in exporting services is in contrast to the experience of most other developing countries.

The trends in exports and production are two sides of the same coin. The higher rate of growth of service exports than of manufactures corresponds to the trends in output.

Higher service exports have, however, also been accompanied by greater imports of services. So trade is becoming more service oriented.[34] An important aspect of this increasing importance of services trade is that more of it is with the developed countries than with developing countries. This, of course, makes India more vulnerable to cycles of economic activity in the developed countries, particularly as many of the service exports are inputs in the production process.

The acceleration of growth has been accompanied, particularly in recent years, by an increase in the rate of investment funded by an increase in domestic savings. For much of the 1980s and 1990s the rate of investment remained at about 24 per cent and savings at just under that figure. In recent years, however, the rates of investment and domestic savings have reached almost 30 per cent providing a more secure basis for maintaining a high rate of growth.[35] There

Table 1.4: The Investors

(*per cent of GDP*)

Plans	*Households*	*Corporations*	*Public Sector*
Sixth (1980–85)	5.8	4.8	10.5
Seventh (1986–90)	8.1	4.5	10.6
Eighth (1992–96)	6.8	8.2	8.4
Ninth (1997–2001)	9.9	6.7	7.0
Tenth (2002–06)	11.6	9.3	6.8

Source: Reserve Bank of India (2008).

[34]In this the Indian experience varies from that of countries in East and South East Asia which depended more on exports of goods rather than services. The growth of service exports is a bit ironic as the Indian Government opposed the inclusion of services in multilateral trade negotiations.

[35]Analysis shows that the capital–output ratio in India has been very stable at about 4 over the last 30 years, a figure which is very similar to that for East and South East Asia. Such a capital–output ratio along with an investment rate of about 30 per cent would enable the Indian economy to grow at about 8 per cent a year.

has been a shift from investment by the public sector to that by the private sector. Since the Sixth and Seventh Plans, the share of investment undertaken by the public sector has declined as a percentage of GDP, while that undertaken by the household, family farms and enterprises and corporations has increased (Table 1.4). As a consequence, public investment which was about 50 per cent of total investment has declined to less than a quarter.

Savings have increased along with the rise in investment. Consequently, the dependence on foreign savings has not increased much. Foreign savings as a percentage of GDP declined from 2.2 per cent in the 1980s, and the dependence was much greater just before the crisis, to 1.2 per cent in the 1990s, and in the initial years of the twenty-first century the country was exporting capital to the tune of 2.8 per cent of GDP.

Table 1.5: The Savers

(*per cent of GDP*)

Plans	*Households*	*Corporations*	*Government*
Sixth (1980–85)	13.2	1.6	3.7
Seventh (1986–90)	16.0	2.0	2.4
Eighth (1992–96)	18.2	3.8	1.5
Ninth (1997–2001)	20.4	4.0	–1.1
Tenth (2002–06)	24.6	6.8	1.5

Source: Reserve Bank of India (2008).

Government savings have been negligible particularly since the early 1990s, and were even negative in the Ninth Plan (Table 1.5). Households are the major savers and account for almost 80 per cent of the country's savings. But a remarkable feature has been that corporate savings as a percentage of GDP, which had been relatively stable before the reforms, increased later at a very rapid growth. A major issue for policy makers is to ensure transfer of savings to the corporate and government sectors where savings have been less than investment. The government has tapped household savings by issuing various instruments that provide some tax incentives. The corporate sector had become increasingly dependent on the capital markets to meet its savings investment. However, the corporate sector has depended more on internal funds in recent years.

Sustainability of Growth of the Indian Economy

We argue in this section that the policy changes have resulted in a more resilient structure that has very significantly reduced the possibility of a crisis. As noted already, growth has been interrupted usually because of a BOP crisis arising from a supply shock or a macro imbalance in the domestic economy.

Imports, particularly energy-related imports, are likely to grow rapidly. The elasticity of energy consumption with respect to GDP is low in India and has been declining. But given the shortfalls in supply and the low absolute level of energy consumption in India, energy consumption is bound to increase with rising incomes. India will have to depend on imports because of limited domestic supplies. Much of these imports are likely to be of oil and oil-related products. Attempts to diversify into using gas for electricity production and to tie in gas imports have not been successful.[36] India might also become an important importer of coal and other mineral products. Furthermore, the relatively stagnant agricultural output has resulted in recent years in increasing imports of agricultural products, mainly vegetable oils, and now wheat and rice. This dependence on energy related and food imports could lead to strains on the BOP, as in the past.

One of the important features of the recent performance of the Indian economy is the increasing interaction with the world economy; and the large increase in service exports is partly the result of this greater interaction. The share of exports of goods and services in GDP, which had decreased in the 1980s, increased from 7 per cent to 20 per cent between 1990 and 2005. Exports of both goods and services have increased as a share of world exports. India's share of world exports of goods has increased to about 1 per cent of world exports, though it remains lower than that in many emerging economies. Furthermore, India runs a current account deficit, again in contrast to many emerging economies. The structure of exports of goods is dominated by manufactures, which account for about 80 per cent of exports. Exports of services in export earnings have performed even better: India's share of world exports has almost quintupled, with exports of IT-related services increasing even more

[36]Attempts to negotiate long-term supply contracts with Bangladesh, Iran and Myanmar, and to build pipelines for the supply of such gas have not been successful.

rapidly.[37] The structure of exports leans towards the more dynamic sectors; this augurs well for future export performance. Also, the trade in services is more with the developed countries than with developing countries. This creates a potential for rapid growth as developing countries integrate IT-related services into their production structures.

The greater flexibility of the exchange rate and the supply responsiveness of exports that has been observed make it extremely unlikely that the current account deficit will spiral out of control so that a BOP crisis would derail the growth process. The structure of Indian exports with their concentration on services trade which has been growing much faster than trade in goods, and, within goods, the dependence on manufactures rather than commodities augurs well for Indian exports. The substantial diversification of India's export and import baskets both in terms of products and partner countries also suggests that Indian trade is not hostage to developments in any particular country or region. This diversification is a further protection against possible disruptions. Such greater integration with the world economy will, however, pose a challenge to policy makers as economic activity in India will be more closely tied to the international business cycle.[38]

The current account deficit is currently more than covered by capital inflows, and reserves have continued to increase. During some years the country even ran a current account surplus. However, the reserve accumulation has to be viewed cautiously. Since there has usually been a current account deficit, unlike in China, the reserves are more likely to be borrowed reserves than owned reserves and thus more vulnerable to a withdrawal. However, an increasing part of private capital inflows is foreign direct investment (FDI) rather than debt creating forms of capital. This provides stability to the capital account. The recent outflows of portfolio capital will provide policy makers with better knowledge about the resilience of the Indian economy in the face of external shocks. The withdrawal of

[37]This increase in exports and within exports, in service exports is in accordance with trends in many other Asian countries, and is in contrast to the trends in developing countries in other regions. Countries in Latin America and Africa have not been as successful in exporting services, particularly IT-related services.

[38]The contagion of the effect of the world financial crisis on the Indian economy has shown that the complacency based on a belief that the Indian economy is de-coupled from the world economy was inappropriate.

funds by foreign investors from the stock market has resulted in a steep fall in the stocks in the market. However, it has also resulted in a large depreciation of the rupee as they have converted their rupee holdings into foreign currency.[39] This depreciation is likely to provide a fillip to exports and so, could have a positive effect. Furthermore, the banking system is still insulated from the stock market and so is not immediately or significantly affected by the turmoil in the stock market. The overall effect on the real economy may be limited.

The usual debt indicators also are very favourable. The debt-to-GDP ratio has fallen from almost 30 per cent at the time of the 1991 crisis to about 15 per cent, and the debt is much lower than the reserves. Also, short-term debt is less than 10 per cent of the total debt. The debt servicing burden has almost halved over the last 15 years and is now about 10 per cent of export earnings.

We now discuss the possibility of the government having to adopt contractionary fiscal and monetary policies for a prolonged period. After remaining low for a considerable period, despite the very large increase in oil prices, the rate of inflation has accelerated in late 2008 and early 2009. Thus, the government has been forced to temporarily tighten monetary policy. This has resulted in a higher interest rate in the economy. The higher interest rate together with the slowdown in the world economy is lowering the rate of growth of the economy. On the other hand, the exchange rate has depreciated providing a boost to exports which would help to raise the rate of growth of the economy. It is unfortunate that the entire burden of controlling inflation has fallen on monetary policy as fiscal policy has been expansionary—partly in view of the elections in mid-2009. It could happen that a period of expansionary fiscal policy because of approaching elections coincides with an expanding world economy so that there is a strong impetus for expansion of the Indian economy. Later fiscal policy would need to be contractionary to compensate for the earlier expansionary phase and this might coincide with a downturn in the world economy so that the growth of the Indian economy declines. If the exigencies of domestic politics coincide with developments in the world economy the result could be greater instability in the Indian economy. But there is no reason to expect that such cyclical fluctuations will significantly reduce the trend rate

[39]The adoption of a market-based floating exchange rate was one of the structural changes that reduced the possibility of a crisis.

of growth. This is particularly so as the government is very sensitive to the rate of inflation and one should expect a tightening of fiscal policy once electoral considerations are over. There is no evidence as yet that liberalization has actually increased instability. Analysis of growth in India shows that the economy is not only growing faster after the reforms but that growth has been more stable. The variation of growth as measured by standard deviation has become smaller after the reforms.

The steadily increasing share of savings in GDP, which now exceeds 30 per cent, implies that a high rate of investment can be maintained without the need to depend excessively on foreign capital. However, the public savings rate has been low in comparison to the East Asian economies, and has been declining. During the Ninth Plan it was actually negative. The lack of public savings has limited investment in infrastructure, health and education. The lack of investment in human capital has acted to prevent the achievement of an even higher rate of growth. It has also skewed the distribution of the benefits of growth which creates problems in political management.[40]

The increasing capital flows, both outward and inward, help in maintaining a high rate of growth. These flows allow for a greater transfer of technology. Some of the foreign investments by Indian companies have been undertaken with the idea of buying high technology sources. A number of transnational companies are relocating some of their research activities in this area to India. This relocation and their operations have a spillover effect (Siddharthan in this volume).

An area which needs attention is the generation of new technologies in agriculture. Raising agricultural output will not only lessen the strains on the BOP but will also substantially influence the rate of reduction of poverty.

Continuation of recent growth trends in India and in other countries would increase India's share of world income from the current 2 per cent to 4–5 per cent in 2025 and 9–10 per cent in 2050. In terms of per capita income, India's per capita income would increase from 1.5 per cent of that in the US in 2004 to 4 per cent of US income in 2025 and 10 per cent in 2050. India would still remain a relatively poor country and its demand pattern would reflect this. India's importance in the world economy would lie between that of

[40]The uneven distribution of the benefits may explain the demand for reservations which could have important implications as discussed in the papers in this volume by Mahajan and Indiresan.

China and the emerging economies of Latin America. India's share of world exports in goods can also be expected to increase to about 2 per cent in 2025 and 4–5 per cent in 2050. The diversification in both commodities and destinations means that India may face few barriers to this export growth. It would be a more important player in international trade but would still rank only about fifth in 2050. India's success in exporting services is also likely to continue as the sector is vigorously removing constraints to its further expansion. It is spreading to newer areas in the country where costs are lower and is also moving up the value added chain.[41] The move up the value chain contrasts with the public perception in India that exports are only of low level services.

We now look at the possible constraints arising from the size of the fiscal deficit. Fiscal policy influences growth through both its macro and micro effects. At the macro level, growth is affected by the size of government expenditures as well as the size of the deficit. At the micro level, there are the direct public expenditures on capital formation as well as on education and health which affect the extent of human capital formation. The argument of this paper is that the deficit is not likely to directly impede long-term growth in terms of its macroeconomic effects. What is more important from the viewpoint of long-term growth is how it affects private sector investment, particularly whether public expenditures crowd out private investment or crowd it in, and the impact of public expenditures on human capital formation.

Arguments about the extent of the fiscal deficit and its impact on the economy have been long standing in India. They have, however, reached greater salience in the last three decades, particularly the last two. Earlier the revenue account was in surplus. This excess was financed mainly by foreign aid and by money creation. The debate centred around the safe limit for money expansion. But the revenue account has been in deficit and the deficit has been large over most of the last three decades. The impact of the deficit in recent years is, however, very different now than it was earlier because the exchange rate is market determined and capital flows have become much more important. In a closed economy a major concern with large deficits is their impact on the rate of inflation. Of course, the presence of any unemployed resources would, it was clearly understood, mitigate

[41]The sector is also trying to remove the constraints posed by lack of a suitable workforce by providing more training to potential entrants.

the inflationary effect. However, in an open economy imports would rise to meet the increased demand and the inflationary impact might be very limited. We find that after the liberalization of the economy the impact of the deficit on the rate of inflation has been limited. A major factor then is imported inflation either because the international prices of imported goods rise or because the exchange rate depreciates. Under a flexible rate system and liberalized capital flows, the effect of the budget deficit on the economy depends on the extent of the capital inflows. The larger the inflow the smaller is the effect on the exchange rate and on the interest rate. In the extreme, the exchange rate may appreciate and the interest may remain constant.

Deficits and Macro Conditions

Over the past three decades there has been considerable stability in the size of the total deficit of the Central and state governments. Over the same period the position of the Central Government has improved and that of the states has deteriorated (Table 1.6).

Table 1.6: Fiscal Deficits

	Gross			*Primary*			*Revenue*		
PLAN	*Total*	*CG*	*SG*	*Total*	*CG*	*SG*	*Total*	*CG*	*SG*
Sixth Plan	7.19	5.78	1.41	4.77	3.74	1.03	0.63	0.86	–0.23
Seventh Plan	8.88	7.51	1.37	5.22	4.41	0.81	2.67	2.36	0.31
Eighth Plan	7.18	5.62	1.56	2.23	1.45	0.78	3.53	2.52	1.01
Ninth Plan	8.33	5.63	2.70	2.89	1.15	1.74	5.37	3.55	1.82
Tenth Plan	8.44	4.93	3.51	2.22	0.58	1.64	5.14	3.49	1.65

Note: CG: Central Government; SG: state government.

Source: Reserve Bank of India Handbook of Statistics, various issues, Reserve Bank of India, Mumbai.

The pattern of behaviour of the three major definitions of the deficit—gross, primary and revenue—is, however, quite different. The combined gross deficit has been almost constant through this period; the fluctuations have been quite minor. Over the Eighth Plan it was cut back, but soon came back to the old level. The gross deficit of the states has deteriorated almost continuously while that of the

Centre has shown an overall, albeit weak, tendency to decline. The combined primary deficit has declined, implying that the interest burden has gone up for both the Central and state governments. Interest payments by the Central Government have increased more in absolute terms, from about 2 per cent of GDP to over 4 per cent. The percentage increase has been higher for the states as it more than quadrupled from 0.38 per cent of national GDP to almost 2 per cent. The improvement in the primary deficit has obviously prevented a further worsening of the fiscal position. But this also implies a cutback in other expenditures.

What is particularly worrisome about the fiscal position is the worsening revenue deficit, both for the Central Government and the state governments. The worsening revenue deficit while the overall gross deficit is constant implies a declining deficit on the capital account. This would not be troublesome if it was achieved by a larger savings effort. But this is not the case. The budgetary position has been maintained by decreasing investments. This is particularly marked in the case of the Central Government. The deficit on the capital account has decreased from almost 4 per cent of GDP to barely 1.5 per cent.

In the context of the very long term, the macro effects of the budget deficit are unlikely to be significant. The deficit is not likely to lead to a situation of hyperinflation given the strong preference of governments to maintain a low rate of inflation as the voters may exact a high price in the elections. The flexibility of the exchange rate is a protection against an exchange crisis. The major effect of the deficit is, as we reasoned, on investments mainly in infrastructure and in social expenditures on education, health etc. The poor state of the infrastructure, particularly power shortages, has pushed up costs and may be a major reason for the relatively poorer performance of the manufacturing sector in India when we compare it with the performance in China. The lack of investment in education and health undoubtedly limits the increase in human capital with adverse effects on productivity increase.

We thus see no particular macroeconomic problems on the horizon which would lead to a prolonged slowdown of the economy. The high rates of savings and the increased flows of FDI augur well for maintaining a high rate of growth and one based on significant increases in productivity.

References

Agarwal, Manmohan (2008), 'The BRICSAM Countries and Changing World Economic Power: Scenarios to 2050', Working Paper No. 39, October 2008, CIGI, Waterloo, Canada.

——— (1997), 'India', in P. Desai (ed.), *Going Global*, M.I.T. Press, Cambridge, Mass.

Bhagwati, J.N. (1978), *Anatomy and Consequences of Exchange Control Regimes*, Ballinger Publishing Company, Cambridge, Mass.

——— (1993), *India in Transition: Freeing the Economy*, Clarendon Press, Oxford.

Bhagwati, J.N. and S. Chakravarty (1969), 'Contributions to Indian Economic Analysis', *American Economic Review*, Vol. 59, Supplement 5.

Bhagwati, J.N. and P. Desai (1970), *India: Planning for Industrialisation and trade Policies since 1951*, Oxford University Press, New York.

Bhagwati, J.N. and T.N. Srinivasan (1975), *Foreign Trade Regimes and Economic Development: India*, National Bureau of Economic Research.

Bhalla G.S. (2007), 'Agricultural Trade Liberalization in India: A Critical Review', in Manmohan Agarwal and Amit Shovon Ray (eds.), *Globalization and the Millennium Development Goals: Negotiating the Challenge*, Social Science Press, New Delhi.

Bhanoji Rao V.V. (2001), *East Asian Economies: The Miracle, A Crisis and the Future*, McGraw Hill, Singapore.

Bowles, C. (1971), *Promises to Keep: My Years in Public Life, 1941–1969*, Harper and Row, New York.

Bumb, B. (1985), *The World Bank's Lending for Agriculture and Rural Development in India*, Development Strategy Division, World Bank, Washington D.C.

Eldridge, P.J. (1969), *The Politics of Foreign Aid in India*, Weidenfeld and Nicholson, London.

Joshi V. and I.M.D. Little (1994), *India: Macroeconomics and Political Economy: 1961–91*, World Bank, Washington D.C.

Kenen P. (2000) *The International Economy*, Cambridge University Press, New York.

Krueger, A. (1978), *Liberalization Attempts and Consequences*, Ballinger Publishing Company, Cambridge, Mass.

Krugman P. (1994), 'The Myth of Asia's Miracle', *Foreign Affairs*, Nov–Dec, pp. 62–78.

Lele, U. and M. Agarwal (1991), 'Four Decades of Economic Development in India and the Role of External Assistance', in U. Lele and Ijaz Nabi (eds) *Transitions in Development: The Role of Aid and Commercial Flows*, International Center for Economic Growth, Institute for Contemporary Studies Press, San Francisco, 1990.

Little, I.M.D., T. Scitovsky and M. Scott (1970), *Industry and Trade in Some Developing Countries*, Oxford University Press for OECD.

Mahalanobis (1953), 'Some Observations on the Process of Growth of National Income', *Sankhya*, Vol. 12, pp. 302–12.

Mahalanobis (1955), 'The Approach of Operational Research to Planning in India', *Sankhya*, Vol. 16, pp. 3–130.

Panagariya, A. (2008), *India: The Emerging Giant*, Oxford University Press, New York.

Rodrik, D. and A. Subramaniam (2005), 'From "Hindu Growth" to Productivity Surge: The Mystery of the Indian Growth Transition', IMF Staff Papers, Vol. 52, No. 2.

Reserve Bank of India (2008), *Handbook of Indian Statistics*.

World Bank (2007), Development Indicators, World Bank, Washington D.C.

Young A. (1995), 'The Tyranny of Numbers: Confronting the Statistical Realities of the East Asian Growth Miracle', *Quarterly Journal of Economics*, Vol. 110 (August), pp. 641–81.

Chakravarty S. (1977), 'Some Reflections on the Growth Process in Indian Economy' in C.D. Wadhwa (ed.), *Some Problems of Economic Policy*, Tata McGraw Hill, Bombay.

2

Emerging Through Technological Capability
An Overview of India's Technological Trajectory

Amit Shovon Ray

Introduction

India's emergence in the world economy over the last decade, has in the popular discourse, been attributed, at least to a large extent, to its sustained efforts towards technological learning and capacity building. In this chapter we present an overview of India's technological trajectory with a view to understanding the nuances of India's technological capability and the role it has played in the economic progress of the country.

Total factor productivity growth (TFPG) has been accorded prime importance in growth analysis ever since Solow's (1957) pioneering work. This is usually taken to mean significant outward shifts in the technological frontier in the case of developed countries. But for developing countries, dispersion, adaptation and application of existing technologies is considered more important. We next discuss different ways of categorizing technological development in developing countries. One method is that as countries become technologically more adept they progress from 'learning by doing' to 'learning by adapting' to 'learning by design' to 'learning by improved design' and finally 'learning by improved new processes'. However, another way of categorizing development of technological capability is by differentiating know-how which is basically knowledge of production engineering and know-why which creates the capacity to generate new technology. Countries usually combine both approaches but in different mixes. From independence till the 1991 reforms India sought to achieve technological self-reliance by developing its capabilities to generate new technologies and to restrict imports of technology whether through licensing or foreign direct investment (FDI). Much of this effort was concentrated in public sector laboratories. Incentives provided to the private sector were for adopting technologies developed by these laboratories. But there has been a sea-change since the 1991 reforms. Greater reliance has been placed on the private sector for generation of new technology. Tax incentives are given for establishment of special private sector organizations to undertake fundamental research and development (R&D). This would imply that technology generation would be more market driven. There is a new division of labour between the public and private sectors with the latter concentrating on consultancy and other services to bring new technologies into the production stream. Detailed comparisons are undertaken between the chemical and electrical and electronic (E&E) industries and between the pharmaceutical and E&E sectors to point out how the nature of technological change, including spillover effects, differ across industries. The chapter then discusses how changes in the patent regime mirror the changing requirements of technological development in India.

Technological Progress And Economic Growth

For a very long time, economic theory highlighted capital and labour, the two primary factors of production, as the key driving forces behind production and growth. It was only in the 1950s that technological advancement was brought into the discussion of mainstream economic theory as an important source of growth. Solow's (1957) pioneering attempt to estimate the contribution of physical factors to growth, by introducing the technique of growth accounting, revealed that only 1/8th of the growth of the US economy during the first half of the present century could be explained by the growth of its endowments of physical factors, leaving the remaining to a 'residual' (termed as technical progress or TFPG). Focus shifted thereafter from physical factors to the role of technology in production and growth. It is fairly well-established now that technological advancement resulting from R&D is the most important factor behind today's productivity growth.

Indeed, the growth experience of most advanced industrial nations has been driven by TFPG than by growth in factor endowments. For these nations, operating essentially on the frontiers of global technology, TFPG necessarily implies an outward shift of the technological frontier. Of course, the contribution of TFPG to economic growth has not been uniform across all industrialized nations. Hayami (1999), for instance, compared the sources of growth in Japan and the USA during their respective high growth periods (1958–70 for Japan and 1929–66 for the USA) and found, not surprisingly, that Japan's growth was attributable to both capital input growth as well as technical progress as opposed to the US experience of predominantly technology driven growth—the TFP contribution being 53 per cent for Japan and 80 per cent for the USA.

Even for the late industrializing countries in East Asia (the so-called East Asian Tigers: South Korea, Hong Kong, Singapore and Taiwan), the contribution of TFP has been observed to be much more moderate than the US experience. According to the World Bank (WB) (1993), approximately two-thirds of the growth observed in these economies may be attributed to the accumulation of physical and human capital and the rest to TFPG. This is not to deny that productivity growth *did* play a very important role in East Asian success, but it was clearly not the sole (or even the dominant) factor.

However, equating productivity growth with technological progress *a la* Solow (1957) can be somewhat problematic in understanding the growth successes of developing nations. Not all productivity growth is derived from 'pure' technological advancement. Rather, a large part of productivity growth may arise out of improvements in the labour force and human capital accumulation; thus, leading to high levels of cognitive skills of the labour force that permit better firm-level adoption, adaptation and mastery of 'given' technologies. In fact, Young (1995) made an exemplary attempt to control for all changes in inputs, including improvement of the labour force as well as sustained capital accumulation, and found that the residual TFP contribution to the growth of the East Asian Tigers between 1966–90 was abysmally low. It was 2.3 per cent in Hong Kong, 2.1 per cent in Taiwan, 1.7 per cent in South Korea and 0.2 per cent in Singapore. Hence, 'technological improvement' in the neoclassical sense was perhaps not *that* important in facilitating the East Asian Miracle.

Beyond Neoclassical Perspectives: Technological Capability of LDCs

In the neoclassical theoretical tradition, technological progress is identified with major breakthroughs in science and technology resulting in a shift of the frontier.[1] As a result, the important contributions to technical progress made in diffusion, adaptation and application of new technologies, which are particularly important in the context of less developed countries (LDCs), have remained underemphasized. However, the evolutionary models of technological progress (Nelson and Winter 1982; Mowery and Rosenberg 1989) are perhaps the only theoretical constructs that consider 'minor', as opposed to 'major', innovations to be the more likely and more conventional research output of any R&D programme. These models have a broader perspective on technology defined as a set of linked capabilities based on different types of knowledge: formal and informal (that is, tacit or experimental). Indeed, the evolutionary models' characterization of technical change as a 'tacit', 'path-dependent' and 'non-linear' movement makes technological progress similar to the process of technological catch-up commonly observed in many LDCs.

Lall (1987) observed that:

> considering technological progress only as a movement of the frontier is a highly simplified neo-classical view because 'major technological innovations' are not the only, perhaps not even the main, source of productivity improvement in the history of industrial development...and...minor changes to given technologies—to equipment, materials, processes and designs—are vital and continuous source of productivity gain in practically every industry.

[1]See, for instance Schumpeter (1934, 1939). Note that Rosenberg (1976) has strongly criticized the Schumpeterian usage of the term 'innovation' on four grounds: '(1) We confine our thinking about innovations to characteristics which are likely to be true only of major innovations, (2) we focus disproportionately upon discontinuities and neglect continuities in the innovative process, (3) we attach excessive importance to the role of scientific knowledge and insufficient importance to engineering and other "lower" forms of knowledge, and (4) we attach excessive significance to early stages in the process of invention and neglect the crucial later stages.'

Therefore, one can argue in line with Bell (1984) that technological effort should ideally be viewed as 'conscious use of technological information and the accumulation of technological knowledge, together with other resources, to choose, assimilate and adapt existing technology and/or to create new technology'. This is what reflects the technological capability of an LDC, defined as the capacity to select, absorb, assimilate, adapt, imitate and perhaps improve given (imported) technologies. Several case studies (country level, industry level and firm level) confirm that the creation of such indigenous technological capabilities requires conscious technological effort and risky investments in R&D.

Accordingly, one must broaden the definition of technological output in the context of a so-called research production function of an LDC. The R&D units in LDCs need not come up with very different products or processes but may still be acknowledged as innovators, albeit of minor rather than major innovations. The distinction between minor and major innovations proves to be extremely important in understanding technological progress in developing countries.[2]

The stages of technological capability acquisition can be described as a process of path dependent evolution.[3] This process begins with learning by doing followed by learning by adapting, aiming at augmenting productivity through efficient utilization and adaptation of technologies at the shop floor. We call this the stage of production engineering. Next comes learning by design and learning by improved design, aiming at replicating processes and designs for better understanding and further improvement of given technologies. This stage is described as Reverse Engineering (RE). All this culminates into learning by setting up complete production systems and learning by designing new processes which ultimately sets the stage for basic (frontier) R&D capabilities.

Following Lall (1985), it is useful to categorize technological capability as know-how and know-why. Know-how is acquired through 'not only the assimilation of imported techniques (which itself can be a lengthy and active learning process) but also quality control

[2]Indeed, instead of recognizing the key role played by the capability to invent around (minor innovations), the rise in competitiveness of Japanese industries in the mid-1960s was initially wrongly attributed to low labour cost advantage (along the lines of the product cycle paradigm) (see Rosenberg and Steinmuller 1988).

[3]Lall (1978).

(which also involves active technical effort), improved plant layout and production practices, slight modifications to equipment and tooling, troubleshooting, the use of different raw materials and so on',[4] all of which can be summarized as production engineering. Know-why is the next stage of technological development, which involves the understanding of the nature of the process and product technologies leading to the development of new improved designs. Applied research and frontier R&D, leading to major innovations, follow this stage.

Broadly speaking, know-how is expected to bring about rapid and immediate productivity growth in LDCs. Know-why, on the other hand, is absolutely necessary (but by no means sufficient) to create and strengthen the technological foundation of LDCs. Without going through this phase of know-why oriented technological learning, LDCs can never aspire to reach the global technology frontier to catch up with the levels of technological advancement of developed countries in the long run. However, there may not be any immediate pay-off of know-why oriented technological effort in terms of immediate productivity gains in the short and medium terms.

What then are the technological options available to LDCs? In very broad and simple terms, there are two alternatives, which are not necessarily mutually exclusive:

One, bring in the latest imported technology (exploit the global frontier) and focus on know-how to reap maximum productivity gains. Two, concentrate on know-why and applied research to create capabilities to generate new technology and attempt to catch up with the advanced nations on their own footing.

Historically, LDCs have usually opted for different combinations of the above alternatives, depending on their initial conditions and policy focus. Accordingly, we may find inter-country variations in the levels of technological capability acquired by LDCs. Evenson and Johnson (1998) have classified developing countries into six levels of technological capability. Countries belonging to the lowest three levels of technological capability generally do not undertake any R&D work. Though a little bit of R&D work is visible in the third level, it is mostly directed towards pirating of trademarks and

[4]Lall (1985), p. 116.

design. In these three levels, production technology is essentially purchased in an 'inter-linked' contractual form. In the fourth and fifth levels of technological capability, the dominant objective of firm-level R&D is to facilitate technology purchase, directly (licencing) or indirectly. Here the role of R&D is to create absorptive capacity to understand, adapt and implement the purchased technology successfully. Some adaptive invention is undertaken, usually stimulated by domestic intellectual property rights (IPR). The technological competence developed through R&D in these countries is instrumental in initiating activities of RE or imitation. In the sixth level of technological infrastructure, imitation is generally taken up as a conscious policy of technology generation through a more structured 'buy-then-imitate' strategy. According to this classification by Evenson and Johnson (1998), India falls into the fifth level of technological capability while Korea belongs to the sixth level.

India's Technology Policy Framework

India is among the very few LDCs that have pursued a well-articulated technology policy providing the broad guidelines for technological development within the country.[5] India's technology policies included both direct policies for indigenous technological development as well as indirect policies for restricting and regulating technology imports and technology transfer. The first *Scientific Policy Resolution* was published as early as 1958 and the latest *Technology Policy Statement* appeared in 2003. Over this fifty-year period, there has been a major shift in India's policy stance towards technology development, roughly coinciding with the economic reforms and trade liberalization in the 1990s. Accordingly, India's technology policy environment has been distinctly different in the pre- and post-reforms period.

Technology Policy in the Pre-reforms Period (pre-1991)

The basic objective of India's post-independence technology policy was 'the development of indigenous technology and efficient

[5]This section draws heavily on my earlier paper, Ray (2004).

absorption and adaptation of imported technology appropriate to national priorities and resources'.[6] Attainment of technological competence and self-reliance was placed at the heart of India's technological development. The aim was to achieve breakthroughs in indigenous technological development 'appropriate to national priorities and resources' (that is, maximum utilization of human resources, efficient use of energy, increasing productivity and maintenance of ecological balance).

In fact, prior to 1990, the Indian economy operated within the broad framework of an inward-looking policy regime of protection and interventions. Restrictions and regulations on trade and industrial production were pervasive. Against this backdrop of overall policy framework, the main focus of India's technology policy was not only to build up *search*, *selection*, *implementation* and *absorptive* capability, but also to acquire technological capabilities of adaptation and minor innovation through RE.

Considerable resources were allocated for this purpose. Indeed, India's share of national R&D expenditure in gross national product (GNP) increased steadily from 0.17 per cent in 1958–59 to 0.98 per cent in 1987–88, the major part being borne by the government.[7] The overwhelming majority of government R&D expenditure was allocated to various public sector research laboratories, under the auspices of the Council of Scientific and Industrial Research (CSIR), engaged in applied research in a wide range of fields including aeronautics, experimental medicine, environment, oceanography and structural engineering.

Apart from spending on R&D, the government also offered specific R&D incentives with the objective of building up domestic technological capability for rapid industrialization. Prior to the 1990s, the main thrust of the R&D incentives was to generate indigenous technologies primarily in the institutional sector (public-funded R&D institutions) and facilitate effective commercialization, transfer and absorption of such technologies in the industrial sector. There were very few incentives at the firm level with the explicit aim of augmenting technology-creating capabilities. In-house R&D

[6] *Technology Policy Statement of 1983*, Government of India (1983), p. 3.

[7] Even as late as 1998–99, 75.5 per cent of the national R&D expenditure in India was borne by the government.

was encouraged only to facilitate acquisition of technological capabilities of absorption, adaptation and assimilation. Special incentives were given to firms using indigenous technologies developed by R&D institutions.

Apart from these direct policies to promote indigenous technology development, the government also adopted indirect policies for restricting and regulating technology imports and technology transfer. Till 1991, import substitution and technological self-reliance constituted the core of India's technology policy, which was in line with its inward looking overall policy regime. Import of technologies in the form of licencing as well as FDI was severely restricted in order to promote indigenous technology. The importer of a technology had to obtain a clearance from the appropriate government authorities after a thorough screening to make sure that there were no objections on grounds of high cost, 'inappropriateness', availability of local substitutes or even the long-term building up of indigenous R&D capability. The onus lay on the prospective importer to show that the technology was necessary (in terms of Plan priorities), not available locally and fairly priced (Lall 1984).

Another indirect policy instrument has been the IPR Regime adopted by India. The Patent Act of 1970 promoted considerable technological learning and acquisition of technological capability through RE activities. This issue of IPR as a determinant of technological development will be discussed at length in a subsequent section.

Thus, India's technology policy in the pre-reforms era was essentially based on building up national level capabilities through public institutions. At the same time the industry (private and public sector) was encouraged to actively engage in R&D activities to develop absorptive and adaptive capabilities of minor innovations.

Technology Policy in the Post-reforms Era (post-1991)

The decade of the 1990s started with the ongoing thrust of integrating the Indian economy with the global economy in the General Agreement on Tariffs and Trade–World Trade Organization (GATT–WTO) framework. From 1991, with the liberalization of the Indian economy, the restrictions on imports, FDI and technology transfer have been progressively removed. The technology policy also had to be moderated, and attuned to meet the new challenges of global competition.

In fact, the *Science and Technology (S&T) Policy 2003* of the Government of India states that:

> It is recognised that these objectives will be best realised by a dynamic and flexible Science and Technology Policy, which can readily adapt to the rapidly changing world order. This policy, reiterates India's commitment to participate as an equal and vigorous global player. ...

The decade of the 1990s saw a departure in the sense that the government attempted to distinguish between fundamental R&D and commercial R&D, both in the private R&D units. It encouraged the creation of the so-called Scientific and Industrial Research Organizations (SIRO) in the private sector for undertaking more fundamental R&D in a non-commercial manner. Such private sector R&D institutions might have existed earlier, but in the late 1980s, they were given renewed attention and emphasis under the new name of SIRO.

One contrasting feature is the shift in focus from national R&D institutions to R&D carried out by the industry either through in-house R&D units or in the SIROs. Industry captured the lion's share of the incentives provided in the 1990s compared to the earlier decade, when the majority of the incentives were directed towards the public R&D institutions. Indeed, post-1991, the thrust of R&D incentives showed a clear shift away from the institutional sector towards the industrial sector. In the post-reforms period, with a market-driven (profit maximizing) framework, industrial productivity and technological capability have perhaps been accorded priority over indigenization (import substitution) of technology and self-reliance. There has also been a move to encourage collaborative R&D between industry and R&D laboratories.

The nature of some of the *non-fiscal incentives* also underwent significant changes in the 1990s, especially with the introduction of the new Patent Act of 2005 (to be discussed later in the paper).

Table 2.1 presents a summary of R&D incentives in India in the 1980s and the 1990s. We notice a clear shift in the structure of R&D incentives and its underlying guiding principles over the period under study.

Table 2.1: A Summary of R&D Incentives in India

Incentives in the 1980s		*Incentives in the 1990s*	
To Promote Institutional R&D	*To Promote In-house R&D in Industry*	*To Promote Institutional R&D*	*To Promote In-house R&D in Industry and SIROs*
• Customs duty exemption • Depreciation allowance* • Investment allowance* • Weighted tax deduction*	• Income tax benefits (100 per cent tax deduction)	• Duty free imports • Depreciation allowance*	• Income tax deduction • Weighted tax deduction on sponsored research • Tax holiday • Excise duty exemption • Weighted tax deduction, industry specific • Customs duty exemption to SIROs • Excise duty exemption on purchases made by SIROs • Income tax exemption for donation to SIROs • Excise and customs duty benefits to biotech and pharmaceutical companies
* granted to firms for using and commercializing technologies developed by institutes		* granted to firms for commercializing technology developed by institutes	

Source: Ray (2004).

India's Trajectory of Technological Capability Acquisition

Against this backdrop of a well-articulated technology policy over the last fifty years, India's share of national R&D expenditure in GNP had increased steadily from 0.17 per cent in 1958–59 to 0.91 per cent in 1988–89. Thereafter it started declining, reaching a low of 0.71 per cent in 1995–96 and finally it has settled around 0.8 per cent as per the latest available information.[8] This is rather alarming, especially in the context of the new economic policy regime of reforms and globalization. In spite of a clear mandate of the S&T Policy of 2003 to strengthen India's in-house industrial R&D in the post-liberalization period by raising the above share to at least 2 per cent of India's GNP by the end of the Tenth Plan, India has not been able to reach even the 1 per cent target. It is worth noting that among the newly industrialized Asian countries, South Korea spends as much as 2.8 per cent of its GNP on R&D, which is at par with industrialized nations such as US, Japan, UK and Germany.

The government's R&D expenditure takes two forms: institutional R&D in Central and state government laboratories and industrial, in-house R&D in public sector enterprises, accounting for 62.6 per cent, 8.5 per cent and 4.5 per cent of total (national) R&D expenditure, respectively. There is a small portion (4.1 per cent) going to higher education, bringing the total share of the government in India's R&D expenditure to 79.7 per cent. The share of private sector R&D remains at around 20 per cent. Industrial R&D (public + private sector) constitutes only 24.8 per cent of total R&D.[9] This share is remarkably low compared to some of the East Asian countries, for example, Singapore (60 per cent in 1992), Korea (around 80 per cent in 1992) and Taiwan (50 per cent in 1993).

Technological Achievements: Outputs and Expenditure in the Institutional and Industrial Sectors

India's post-independence, inward looking policy regime did manage to generate a considerable amount of technological effort and development. To understand the trajectory of technological learning and technological capability acquisition, let us first take a quick look at the technological achievements in terms of R&D output. As already noted, the public sector (institutional R&D) played the dominant role, especially during the pre-reforms period (pre-1990). In this phase, much of the technological effort went into creating technologies first time in the country rather than breakthroughs first time in the world and that too predominantly in the public sector

[8]R&D Statistics, Department of Science and Technology, Government of India.

[9]See R&D Statistics 2004–05, Department of Science and Technology, Government of India.

institutions.[10] This is perhaps expected as it conformed to the broad objective of creating technological self-reliance in the pre-reforms period. However, it is doubtful whether the effort of the public research laboratories has had 'much impact on technological development in large scale organized industry, though it claims to have provided hundreds of technologies for use to small scale enterprises'.[11] More importantly, it is doubtful how efficient these indigenously developed 'new' technologies were according to international standards of costs and quality.

As far as in-house industrial R&D is concerned, this import-substituting policy regime typically fostered several conditions—no direct need to keep up with the global frontiers of technology, small size of operations, various input scarcities and lack of adequate competitive pressures with respect to cost and quality—all of which dampened the effort to build up sustained technological capability at the frontier. The absence of competition in any of the three key dimensions (domestic or internal competition, import competition and export rivalry) encouraged conservative technological behaviour on the part of the Indian firms preventing technological upgrading, let alone major innovations and breakthroughs. Moreover, restrictions on technology imports resulted in failure to promote effective transfer and absorption (know-how) of latest global technologies. Although, many Indian firms did manage to assimilate a lot of basic technology and even improve upon it, they remained far behind the global frontiers of technology.

We have already seen that fiscal incentives for R&D have taken a new turn in the era of globalization with the focus shifting from institutional to industrial R&D. Ray (2004) takes a closer look at the profile and composition of R&D expenditure and outputs in terms of institutional versus industrial R&D over the period 1986–2000 and attempts to relate this with the structural changes in incentives.

The Department of Science and Technology (DST) identifies various technological outputs and publishes the same in its biennial R&D Statistics volumes. We have categorized these outputs in two groups: Type-1 output includes R&D outcomes like patents, product

[10]In the very few cases where 'pioneering' technologies were created, typically Indianized raw materials were used, for example, Amul Spray, a baby food technology from buffalo milk.

[11]Lall (1984), p. 233.

Table 2.2: Type-1 and Type-2 Outputs by Institutes and Industry

Year	*Institute Type-1*	*Institute Type-2*	*Industry Type-1*	*Industry Type-2*	*Ratio Inst.: Indy Type-1*	*Ratio Inst.: Indy Type-2*	*Ratio Type1: Type2 Industry*	*Ratio Type1: Type2 Institute*
1987	951	42,083	16,273	5916	0.06	7.11	2.75	0.02
1991	3670	23,527	13,430	5609	0.27	4.19	2.39	0.16
1993	2111	29,778	11,933	8342	0.18	3.57	1.43	0.07
1995	1335	22,290	9687	4283	0.14	5.20	2.26	0.06
1997	2172	70,849	13,783	10,690	0.16	6.63	1.29	0.03

Source: Ray (2004).

development, process development, development of new designs and import substitutes, which directly *augment firm-level productivity and profitability*. Type-2 output consists of R&D outputs like consultancy services rendered and publication of books, papers and reports, which reflect technological capability through augmenting the knowledge base, but do not directly enter the firm's production function, at least, in the short run. Table 2.2 shows the profile of R&D output.

While the institutional sector places greater emphasis on type-2 output, industry puts more emphasis on type-1 output. The industry is more concerned with type-1 output for immediate gains in profitability and productivity. But the institutional sector during the 1980s perhaps followed a social mandate of enriching the public domain of R&D knowledge by producing and disseminating type-2 output. The situation has changed somewhat in the last decade. We find that industry's share of type-2 output in total R&D output is

Table 2.3: Share of Import Substitutes in Type-1 Output

Year	*R&D Institute*	*Industry*
1987	0.81	0.22
1991	0.21	0.25
1993	0.40	0.24
1995	0.26	0.34
1997	0.39	0.24

Source: R&D Statistics, DST (various years).

increasing. This increase can be attributed to the changes in the R&D incentive structure, which does not intend to portray the public sector R&D institutes as the sole source of indigenous technologies and knowledge-base. In the changed scenario, industry has to appreciate the complementarities between the two types of R&D outputs—instant productivity gains through type-1 and augmenting knowledge base through type-2.

One interesting finding relates to the relative importance of import substitutes developed by the institutional and industrial sectors (as revealed in Table 2.3). The share of import substitutes in type-1 output produced by the institutional sector declined from around 0.81 per cent in the 1980s to around 0.3–0.4 per cent in the 1990s. The industry has, however, maintained its share of import substitutes (with perhaps a marginal increase) in type-1 output at 0.2 per cent. Note that the decade of the 1980s had a clear mandate to develop import substitutes in both sectors which was removed in the 1990s. We, however, conclude that the scope of cost effective import substitution by industry, especially in a profit-maximizing framework, continues even with globalization and economic reforms.

A comparison of aggregate nominal R&D expenditure also reveals some interesting turnarounds (Table 2.4). While every sector has witnessed growth in the nominal R&D expenditure, their growth rates are far from uniform. Moreover, there is also evidence of contrasting growth rates of a particular sector during the two sub-periods under consideration. Overall during the entire period, the growth rate of the private sector R&D expenditure has been the highest followed by the growth of the state, Central and public sectors.

However, as shown in Table 2.4, during the 1980s, the state sector witnessed the highest rate of increase in R&D expenditure followed by the private sector, public sector and central institutes. The decade

Table 2.4: Rate of Increase in Nominal R&D Expenditure

	Central	*State*	*Inst–Agg*	*Public*	*Private*	*Ind–Agg*
Inc 86–98	2.95	5.24	3.12	1.76	7.35	4.75
Inc 90–98	2.05	1.81	2.02	0.57	3.30	2.09
Inc 86–90	0.30	1.22	0.37	0.76	0.94	0.86

Notes: (1) Inc 86–90=(R&D1990–R&D1986)/R&D1986; (2) Inc 90–98 = (R&D1998–R&D 1990)/R&D1990; Inc: rate of increase.
Source: R&D Statistics, DST (various years).

of 1990s saw a reversal in this trend. The private sector emerged as the fastest growing sector, followed by the Central R&D institutes. The rate of increase of public sector R&D expenditure fell from 0.75 per cent in the 1980s to 0.57 per cent in the 1990s. This picture seems to be compatible with the overall decline in policy attention towards public sector enterprises. On the other hand, co-operative R&D between the private sector and Central R&D institutes seems to have taken off, resulting in high growth rates of R&D expenditure in both the sectors. State sector growth rate also increased marginally.

The impact of structural change in the R&D incentive structure is also visible in the pattern of the R&D expenditure by different sectors. The relative share of R&D expenditure by the institutional sector has been declining steadily. Indeed, the government R&D expenditure (especially in the state sector) witnessed high growth in the decade of 1980s, while the private sector R&D expenditure achieved the highest growth rate in the 1990s, perhaps due to the positive encouragement offered in the new R&D incentive regime. It also appears that Central R&D institutes may have performed better than the state institutes in the decade of 1990s due to better inflow of sponsored research, which has been a key feature of the R&D incentive structure in the 1990s.

Total Factor Productivity Growth in Indian Industry

Against the backdrop of India's technological effort as described above, we now explore its experience with TFPG. There have been several attempts to measure TFPG in Indian industry for different time periods. Ahluwalia (1991) summarizes the results pertaining to the period up to the mid-1980s. Long-term TFPG in this period was negligible. Later studies extended the period and came up with similar pessimistic conclusions. Balakrishnan and Puspangadan (1994), for instance, found TFPG to be 0.33 during the period 1970–71 to 1988–89. Unfortunately, most of these estimates relate to TFPG at the aggregate industry level.

In a study undertaken for the DST, Government of India, we attempted a more disaggregated analysis at the level of 29-industry classification.[12] Using a panel of 29 industries over the period 1975–76 to 1994–95, we estimated the following robust random effects model of the Cobb-Douglas production function corrected for multi-

[12]Ray et al. (1999), Ray and Bhaduri (2002).

collinearity (using the ratio form) after confirming the hypothesis of constant returns to scale:

$$\text{Log } (Q/L)_{it} = \alpha + \beta \text{ Log } (K/L)_{it} + \lambda t + v_i + u_{it}$$

The estimated values of the coefficients are: $\alpha = -5.48$, $\beta = 0.26$, $\lambda = 0.024$, all statistically significant at the 1 per cent level. Our estimation thus revealed an overall TFPG of 0.024 (2.4 per cent) during this period. However, we also noticed substantial variation of TFPG across industries and over time and sought to explain this variation in terms of R&D effort by estimating a panel model of the following form:

$$\text{TFPG}_{it} = a + b\,\text{RD}_{it} + \gamma t + v_i + u_{it}$$

R&D came up as a significant determinant of TFPG. The time variable appears negative and significant over this entire period. This is indeed alarming. But we intended to explore whether this reflects a secular decline in TFP throughout the period or if there been any structural break in the growth of TFP. To this end we used time dummy for each year beginning 1978 to estimate the following models:

$$\text{TFPG}_{it} = a + b\,\text{RD}_{it} + \gamma t + \delta\, t^{*}d + v_i + u_{it}$$

where d=0 if t<x; 1 otherwise. This is to identify possible structural breaks at year x. We find a distinct structural break in the growth of TFP in 1982. After a long period of decline and stagnation, productivity in Indian industry displayed an upward movement. This break coincided with a similar break identified by Ahluwalia (1991) in a Cobb-Douglas production function estimation of the Indian industry.

More importantly, we also observed wide variations in the TFPG experience of different industries in our 29 classification structure. Only 8 out of 29 industries recorded positive TFPG. Among these, E&E achieved a phenomenal 137 per cent growth in TFP during this period. TFPG in fertilizer and telecom sectors was 73 per cent and 50 per cent, respectively. Sugar and fermentation industries displayed moderate TFPG of around 30 per cent. It may be worth noting that almost all sectors constituting the chemical industry experienced negative TFPG with the exception of fertilizers. Interestingly, in the three sectors registering the highest TFPG (E&E, fertilizers and telecom), the contribution of the public sector in total R&D expenditure is fairly high (43 per cent, 82 per cent and 69 per cent, respectively).

We then took a closer look at two of the sectors reported above, namely, chemicals (including pharmaceuticals) and E&E. We selected these two sectors as they are two of the most R&D intensive sectors in India as composite groups, but have had divergent experience in TFPG during this period. The E&E experienced a consistently high growth in TFP, which contributed to 96 per cent of the output growth of this sector. The chemical sector, on the other hand, had a negative and declining TFPG. Output growth in chemicals has, therefore, been primarily factor driven and is observed to be generally lower than that of E&E.

Posing the findings on India's TFPG experience in these two sectors against the Krugman thesis,[13] one may be *tempted* to conclude that the technological experience of the E&E sector has been ideal for sustained growth while the technological effort in chemicals has not been that successful in India. But this completely contradicts the results that we obtained from our estimation of production functions for these two sectors with R&D as a third factor of production (apart from labour and capital). R&D appeared to be a significant third input in the production of chemicals but not in the E&E sector. This is perhaps due to the fact that in the E&E industry technology is largely embodied in capital equipment and is, therefore, not significant as a separate input in the production process. This is not the case in chemicals, where technology (R&D) is mainly disembodied and acts as a distinct third input. Indeed, the chemical industry, by its very nature, requires substantial adaptation and modification for making the product/process suitable to local conditions (taste, temperature, climate etc.), which calls for a deeper understanding of the underlying technological process. By contrast, the E&E sector in India is characterized by the so-called 'screw-driver' technology. Accordingly its technological effort is primarily geared towards better implementation of given technologies with little or no modification/adaptation in order to achieve a greater degree of operational efficiency.

Clearly then, the process of technological capability acquisition and the trajectories of technological learning have been very different

[13]The so-called Krugman (1994) thesis on *the myth of Asia's miracle* suggests that the East Asian growth experience is bound to slow down as it has been fuelled essentially by mobilizing resources (capital) rather than through productivity growth and efficiency gains.

in these two sectors. It is hardly surprising that each sector will follow its own distinct learning trajectory and generate distinct patterns of capability and technological advantages.

Technological Learning in Indian Industry: Pharmaceutical versus Electronics Sector

As discussed in the section titled 'Beyond Neoclassical Perspectives: Technological Capability of LDCs', the literature on technology in LDCs—pioneered by Nelson, Katz, Lall, Bell and others—recognized two principal characteristics of technological activities in LDCs. First, their R&D effort is geared towards minor as opposed to major innovations. Second, technological learning, in some form or the other, constitutes an integral part of their research thrust. In an earlier paper (Ray and Bhaduri 2001), we examined the process of technology generation and learning in Indian industry by estimating a comprehensive research production function incorporating the role of learning, using Indian firm-level data for the pharmaceutical and electronics sectors.[14]

There has been little explicit theorization of the role of learning in the research production process. Arrow (1962) is perhaps the only theoretical construct that introduces the concept of learning by doing in the neoclassical theoretical literature, but 'there is little discussion even in that article regarding the nature of the process involved'.[15] In the context of developing countries, Bell (1984) distinguished between two dimensions of the learning process: (i) 'doing based' learning and (ii) 'learning by training' or 'learning by hiring' or 'learning by searching' or 'spillover'. Both types of learning are equally important in the research production process in an LDC. Learning by doing, for instance, may not result in a research outcome which is altogether new (a major innovation), but it certainly contributes to the acquisition of technological capability (absorptive, adaptive) and the consequent minor changes or *inventing around*, which are crucially important in LDCs. We also expect that firms with longer experience will spend more on R&D. The justification comes from an evolutionary framework, where firms, which are

[14]Such exercises have produced rich and useful results for developed industrialized nations. See Kamien and Schwartz (1975) and Cohen and Levin (1989) for comprehensive surveys of this empirical literature.

[15]Nelson (1987), p. 81.

successful in research, continue with their research activity and enlarge their R&D outfit. Learning through experience also raises the efficiency with which R&D inputs are converted into outputs. It thus has a positive impact on the *amount* of technological output by raising the marginal productivity of R&D inputs.[16] We, therefore, expect that *ceteris paribus* firms with a longer history of learning (or with more experience) would produce greater research output.

With regard to the role of learning through spillover, the neoclassical literature is less precise as it assumes instantaneous diffusion.[17] However, later developments have recognized diffusion as a complex process requiring explicit effort and investment.[18] This is true even for acquiring knowledge freely available in the public domain. Spillovers would then enter the research production process in a significant manner. They would augment technological output in the same manner as learning by doing, but their impact on research effort would be less obvious. We define two distinct sources of spillover: national and international, both of which could act as important inputs in the research production function.[19]

The econometric results obtained by Ray and Bhaduri (2001) presented new and interesting insights into the process of technology generation and learning in the Indian pharmaceutical and electronics sectors. We made a clear distinction between R&D inputs and R&D outputs in a research production function framework to understand the process of technology generation. We found that the conventional determinants of R&D such as firm-size, technology import or ownership, appeared significant in explaining R&D effort only in line with existing empirical studies. However, when we sought to explain the variations in research output, none of these factors, not even research effort on its own, appeared to be statistically significant. Here, in fact, learning, both

[16]This is in line with the time–cost trade-off analysis by Scherer (1967) showing that curtailment of the learning period makes the research production process less efficient by reducing the scope of trial and error.

[17]If at all, spillover was believed to have an adverse effect on the incentive to innovate. See Spence (1984).

[18]See, for instance, Cohen and Levinthal (1989).

[19]The theoretical literature is less precise about the pattern of both types of learning (through experience or through spillovers). It is evident from several empirical studies (Katz 1987 for Latin American firms, Lall 1984 for Indian firms and Jomo, Felkar and Rasiah 1999 for Malaysian firms) that the learning pattern and its importance vary across industries as well as according to the ownership structure.

experience-based as well as interaction (or spillover) based, proved to be the only important determinant of the research production process. According to Ray and Bhaduri (2001), therefore, technological learning has been the most important determinant of technology generation in the Indian industry.

First of all, learning through interaction (spillover) proved to be important in the research production process for both sectors. The effect of spillover on research output appeared to be non-linear. In both industries there was evidence of an optimum level of spillover (national as well as international).

Learning through experience also entered the research production function for both sectors, although the way in which it augments research output differs across the two industries. In the pharmaceutical sector, it entered interactively with research effort, implying that firms with older R&D outfits spend on R&D more efficiently. In other words, experience based learning augments the efficiency of R&D effort in the pharmaceutical sector, which is mainly reverse engineering (through trial and error). Research experience helps the firm to decode the technology faster, reducing its cost of trial and error and thereby making its R&D effort more efficient. In the electronics sector, on the other hand, learning through experience entered the production function as an independent input. Given that the electronics industry in India is driven by the so-called 'screw-driver' technology, simple, experience-based knowledge (of assembling) proves to be important in the R&D process.

Indeed, the two sectors have followed two distinct trajectories of technological learning, resulting in different kinds of technological capability generation. In the electronics industry in India, assembly operations, production engineering, shop-floor practices and quality control could prove to be the key elements of technological effort. In-depth technological learning of product designs and processes have perhaps been less important for electronics firms in India. Their technological effort lay primarily in gaining operational efficiency and productivity augmentation through shop-floor practices, day-to-day trouble shooting and customer servicing. Hence, it is know-how rather than know-why that best describes the learning trajectory of the electronics industry in the country.

The pharmaceutical industry, on the other hand, followed a rather different trajectory of technological learning based on reverse engineering.[20] This essentially implies decoding an original process for producing a bulk drug. It involves a detailed understanding of the chemical properties of the active molecule, the excipients used and the chemical process of conversion from the active molecular compound to the final bulk drug. A chemical process incorporates a complex set of parameters, for example, solvent conditions, temperature, time, stirring methods, use of various chemical and physical substances with different levels of purity etc., all of which have to be simultaneously optimized in order to arrive at the optimum process specification. It is possible to decode all the parametric specifications of a process through reverse engineering.

Indeed, beginning in the 1970s, the industry acquired substantial technological capability of process development through reverse engineering, both infringing processes for off-patented molecules and non-infringing processes for patented molecules. This phenomenon has been often been referred to as the *process revolution in the Indian pharmaceutical sector.*

Effectively then, the learning process has been largely know-why oriented in the pharmaceutical sector, while in electronics, it has perhaps been simpler and more know-how oriented. We may expect a significant role of formal R&D in the learning process of the former. Learning in electronics, on the other hand, is likely to be less dependent on formal R&D;[21] it is more learning by doing and learning through experience.

Exporting through Technological Capability

India's technological effort has been primarily directed towards creating assimilative and adaptive capacities rather than generating new technologies.[22] Although some technology generation took place at the institutional level, India remained far behind the global frontiers of technology in most industrial areas. The inward looking, protectionist policy environment till 1990 further bolstered India's inability to use the latest developments in global technologies though liberal and unrestricted imports. As a result, notwithstanding its

[20] Ray (2005).

[21] The results of the estimated production functions with R&D as the third input for the two sectors reported above vindicate this hypothesis.

[22] This subsection draws heavily on an earlier work: Bhaduri and Ray (2004).

impressive track record of technological learning, India continued to be 'technologically backward' throughout most of the five decades post-independence. According to the conventional product-cycle or technology-gap paradigms of international trade, therefore, the technology factor is unlikely to be a key determinant of India's comparative advantage and export competitiveness. In a recent paper (Bhaduri and Ray 2004), we have, however, argued that India does enjoy technological advantages in exporting, but these advantages rest on a very different foundation—technological capability as opposed to major technological advancements or breakthroughs.

To explain India's technological advantages in exporting, we again refer to the distinction between know-how and know-why capabilities. Know-how is acquired through 'not only the assimilation of imported techniques (which itself can be a lengthy and active learning process) but also quality control (which also involves active technical effort), improved plant layout and production practices, slight modifications to equipment and tooling, troubleshooting, the use of different raw materials and so on',[23] all of which can be summarized as production engineering. Hence, know-how oriented technological effort leads to greater production efficiency and, therefore, reduced marginal costs. Know-why is the next stage in technological development, which involves understanding the nature of the process and product technologies, ultimately, leading to the development of new improved processes and designs. Clearly, the reduction of marginal cost may not be the overriding (or even an important) consideration for such know-why oriented technological activities, at least initially.

In explaining the technological advantages for export success in LDCs, it is know-how rather than know-why, which has been highlighted in the literature as the key determinant. It is generally argued that know-how oriented technological learning (production engineering) enhances firm-level competitive advantage by augmenting production efficiency. On the other hand, technology creating know-why capabilities (reverse engineering) may actually reduce export competitiveness since reverse engineered processes and designs do not usually lead to greater production- and cost-efficiency, at least in the short run.

[23]Lall (1985), p. 116.

However, sustained effort towards know-why activities may eventually lead to technology creating capabilities to *invent around* cost-effective processes or designs.[24] This could then provide a major fillip to the LDC firms' competitive edge in the long run and prove to be a key determinant of their export success. Indeed, the international competitive strength of Japan's automobile industry and Korea's semi-conductor industry was hidden in their capability to invent around, which evolved from conscious long-term research effort on creating know-why capabilities.[25]

According to this conceptual framework, therefore, both know-how and know-why would act as important determinants of comparative advantage of LDCs. However, the relative importance of these two forces will perhaps vary across industries depending on their technological characteristics and learning trajectories.

To capture the precise nature of the impact of technological capability on export performance, Bhaduri and Ray (2004) introduced quantifiable (measurable) definitions of various facets of technological capability. In particular, we made a distinction between know-how and know-why oriented capabilities. Our econometric results, capturing the impact of these various facets of technological capability on export performance, revealed striking inter-industry differences.

We found that know-how (or production engineering) augments export performance in both sectors. Know-why (or reverse engineering), on the other hand, was important for pharmaceutical exports but not for E&E. Indeed, as argued earlier, it is know-how oriented capabilities (production engineering and quality control for instance) that augment production efficiency and enable an LDC firm to remain internationally competitive. Know-why capabilities raise export competitiveness only in the long run after a gestation lag of successful learning.

One may, of course, ask why the E&E firms in India, unlike pharmaceuticals, are unable to augment exports through know-why capabilities. The reason perhaps lies in the different character of the two products. While in both cases the global technological frontier is moving fast, in E&E the rate of product obsolescence is very high,

[24]Dore (1984).

[25]See Ungson et al. (1997).

whereas an old drug is never quite pushed out of the market even in the long run when a new and 'better' replacement arrives. Therefore, there is ample scope and incentive to carry out sustained know-why activities of inventing around cost efficient processes and designs keeping in mind the off-patent segment of the international pharmaceutical market. Such long-run prospects of pay-off from know-why do not exist in the case of E&E—characterized by a very high rate of product obsolescence.

The Role of IPR in Technological Capability Building

We have already described technological capability acquisition as a path dependent process, which begins with simple production engineering (know-how) capabilities, followed by the acquisition of know-why or reverse engineering capabilities that sets the stage for a paradigm shift onto basic research. The transition from know-how to know-why capability acquisition entails a trade-off between short-run gains in term of productivity augmentation (through know-how) versus long-run benefits of creating a sound foundation for advanced technological capability of basic and frontier innovations (through know-why).

It is now widely recognized in the literature that IPR policy has very significant implications for technological learning and technological capability accumulation in developing countries (Lall 2001; IPR Commission 2002; Dutfield and Sutharsanan 2005). However, designing an appropriate IPR policy to move the economy onto an optimum learning trajectory involves a complex public choice problem due to the trade-off between innovation and the diffusion that it entails.

Economists belonging to the neo-liberal tradition unequivocally endorse the importance of incentives in innovation[26] and believe that a strong IPR regime that fosters such incentives (but restricts diffusion and learning through imitation and RE) would be the best policy option for a developing or emerging economy to embrace globalization. Others, however, believe that developing countries are

[26]Note, however, that the strength of an IPR regime may not always raise the incentive for innovation in a linear fashion, especially if innovation is a cumulative process based on a pioneer invention. See, for example, Nordhaus (1969), Scotchmer (1991), Lerner (2001) and Gallini (2002).

likely to lose out under strong IPR due to shrinking opportunities of imitative R&D; and hence a weak IPR that facilitates diffusion and learning, could prove to be most important, for know-why type technological learning and catch-up (Helpman 1993; UNCTAD 1996; Lall 2001; Maskus 2000).

While the debate on an optimum IPR policy continues, one is tempted to conclude that a weak IPR policy would perhaps be preferred over a stronger one in the initial stages of technological learning and economic development. But, once a country reaches technological maturity to achieve major breakthroughs, the benefits of protecting knowledge through strong IPR (incentive to innovate) might outweigh the benefits of diffusion. Hence, a strong IPR policy that encourages innovation may be necessary at a later stage after the country in question acquires innovative capability through learning.

This essentially reflects that IPR policy cannot remain static or invariant over time. It needs to be modified, fine-tuned and adjusted at various points in the technological learning trajectory of a nation, according to the nature and level of technological capability already acquired through this learning process. At the same time, the nature and extent of technological learning will also be definitely shaped by the IPR policy adopted. In other words, technological learning and IPR policy have a strong mutual interface in the way they evolve. There is significant historical evidence of this phenomenon. Dutfield and Sutharsanan (2005), for instance, document 'numerous instances of how today's developed countries often ensured they had weaker IP regimes than those of the technologically more advanced countries with which they were seeking to catch up'.

Ray and Bhaduri (2008) attempt to provide a theoretical understanding of the interface between technological learning and IPR policy, using tools of applied microeconomics. We develop a game theoretic model to explain the optimum IPR policy and the corresponding technological learning in a developing country. Our model identifies the nature and extent of domestic technological learning under different IPR regimes, both being endogenously determined.

Our model, although neoclassical in character, and based on rational behaviour and optimization, arrives at a *Nelsonian* conclusion of co-evolution of technology (learning) and institution (IPR regime) with a strong interface between the two in their evolutionary process (Nelson 1994). In this co-evolutionary framework, the technological learning begins with know-how oriented production engineering followed by know-why oriented reverse engineering under weak IPR till sufficient innovative capability is acquired for basic research. At this point, the IPR regime is made stronger to enable firms to adopt basic research as a viable (and sustainable) strategic option. Without the introduction of a strong IPR as a negotiated order at this juncture, the transition to basic research will perhaps prove to be difficult and unsustainable.[27]

As already noted, the technological learning trajectory has not been uniform across all sectors in India. The technological trajectory of the E&E sector has essentially been targeted towards the achievement of high TFP (based on know-how capabilities) with little emphasis on the acquisition of adaptive and designing (know-why) capabilities and, therefore, IPR policy perhaps had little role to play in this regard.

The pharmaceutical industry, on the other hand, focused on building up know-why oriented technological capability, even at the cost of immediate productivity gains in the short- or medium-terms. Here the IPR regimes did matter. Indeed, the process revolution in the Indian pharmaceutical industry, reflecting significant learning and technological catch up, can be largely attributed to the Patent Act of 1970 allowing only process (and not product) patents for pharmaceutical substances. One may, of course, further argue that India's transition in 2005 into a stronger IPR regime, compatible with the TRIPS agreement under the WTO, is perhaps the right moment to leverage its innovative capacity to take a leap towards basic research (new drug discovery).

Conclusion

If one looks at India's economic progress in the last decade or so, it is quite evident that knowledge-intensive sectors have been driving India's growth, be it IT, Biotech or Pharmaceuticals among many more skill intensive service sectors. India's technological advantages in these areas have, by and large, remained confined to the domain of minor as opposed to major innovative capabilities. India has

[27]However, a premature imposition of strong IPR, suppressing the evolutionary interface between TC and IPR, will not merely halt the technological catch-up process but will actually reverse the learning trajectory to the stage of production engineering.

demonstrated significant competitive strength in routine (through skill intensive) tasks like coding (in software) or process development (in pharmaceuticals), and perhaps less so in creativity and innovativeness. Transition to a stronger patent regime raises strong hopes that it will stimulate such creative and innovative technological capability in India's knowledge-based industries.

However, to carve out an appropriate (optimum) technology strategy, one cannot afford to ignore the other sectors of the economy, especially the labour–intensive mass manufacturing where productivity augmentation through know-how capabilities may prove to be crucially important for sustained TFPG and industrial development. While India has nurtured, and succeeded (to a large extent) with high-end human capital for technological capability, it has been accompanied with a tragic neglect of low-end human capital investment (in primary education and health) for productivity gains in the mass manufacturing sectors.[28] By stimulating broad-based expansion of these sectors through low-end human capital and technological capability building, India could bring on board its 300 million poor who have been completely left out of the prosperity through its emergence as a major economic player in the world economy. Such an 'inclusive' technology strategy would be of critical importance for the sustainability of the country's growth process.

References

Ahluwalia, I.J. (1991), *Productivity and Growth in Indian Manufacturing*, Oxford University Press, Delhi.

Arrow, K.J. (1962), 'The Economic Implications of Learning by Doing', *Review of Economic Studies*, Vol. 29, No. 3, pp. 155–73.

Balakrishnan, P. and K. Puspangadan (1994), 'Total Factor Productivity Growth in Manufacturing Industry: A Fresh Look', *Economic and Political Weekly*, July, Vol. 29 No. 31.

Bell, M. (1984), 'Learning and the Accumulation of Industrial Technological Capacity in Developing Countries', in M. Fransman and K. King (eds), *Technological Capability in the Third World*, Macmillan, London.

Bhaduri, S. and A.S. Ray (2004), 'Exporting through Technological Capability: Econometric Evidence from India's Pharmaceutical and

[28]Guha and Ray (2004); Ray (2006).

Electrical/Electronics Firms', *Oxford Development Studies*, Vol. 32, No. 1, pp. 87–100.

Cohen, W.M. and R.C. Levin (1989), 'Empirical Studies of Innovation and Market Structure', in R.C. Schmalensee and R.Willig (eds), *Handbook of Industrial Organization,* Vol. II., Elsevier Science Publishers, B.V., Amsterdam.

Cohen, W.M. and D.A. Levinthal (1989), 'Innovation and Learning: The Two Faces of R&D', *Economic Journal,* Vol. 99, pp. 569–96.

Dore, R. (1984), 'Technological Self Reliance: Sturdy Ideal or Self Serving Rhetoric', in M. Fransman and K. King (eds), *Technological Capability in the Third World*, Macmillan, London.

Dutfield, G. and U. Sutharsanan (2005), 'Harmonisation or Differentiation in Intellectual Property Protection? The Lessons of History', *Prometheus,* Vol. 23, No. 2, pp. 131–47.

Evenson, R.E. and D.K.N. Johnson (1998), 'Invention in Developing Countries' (unpublished mimeo).

Gallini, N.T. (2002), 'The Economics of Patents: Lessons from Recent US Patent Reforms', *Journal of Economic Perspective*, Vol. 16, No. 2, pp. 131–54.

Guha, A. and A.S. Ray (2004), 'India and Asia in the World Economy: The Role of Human Capital and Technology', *International Studies,* Vol. 41, No. 3, pp. 300–11.

Hayami, Y. (1999), *Development Economics: From the Poverty to the Wealth of Nations*, Oxford University Press, Oxford.

Helpman, E. (1993), 'Innovation, Imitation and Intellectual Property Rights', *Econometrica*, Vol. 61, pp. 1247–80.

IPR Commission (2002), *Integrating Intellectual Property Rights and Development Policy*, Report of the Commission on International Property Rights, London.

Jomo, K.S., G. Felker, and R. Rasiah (eds) (1999), *Industrial Technology Development in Malaysia: Industry and Firm Studies*, Routledge, London.

Kamien, M.I. and N.L. Schwartz (1975), 'Market Structure and Innovation: A Survey', *Journal of Economic Literature*, Vol. 13, pp. 1–37.

Katz, J.M. (1987), *Technology Generation in Latin American Manufacturing Industries*, Macmillan, London.

Krugman, P. (1994), The Myth of Asia's Miracle, *Foreign Affairs.*

Lall, S. (1978), 'Developing Countries as Exporters of Technology: A Preliminary Analysis', in H. Giersch (ed.), *International Economic Development and Resource Transfer Workshop*, J.C.B. Mohr, Tubingen.

______ (1984), 'India's Technological Capacity: Effects of Trade, Industrial, Science and Technology Policies', in M. Fransman and K. King (eds), *Technological Capability in the Third World*, Macmillan, London.

______ (1985), *Multinationals, Technology and Exports*, Macmillan, London.

_____ (1987), *Learning to Industrialize: The Acquisition of Technological Capability by India*, Macmillan, London.

_____ (2001), *Indicators of the Relative Importance of IPRs in Developing Countries*, Draft Report for UNCTAD.

Lerner, J. (2001), '150 Years of Patent Protection', Harvard Business School Working Paper.

Maskus, K. (2000), *Intellectual Property Rights in the Global Economy*, Institute for International Economics, Washington, DC; available at *www.iie.com/publications/*

Mowery, D.C. and N. Rosenberg (1989), *Technology and the Pursuit of Economic Growth*, Cambridge University Press, Cambridge.

Nelson, R.R (1987), 'Innovation and Economic Development: Theoretical Retrospect and Prospect' in J.M. Katz (ed.), *Technology Generation in Latin American Manufacturing Industries*, Macmillan, London.

_____ (1994), 'The Co-evolution of Technology, Industrial Structure, and Supporting Institutions', *Industrial and Corporate Change*, Vol. 3, No. 1, pp. 47–63.

Nelson, R.R. and S.G. Winter (1982), *An Evolutionary Theory of Economic Change*, Belknap Press, Cambridge, MA.

Nordhaus, W. (1969), *Invention, Growth and Welfare: A Theoretical Treatment of Technological Change*, MIT Press, Cambridge, MA.

Ray, A.S. (2004), 'The Changing Structure of R&D Incentives in India: The Pharmaceutical Sector', *Science Technology and Society*, Vol. 9, No. 2, pp. 297–317.

_____ (2005), 'The Indian Pharmaceutical Industry at Crossroads: Implications for India's Health Care', in Amiya Bagchi and Krishna Soman (eds) *Maladies, Preventives and Curatives: Debates in Public Health in India*, Tulika Books, New Delhi.

_____ (2006), 'Going Global: India's Economic Aspirations and Apprehensions in the New Millennium' in F. Villares (ed.), *India, Brazil and South Africa: Perspectives and Alliances*, Editora UNESP, Sao Paulo.

Ray, A.S. and S. Bhaduri (2001), 'R&D and Technological Learning in Indian Industry', *Oxford Development Studies*, Vol. 29, No. 2, pp. 155–71.

_____ (2002), 'Technological Development in Indian Industry: Challenges and Options after the East Asian Crisis', Richard Hooley and J.H. Yoo (eds), *The Post Financial Crisis Challenges for Asian Industrialization*, Elsevier Science, Oxford.

_____ (2008), 'Co-evolution of IPR Policy and Technological Learning in Developing Countries: A Game-theoretic Model', Paper for Globelics 6th International Conference, Mexico City, September 2008.

Ray, A.S. and V. Upadhyay (1999), 'The Role of In-House R&D in Indian Industry', Report prepared for the Department of Science and Technology, Govt. of India, July.

Rosenberg, N. (1976), *Perspective on Technology*, Cambridge University Press, New York.

Rosenberg, N. and W.E. Steinmuller (1988), 'Why are Americans Such Poor Imitators?', *American Economic Review Proceedings*, Vol. 78, pp. 229–34.

Scherer, F.M. (1967), 'Market Structure and the Employment of Scientists and Engineers', *American Economic Review*, Vol. 57, No. 3, pp. 524–31.

Schumpeter, J.A. (1980 [1934]), *The Theory of Economic Development*, Oxford University Press, London.

——— (1939), *Business Cycles*, McGraw-Hill, New York.

Scotchmer, S. (1991), 'Standing on the Shoulders of Giants: Cumulative Research and the Patent Law', *Journal of Economic Perspective*, Vol. 5, No. 1, pp. 29–41.

Solow, R.M. (1957), 'Technical Change and the Aggregate Production Function', *Review of Economics and Statistics*, August, Vol. 39, No. 3, pp. 312–20.

Spence, A. (1984), 'Cost Reduction, Competition and Industry Performance', *Econometrica*, Vol. 52, pp. 101–21.

UNCTAD (1996), *The TRIPS Agreement and Developing Countries*, United Nations, New York and Geneva.

Ungson, G.R. et al. (1997), *Korean Enterprise*, Harvard Business School Press: MA.

World Bank (1993), *The East Asian Miracle: Economic Growth and Public Policy*, Oxford University Press, Oxford.

Young, A. (1995), 'The Tyranny of Numbers: Confronting the Statistical Realities of the East Asian Growth Experience', *Quarterly Journal of Economics*, August., Vol. 110, No. 2.

3

Determinants, Constraints and Impact of Foreign Direct Investment
India–China Comparison

N. S. SIDDHARTHAN

Both China and India have been wooing foreign direct investment (FDI) inflows and have been successful in attracting FDI inflows and foreign portfolio investments.* China has been the most preferred destination (apart from the US) for FDI for more than two decades and India has emerged as an important destination during the last few years. However, only a few regions in China and India receive FDI and a vast majority of the regions in both countries receive very little or virtually no FDI. This chapter argues that infrastructure, socio-economic environment and governance constraints have stood in the way of FDI inflows to most of the regions in the two countries. The chapter is divided into two parts: the first part develops the hypothesis relating to the determinants of inter regional distribution of FDI and tests the hypothesis for Chinese and Indian data. The second part deals with the impact of FDI, particularly on technology and productivity spillovers on the local firms. It analyses the main

*An earlier version of this paper was presented at the international workshop on *The Rapid Development of China and India: Domestic and International Consequences*, organized by the Centre for International Management and Development Antwerp, University of Antwerp, Antwerp, 31 March–1 April 2006. My thanks to G. Lakshmana Rao for research assistance and to Sriram Natarajan for introducing me to the Chinese data sources.

determinants of the spillovers and stresses the importance of in-house R&D and corporate governance as seen from the ownership pattern of the local enterprises.

In the case of India, the results of studies covering the nineties show that during the initial years of liberalization, the spillover effects were modest but later increased sharply and stabilized towards the end. However, not all domestic firms gained equally from the spillovers—those that possessed higher labour productivities and had lower productivity gaps with multinational enterprises (MNEs) were able to enjoy higher spillovers while those with larger productivity gaps could not benefit much. Consequently, firms with better endowments in terms of productivity and technology benefited from liberalization and FDI presence. Firms with large productivity gaps became the victims.

Determinants of FDI Inflows: Infrastructure and Governance Constraints

Introduction

Several studies analyse inter-country differences in FDI, emphasizing location advantages (for example, Wei 2000; Habib and Zurawicki 2002; Globerman 2002; and Globerman and Shapiro 2003). These studies have identified various location advantages such as size of the market, income and its growth rate; membership of a regional union; labour and skill content of the population; infrastructure facilities like transport, tele-density, electricity, and port facilities; and variables representing good governance such as legal dispute settlement, the rule of law, spending on social sector to enhance the skills of the population, improving the health of the people by spending on sanitation, preventive medicine and potable water and, in general, all expenditures directed towards increasing the well-being of the citizens. More recent studies have focused on such factors as technological status, brand name, openness of the economy, macro trade policies of the government and intellectual property protection. Some of these variables are country specific rather than pertaining to a specific region or a state within a country. However, there are very few analytical studies on the inter-state or inter-province differences in FDI inflows.

Though there are very few studies that explain inter-state differences in FDI, some of the studies on the emergence and development of industrial clusters and the role of FDI have identified a number of variables that are specific to a state or a region within a country (He 2002; Belderbos and Carree 2002; Tuan and Linda 2003; Eaton, Lipsey and Safarian 1994; WeiY. 1999 ; Jianping 1999). These studies emphasize the roles of infrastructure, international orientation (proxied by volume of total trade—exports and imports), high regional income, especially industrial income, and the presence of MNEs in attracting FDI. Certain other studies (Zucker et al. 1998; Cooke 2001; Breschi and Malerba 2001; Audretsch and Lehmann 2005; Ronde and Hussler 2005) emphasize the role of educational institutions—schools and universities, research and development (R&D) laboratories, and qualified labour force. Nevertheless, the objectives of these studies are not to explain inter-provincial differences in FDI inflows. Unlike the case of inter-country differences in FDI inflows, the econometric studies on inter-provincial differences in FDI inflows are scarce.[1] This chapter attempts to fill this important gap in the literature. In trying to fill this gap, the chapter uses the empirical results of inter-country studies as well as studies that explain agglomeration benefits to develop testable hypothesis.

During the last two decades, both China and India have been experiencing very high growth rates of national income and have been attracting massive inflows of FDI.[2] Nevertheless, for both China and India, the aggregate figures of FDI inflows are misleading as only a few regions account for the bulk of FDI inflows. This high regional concentration could pose long-term problems for the two countries. Hence, it is vital to analyse the important determinants of regional differences in FDI. Such an analysis will bring to light the main constraints for development.

As seen from Table 3.1, during 2003, out of 32 provinces in China, eight provinces accounted for about 80 per cent of FDI flows: Jiangsu (20 per cent), Guangdong (15 per cent), Shangdong (11 per cent),

[1]However, for China Broadman and Sun(1997) analysed inter-provisional differences of FDI inflows for one year.

[2]FDI inflows to China have been several times that of India, however, the two data sets are not comparable as China includes the entire project cost including reinvestments in FDI while India includes only the foreign exchange inflows. Furthermore, most of Chinese FDI inflows come from Hong Kong and overseas Chinese. If we compare FDI inflows from OECD countries then Chinese inflows though larger are comparable to those of India.

Table 3.1: China: Share of Regions in FDI

Province	*FDI 2003*	*FDI (per cent) 2003*	*Province*	*FDI 2003*	*FDI (per cent) 2003*
Beijing	219,126	4.10	Henan	53,903	1.01
Tianjin	153,473	2.87	Hubei	156,886	2.93
Hebei	96,405	1.80	Hunan	101,835	1.90
Shanxi	21,361	0.40	Guangdong	782,294	14.62
Inner Mongolia	8,854	0.17	Guangxi	41,856	0.78
			Hainan	42,125	0.79
Liaoning	282,410	5.28			
Jilin	19,059	0.36	Chongqing	26,083	0.49
Heilongjiang	32,180	0.60	Sichuan	41,231	0.77
			Guizhou	4,521	0.08
Shanghai	546,849	10.22	Yunnan	8,384	0.16
Jiangsu	1,056,365	19.74	Tibet	0	0
Zhejiang	498,055	9.31			
Anhui	36,720	0.69	Shaanxi	33,190	0.62
Fujian	259,903	4.86	Gansu	2,342	0.04
Jiangxi	161,202	3.01	Qinghai	2,522	0.05
Shangdong	601,617	11.24	Ningxia	1,743	0.03
			Xinjiang	1,534	0.03
			Regional Total	5,294,028	98.95

Note: FDI in US$10,000.
Source: *www.stats.gov.cn/english/statisticaldata/yearlydata/*

Shanghai (10 per cent), Zhejiang (9 per cent), Liaoning (5 per cent), Fujian (5 per cent) and Beijing (4 per cent). Except for Guangdong which has shown a decline in share in recent years, all other regions exhibit the same trend in FDI share. This indicates that the regional differences are likely to persist and a convergence might not take place. Furthermore, these provinces also happen to be the ones enjoying higher socio-economic indicators like per capita income, industrialization and infrastructure.

The Indian scene with regard to regional differences in FDI is not very different. As shown in Table 3.2, about six states in India account for more than 55 per cent of FDI receipts. These six states also account for more than 57 per cent of the total industrial output in India. However, some states such as Uttar Pradesh, Bihar and

Table 3.2: India: Share of States and Union Territories in FDI and Industrial Output, 2004

State/UT	*FDI Approvals (Rs 10 million)*	*FDI (per cent)*	*Gross Value Added by Industry (per cent)*
Andhra Pradesh	11658.71	4.61	7.03
Assam	2.41	0.001	0.67
Bihar	739.71	0.29	0.42
Gujarat	12748.98	5.04	13.42
Haryana	3928.34	1.55	4.48
Himachal Pradesh	1226.64	0.48	0.87
Jammu&Kashmir	8.41	0.003	0.12
Karnataka	19202.55	7.60	6.71
Kerala	1812.45	0.72	2.20
Madhya Pradesh	9271.41	3.67	4.02
Maharashtra	37250.67	14.75	19.71
Orissa	8235.45	3.26	1.52
Punjab	2213.65	0.88	3.50
Rajasthan	2911.21	1.15	3.35
Tamil Nadu	22872.18	9.06	9.94
Uttar Pradesh	4846.22	1.91	6.93
West Bengal	8016.87	3.17	4.39
Delhi	30843.14	12.21	1.33
Goa	999.38	0.40	1.03
Pondicherry	1286.21	0.51	0.95

Source: *www.indiastat.com*

Rajasthan that account for a large share of the Indian population as well as the number of seats in the Indian Parliament receive very little FDI (Siddharthan and Rajan 2002). The two maps (Map 3.1 on the regional distribution of FDI in India and Map 3.2 on the regional distribution of industrial output) reveal the industrial concentration in India. In Map 3.2, we see that Uttar Pradesh has a share of more than 5 per cent in industrial output. However, this is misleading, as most of the output comes from the National Capital Region (NCR), namely, areas in and around Delhi, that include some districts of Uttar Pradesh that border Delhi. In the FDI map (Map 3.1), however, these areas are shown as belonging to the NCR.

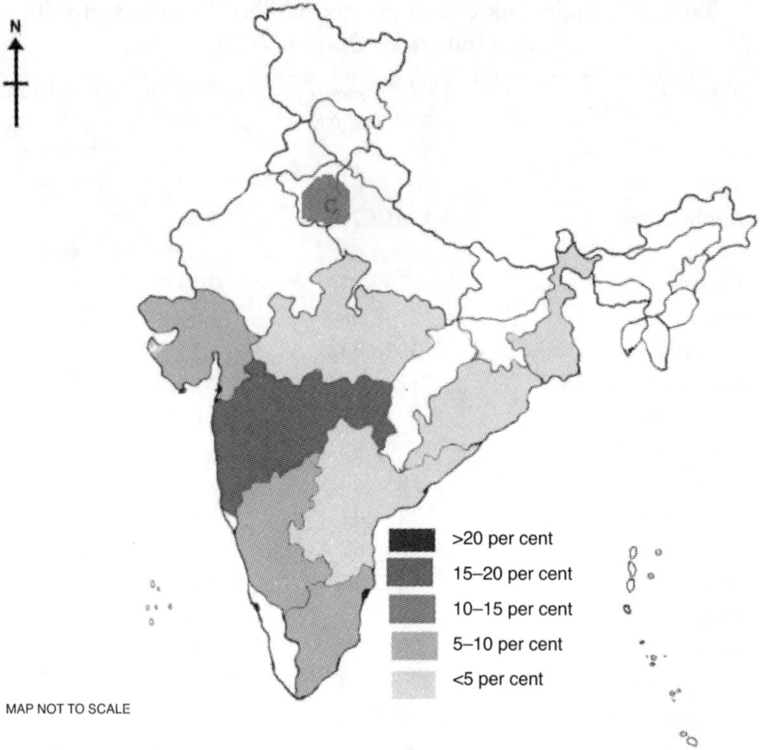

Map 3.1: Regional Distribution of FDI in India

Thus, the extreme inequalities in the regional distribution of industrial production and FDI are important problems for both China and India. The second section examines the literature that deals with the factors that are responsible for the location of FDI across countries. The third section deals with the Chinese case and the fourth section with the Indian case. The fifth section brings out the main findings of the study.

Lessons from Inter-country Studies

Empirical studies analysing the determinants of inter-country differences in FDI inflows indicate the importance of gross domestic product (GDP), macroeconomic policies of the government, trade

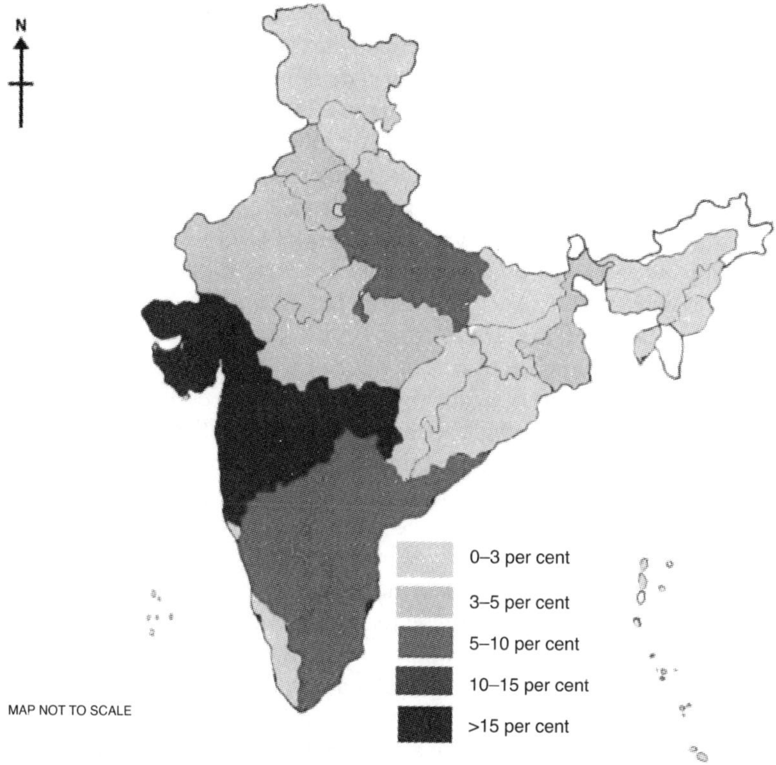

Map 3.2: Regional Distribution of Industrial Output in India

policies, corruption, good governance and skill content of the work force in influencing FDI. This section presents the findings of some of the studies that are relevant for the present paper. Wei's (2000) study analyses the determinants of the bilateral stocks of FDI from 12 source countries to 45 host countries. The source countries include the US, Japan, Germany, UK, France and Italy. In analysing FDI, the following explanatory variables are used: tax rate, corruption, tax credit, political stability, GDP, population, distance between the two countries, linguistic ties between countries and the wage rates. Habib and Zurawicki (2002) also use similar variables: population, GDP growth, per capita GDP, unemployment rate, openness of the economy as measured by the ratio of trade to GDP, science and technology indicators, cultural distance and political stability to analyse FDI inflows. Their findings suggest that the absence of good governance is a serious obstacle for investment. Apart from governance indicators, geographical distance and economic ties also emerge as important determinants of FDI.

Globerman and Shapiro (2003) examine the statistical importance of government infrastructure as a determinant of FDI. They conducted the analysis in two stages. In the first stage the probability that a country was a recipient of US FDI was estimated. In the second stage their analysis was restricted to those countries that received FDI flows and estimated equations focused on the determinants of the amount of FDI received. These measures included the following: (i) rule of law index, which measures contract enforcement, property rights, theft and crime; (ii) political instability and violence index, which measures armed conflict, social unrest, ethnic tension and terrorist threats; (iii) regulatory burden index, which measures government intervention, trade policy and capital restrictions; (iv) government effectiveness index, measuring red tape and bureaucracy, wastes in government and public infrastructure; (v) graft and corruption index, measuring corruption among public and private officials and the extent of bribery; and (vi) voice and accountability index, which measures civil liberties, political rights, free press, and fairness of the legal system. Their results consistently show that governance infrastructure is an important determinant of whether a country will receive any US FDI, and, if so, how much. All the governance variables considered in the study are relevant for inter-state analysis in India as these indicators differ significantly across the Indian states.

Cuervo-Cazurra (2006) examined the effect of corruption on FDI and in doing so argued that corruption did not have the same impact on all the investors. In particular, investors from countries that had strict laws against bribery are likely to be more adversely affected in countries with high levels of corruption than investors from countries that had similarly high levels of corruption. Since investors from countries with high levels of corruption have experience in dealing with corruption, they may not be deterred from investing in countries with high levels of corruption. In other words, corruption discourages FDI from countries that have signed the Organization for Economic Co-operation and Development (OECD) Convention and does not prevent high corruption countries from investing. In addition to introducing corruption in the host and home countries, the model also introduced the following determinants: GDP, population, distance, island, landlocked country, common border, common language, colonial link and restrictions on FDI and trade.

Several studies on FDI and industrial clusters show that MNEs favour locations that minimize information costs and offer a variety of agglomeration economies (He 2002). Belderbos and Carree (2002) analyse the locational choices of Japanese electronics manufacturers in China's regions and provinces during the period 1990–95 and confirm the major impact of regions in promoting industry, and Japanese *keiretsu*-specific agglomeration benefits. International orientation of provinces in terms of exports and imports orientation, and the presence of seaports also appear to attract FDI.

For China, Y. Wei (1999) finds that provinces with a higher level of international trade, lower wage rates, more R&D manpower, higher GDP growth rates, quicker improvement in infrastructure, more rapid advances in agglomeration, more preferential policies and closer ethnic links with overseas Chinese attract relatively more FDI. Similarly, Jianping's (1999) study on agglomeration effects of the location of US and Japanese manufacturing firms within China's 30 administrative regions during the period 1981–96 shows that these effects are important in the choice of provinces. Likewise the study by Broadman and Sun (1997) analysed the accumulated FDI stock in each province at the end of 1992. They used provincial GNP for 1992, average annual provincial wages, adult illiteracy rates, total length of transportation routes within a province, and coastal location as determinants. In their study, only provincial GDP and coastal location emerged as significant at the 5 per cent level.

The studies reviewed indicate that four possible sets of factors influence the interregional distribution of FDI in a given country. They are: (i) international orientation, (ii) infrastructure, (iii) education and social indicators and (iv) prosperity and industrial development of the region. Each one of the factors could be represented by a collection of variables. The exact variable that is ultimately used in the model will depend on the availability of data, its appropriateness for the country and its statistical significance. Furthermore, while comparing different regions with varying sizes, it is important to normalize them for the size factor. In this study the variables are normalized for population and introduced in per capita terms. The state domestic product (SDP) could also be used to normalize for size but in this study population has been preferred as SDP enters as an explanatory variable in the equations.

FDI and Inter-province Differences in China

In China, the provinces belonging to the Eastern Zone have been attracting FDI and they also have higher per capita incomes (see Yao and Zhang 2001). The provinces belonging to the Western Zone have not been attracting FDI and they are also the poorer provinces. Thus, the provinces with high FDI also enjoyed high per capita income. These provinces also had better socio-economic indicators. Table 3.3 presents the main indicators for 2003.

Table 3.3: China: Per Capita FDI, Inter-province Differences, 2003

	PCFDI	*PCTRADE*	*SS*	*PCY*	*PCELEC*	*FREIGHT*
Shanghai	319.61	6459.1444	5.53	46718	0.44	8492.3
Tianjin	151.76	2969.4848	6.79	26532	0.30	6521.1
Beijing	150.46	2151.4769	9.98	32061	0.32	462.5
Jiangsu	142.64	1637.6835	3.41	16809	0.20	1772.6
Zhejiang	106.43	1417.1890	4.22	20147	0.26	2047.2
Guangdong	98.35	3636.1823	5.63	17213	0.26	3158.0
Fujian	74.51	1105.5797	4.23	14979	0.17	1222.9
Liaoning	67.08	709.2962	6.43	14258	0.22	2385.2
Shangdong	65.93	541.4922	2.93	13661	0.15	3908.9
Hainan	51.97	235.8375	4.48	8316	0.07	250.7
Jiangxi	37.89	69.5035	2.45	6678	0.07	768.6
Hubei	26.14	96.7777	4.09	9011	0.10	1212.6
Hunan	15.28	70.5251	4.18	7554	0.08	1350.6
Hebei	14.24	143.0825	2.51	10513	0.16	3223.2
Shaanxi	8.99	96.3463	3.13	6480	0.11	849.1
Guangxi	8.62	66.3306	2.42	5969	0.09	863.4
Heilongjiang	8.44	162.9132	3.36	11615	0.13	991.4
Chongqing	8.33	81.7658	6.44	7209	0.09	367.7
Jilin	7.05	248.9266	2.57	9338	0.13	531.0
Shanxi	6.45	156.2705	2.74	7435	0.22	1259.1
Anhui	5.73	88.5333	3.26	6455	0.07	1328.6

(contd...)

Table 3.3 (contd...)

	PCFDI	*PCTRADE*	*SS*	*PCY*	*PCELEC*	*FREIGHT*
Henan	5.58	57.7483	3.07	7570	0.11	1891.6
Sichuan	4.74	66.4326	3.36	6418	0.09	768.3
Qinghai	4.72	64.2131	2.59	7277	0.28	124.2
Inner Mongolia	3.72	135.5818	2.99	8975	0.18	1160.3
Ningxia	3.00	128.3198	2.29	6691	0.37	244.5
Yunnan	1.91	62.1640	2.57	5662	0.08	612.2
Guizhou	1.17	40.1440	3.02	3603	0.10	547.0
Gansu	0.90	49.6327	1.78	5022	0.15	738.7
Xinjiang	0.79	251.0209	3.10	9700	0.12	636.6

Notes: PCFDI: per capita foreign direct investment flows, FDI in US$ 10,000 and population in 10,000 persons;
PCTRADE: total exports and imports in US$10,000;
SS: expenditure on social services;
PCY: per capita income, gross regional product in 100 million yuan and population in 10,000 persons;
PCELEC: per capita electricity consumption by region in 100 million kw and population in 10,000 persons;
FREIGHT: freight 100 million ton-km by region (total of roads and railways and waterways).
Source: www.stats.gov.cn/english/statisticaldata/yearlydata/

Table 3.3 presents the data for different variables for the year 2003 for China. In all six variables have been selected for presentation in the table after trying several permutations and combinations. The table lists the provinces in the descending order of per capita FDI inflows. Column 1 lists the per capita FDI inflows. Per capita trade (total exports and imports) represents the international orientation of the province. Infrastructure facilities are represented by two variables, per capita electricity consumption and freight by roads and railways. Expenditure on social services has been used to represent the quality of life and social infrastructure. It could also represent governance indicators. Certain other variables such as death rate, expenditures on health and education were also tried but they did not emerge as significant. Following the standard practice, per capita income has also been introduced. In addition, the share of industry was also introduced but it did not emerge significant.

As seen from Table 3.3, Shanghai has the highest per capita FDI inflows and the highest per capita income. Its per capita income is almost 13 times higher than that of Guizhou.[3] By and large, the provinces that have high per capita FDI also have high per capita income levels. The higher FDI provinces also have better infrastructure facilities in terms of electricity and rail and road networks. They are also internationally better oriented in terms of their per capita international trade. Furthermore, they also spend more on social services.

To test for the statistical significance of these variables in determining FDI inflows, a time series-cross section pooled data set was prepared for the period 2000 to 2003 (four years) for a cross-section of 30 provinces. Table 3.4 presents the Generalized Least Square (GLS) estimates (with cross-section weights, corrected for heteroskedasticity) of the coefficients.[4]

As anticipated from the literature survey and the data set presented in Table 3.3, all the variables introduced in the regression equation emerge significant (at the 1 per cent level) in Table 3.4.

Table 3.4: China: Determinants of Inter-province Differences in FDI (2000–03) GLS Estimates (with cross-section weights, corrected for heteroskedasticity)

(Dep. Variable: Per capita FDI)

Variable	*Coefficient*	*'t' Stat*
Constant	–13.81819***	–17.62173
Per capita trade	0.035120***	11.50093
Social Security	2.084534***	13.43053
Per capita income	0.001635***	8.607487
Freight	0.003469***	5.648421
NOBS 120 (4 years * 30 regions)		
R^2 (weighted)	0.8856***	

Note: *** significant at 1 per cent level.

[3]Perhaps a comparison of Guizhou with Shanghai may not be proper as Shanghai is a city province. However, while dealing with India, Delhi, a city State has also been compared with Bihar.

[4]Fixed effect models were tried but could not be estimated as some of the variables exhibited very little intra-cross section variability while exhibiting significant inter-cross section variability. As a result, fixed effect models, which in effect use cross section dummies, showed a near singular matrix due to high correlation between cross section dummies and some of the independent variables.

The socio-economic indicators that were found significant in the inter-country differences in FDI inflows also emerge as significant in explaining inter-regional differences in FDI inflows in China. This feature is captured through the use of social security expenditures. In addition, per capita province income could also capture the general well-being of the province. In inter-country studies, per capita income is used to capture the market size, but in the intra-country case this interpretation may not be relevant as the market is for the whole country and not for a particular region. Per capita foreign trade, another variable that had emerged important in the inter-country studies, has also emerged as significant in the Chinese inter-provinces case. For physical infrastructure facilities, freight by rail, road and waterways has emerged significant. This variable was also significant in the inter-country studies. All the variables used in the inter-country studies may not be relevant for intra-country studies as they include many variables that are macroeconomic in nature—affecting the entire country. However, the variables that show inter-province differences and, therefore, were introduced in this study have emerged as important.

FDI and Inter-state Differences in India

As Table 3.5 indicates, the top six states that received high levels of FDI inflows are also at the top in terms of high industrial output. By and large, most investments went to the coastal areas and the NCR (Delhi and surrounding areas). As Map 3.1 shows, the rest of the states received very little investment, domestic or foreign. Moreover, the states that received higher inflow of FDI also show higher levels of per capita income than the Indian average.

Table 3.5 presents the per capita FDI for states in descending order for the year 2004. It also presents certain other variables that are used in the regression equation, such as socio-economic index, human development index, enrolment ratio in schools, per capita income at current and constant prices, percentage of urban population to total population, per capita consumption of electricity, per capita industrial output, overall tele-density and life expectancy. Some of the earlier studies have found urbanization to be an important determinant of FDI inflows. This variable was not readily available for China and hence could not be used in the Chinese sample. Physical infrastructure features are represented by tele-

Table 3.5: India: Per Capita FDI, Inter-state Differences

	PCFDI	*SEI*	*HDI*	*EDENR*	*PCY*	*URBPP*	*PCELEC*	*PCINDO*	*PCYCP*	*TELE*	*LIFEEX*
Maharashtra	362.8924	112.80	0.523	87.55	29204	42.40	17281.78	19470	16050	9.498	66.2
Tamil Nadu	353.8177	149.10	0.531	100.41	23358	43.86	19447.53	16763	13423	10.911	65.2
Karnataka	346.4661	104.88	0.478	76.20	21696	33.98	8334.04	8829	11799	11.803	64.5
Orissa	216.9032	81.00	0.404	54.01	12388	14.97	7816.70	3628	6427	3.646	58.5
Gujarat	211.3817	124.31	0.479	70.40	26979	37.35	12097.61	25496	16779	12.065	63.4
Haryana	174.9299	137.54	0.509	65.51	29963	29.00	8969.80	21391	15721	10.163	65.2
Andhra Pradesh	146.8943	103.30	0.416	64.86	20757	27.08	16182.17	8161	11333	9.185	63.5
Madhya Pradesh	145.5653	76.79	0.394	63.30	14011	26.97	12163.07	6150	8284	4.830	56.9
West Bengal	93.7230	111.25	0.472	64.28	20896	28.03	7649.71	4914	10952	2.776	63.9
Punjab	84.3017	187.57	0.537	60.06	27851	33.95	7969.17	14530	15800	21.861	68.5
Kerala	54.4352	178.68	0.638	93.64	24492	25.97	6553.02	8424	12109	17.846	73.5
Rajasthan	48.8218	75.86	0.424	61.54	15486	23.38	10521.79	5507	8571	5.777	61.1
Uttar Pradesh	27.5089	101.23	0.388	48.64	10817	20.78	22439.20	3948	5610	3.882	59.1
Bihar	8.4865	81.33	0.367	25.33	5780	10.47	5456.02	883	3707	2.014	60.8
Assam	0.0535	77.72	0.386	56.22	13139	12.72	2510.63	3313	6520	2.706	57.9

Notes: PCFDI: Per capita stock of FDI approvals since 1991 (liberalization). FDI figures are in Rs 10 million and population figures are in million persons; SEI: Socio-economic index presented by the government; HDI: Human development index prepared by the government; EDENR: Enrolment ratio in schools in the age group 11–14 years; PCY: Per capita income at current prices; URBPP: Percentage of urban population in total population; PCELEC: Gross annual per capita consumption of electricity; PCINDO: Per capita gross industrial output in rupees; PCYCP: Per capita income at constant prices; TELE: Overall teledensity; and LIFEEX: Life expectancy at birth.

Source: *www.indiastat.com*

density and electricity consumption. Road density was also used but it has not been reported in the table. Socio-economic features are captured by the socio-economic index, human development index, school enrolment ratio and life expectancy. In addition to per capita income, per capita industrial output has also been introduced as industrialization could have a direct link with FDI inflows. The table does not include Delhi. The FDI inflows are usually classified as per the registered offices of firms. Although Delhi has the registered offices of many firms, their manufacturing units are located in the adjoining areas of Haryana and Uttar Pradesh.

As in the case of China, in India also, the states with high per capita FDI flows are those that also have high per capita income. Bihar has the lowest per capita income (Rs 5780) and Maharashtra and Haryana have the highest (Rs 29,240 and Rs 29,963, respectively); and the difference between Bihar and the high income states is five-fold. Delhi (not shown in Table 3.5) has a per capita income (Rs 51,664), which is more than eight times higher than that of Bihar. Nevertheless, the differences in per capita incomes in India are less than those in China.

States with higher FDI levels also have higher per capita industrial output. However, Orissa happens to be an exception in this respect. It has very low levels of industrialization and yet has obtained a reasonable amount of FDI. This is mainly due to the differences in the nature of FDI obtained by Orissa and other states. Unlike the rest of India, Orissa has been attracting FDI aimed at exploiting its natural resources such as ores and minerals. Again with the exception of Orissa, most of the states with high FDI levels are also urbanized. Orissa also happens to be an exception when infrastructure variables such as tele-density and per capita electricity consumption are considered. According to these indicators, the rank of Orissa in FDI inflows should be very low.

When we consider socio-economic variables, two states emerge as exceptions—Kerala and Orissa. Kerala attracts very low FDI but enjoys very high values of socio–economic indicators. Kerala ranks first in the socio-economic index, human development index, tele-density and life expectancy. However, it does not attract much FDI and also shows relatively low levels of industrialization. The opposite is the case of Orissa—it has relatively high FDI inflows but ranks very low in socio-economic and human development indices, as also in life expectancy and tele-density. It also shows a low level of

Table 3.6: India: Determinants of Inter-state Differences in FDI, (2000–04) GLS estimates (with cross-section weights, corrected for heteroskedasticity)

(dep. variable: per capita FDI)

Variable	*Coefficient*	*'t' Stat*
Constant	–383.7504***	–5.268220
Socio-economic Index	–3.224413***	–8.869783
Education-Enrolment	0.954087***	3.688089
Percentage of Urban Population	10.99286***	20.22645
Per Capita Industrial Output	0.004445***	14.84318
Tele density	3.358361***	2.829902
Life expectancy	7.293228***	4.204932
NOBS 75 (years 5 and states 15)		
R^2 (weighted)	0.9887***	

Note: *** significant at 1 per cent level.

industrialization. Apart from these two states, the other states in India follow the expected pattern of behaviour of FDI being in line with the socio-economic variables.

Table 3.6 presents the GLS estimates (with cross-section weights, corrected for heteroskedasticity) of the determinants of inter-state differences in FDI for 15 Indian states over a five year period (2000–04). Except for the socio-economic index, all the other coefficients have the expected signs and all the coefficients are significant at the 1 per cent level. The negative sign for the socio-economic index could be due to the effect of Kerala (discussed earlier). However, the other two variables representing social and health indicators, namely, enrolment ratio and life expectancy have the expected positive signs. Urbanization and per capita industrial production have the highest 't' values. The infrastructure variable—tele-density, is also significant in explaining FDI.

Main Findings of the Study

Earlier studies have compared FDI inflows to China and India (Siddharthan and Rajan 2002; Wei and Balasubramanyam 2004; and the references therein). However, there is no study comparing the regional differences in FDI inflows in the two countries. In fact, there are very few studies on regional differences in FDI inflows. This paper makes an attempt to fill this gap. Recent literature, in this field, concentrates on the determinants of inter-country differences in FDI inflows. The results of these studies show that FDI mainly goes to countries that are rich, are endowed with a good physical and institutional infrastructure, have a highly skilled workforce and are technologically advanced. These countries also follow more open trade policies and concentrate on good governance, including the rule of law. Most of the developed countries have these characteristics and consequently the bulk of FDI flows to the rich and developed countries. Most of the low-income countries receive very little or no FDI. Nevertheless, some of the larger developing countries like China, Brazil, Mexico, ASEAN member countries and more recently, India, have also been receiving FDI. However, as shown, FDI inflows in China and India have been confined to a few states and provinces.

The main finding of this chapter is that the determinants of regional distribution of FDI flows in China and India are very similar to the pattern influencing inter-country FDI flows, that is, FDI flows to relatively developed regions; and regions that are poor in physical, institutional and social infrastructure receive very little FDI. Exceptions apart, by and large, regions that are bypassed by FDI are also those that have lower life expectancy, are low in human development and socio-economic indicators, and poor in governance indicators. Furthermore, these regions do not even attract domestic investments. Therefore, the main constraint for industrial development and FDI inflows appear to be infrastructure and governance constraints. These two are related. Heavy investment is needed in human infrastructure to improve socio-economic indicators and attract industrial investment. In addition, the rule of law also plays a crucial role. Fiscal and tax incentives play only a marginal role in attracting investments.

The findings of this study also raise several issues. The question of the role of FDI in economic development in developing countries assumes importance, that is, does FDI promote development or does it accentuate regional inequalities further by flowing to the already developed regions. The process of development does not seem to result in a convergence of the level of development of different regions. Instead it could result in a divergence. The crucial concern is one of rapidly developing infrastructure and promoting good governance. These two matters are related—good governance is crucial for developing infrastructure in the fields of social services, health, education and physical infrastructure. Certain far-reaching reforms, including institutional reforms are needed to achieve this goal. Part I of this chapter, identifies these issues for further work. China and India must evolve an action plan to develop their less developed regions urgently before the problem gets out of hand.

FDI Spillovers

This part will concentrate on the impact of FDI on domestic firms and industry. In particular, it will concentrate on spillovers. The literature on spillovers is very rich but the scope of the chapter does not allow us to cover all the major studies. Nevertheless, selected studies that have used Chinese and Indian data are discussed. In recent years, studies have been concentrating on R&D spillovers in addition to FDI spillovers. It is proposed to cover both these in this part.

Evidence from Chinese Studies

Before discussing the evidence on FDI spillovers for domestic Chinese firms, it would be worthwhile to present some unique features of the changing nature of the Chinese industries and ownership of firms. In recent times, there has been much debate relating to China's transition to the market economy and the role of the private sector. A recent study (Dougherty, Herd and He 2007) shows that currently the private sector accounts for more than half of the industrial output compared with less than a quarter in 1998. Small and medium firms have been dominating the private sector and they account for 81 per cent of the firms employing less than 1000 workers. Their study further shows that the total factor productivity of private enterprises after controlling for size, location and industry is more than double that of government-controlled firms. Further, productivity is not only higher in the private sector, it has also been increasing at a faster rate. This background information is relevant for the discussion on spillovers as corporate governance and ownership pattern of firms are important determinants of spillovers.

In analysing the FDI spillovers on local Chinese firms, it is important to take into account several China-specific peculiarities. China has three main sources of FDI inflows and three broad groups of firms (based on ownership pattern). The main FDI sources are: (i) OECD countries, (ii) overseas Chinese and (iii) Hong Kong. Likewise, Chinese enterprises can be classified as (i) government-owned, (ii) private (including collectively owned) and (iii) MNEs. Buckley et al. (2002) analysed the impact of the three sources of FDI on the three groups of firms. In addition to analysing productivity spillovers their study also analysed exports and the introduction of new products.

Their study shows that overseas Chinese capital did not enhance the productivity of Chinese firms but the non-Chinese (OECD) investments did. Their results further show that while OECD capital generated both technological and market access (exports) spillovers, the overseas Chinese capital enabled only market access benefits. The OECD investments also contributed to the creation of new products by the local Chinese firms. The study also reveals that FDI did not contribute to productivity and export spillovers for the government-owned enterprises. Consequently, the spillovers were limited to privately-owned enterprises and collective enterprises. Thus, spillovers depend on the nature of FDI—whether overseas Chinese or OECD investments, and the nature of the Chinese firms—government-owned or privately-owned. Corporate governance, as seen from the ownership pattern, does play an important role in spillovers.

Another important issue relates to the role of R&D intensity in FDI enterprises. In particular, it is important to examine whether FDI per se contributes to spillovers or the R&D intensity of FDI firms contributes to spillovers. Todo et al. (2006) analyse this problem using firm-level panel data from a Chinese science park, where spillovers are more likely to occur compared to national level studies, due to geographical proximity of the firms. Their results indicate that the effect of foreign R&D stocks on domestic value added is positive, statistically significant, and quantitatively large, whereas the effect of foreign capital stocks is insignificant. In addition, they do not find spillovers originating from Hong Kong, Macau or Taiwan. If it is true that spillovers from R&D intensive FDI enterprises are more important than those from the rest, then the next question to ask would be on the motivation of FDI enterprises for doing R&D

in China. Motohashi (2006) analyses the motivation of R&D by multinationals by using Chinese firm level data and finds that the major motivation of foreign R&D in China is 'market driven' instead of 'technological driven' or 'human resource driven'. He also finds that MNEs in China spent less on R&D as compared to domestic firms. Nevertheless, there were large regional variations.

Spillovers not only depend on the nature and source of FDI but also on the technological gap between the MNEs and domestic firms. In this context, most of the studies dealing with South American and Indian data (Kathuria 2000, 2002; Kokko, Tansini, Zejan 1996; and Kokko, Zejan and Tansini 2001) find spillovers to be greater among firms with low technology gaps. However, the Chinese experience appears to be different from the Indian and Latin American experience. Guo and Veugelers (2006), on the basis of a sample of Chinese high-tech industries for the period 1997–2003, find the technology gap as having a significant positive relationship with the total factor productivity of Chinese domestic firms. Unlike India, China has not been importing technology against royalty and technical fee payments. This could be one of the reasons for the differences in the results. However, they did not find a strong positive effect of foreign owned R&D on domestic productivity. This result in a way contradicts the findings of Todo et al. (2006). By contrast, domestic firms' own R&D was a significant determinant of the productivity growth. In their study they considered mainly high-tech industries, as the share of foreign firms in these Chinese industries is very high (73 per cent for electronics and telecommunication equipment and 62 per cent for instruments and office machinery).

The results of these studies raise the important question regarding the relationship between FDI and domestic in-house R&D effort. Fan and Hu (2007) find Chinese firms' R&D expenditure decreasing with the FDI they receive. They find the net effect of FDI on indigenous R&D effort to be negative. Nevertheless, they find some evidence in favour of a positive impact of FDI on the productivity growth of Chinese firms. On the other hand, there is evidence (Hu, Jefferson and Jinchang 2005) that technology transfer becomes more productive if the local Chinese firm also spends on in-house R&D. Hu, Jefferson and Jinchang (2005) also find a positive return for in-house R&D expenditures for Chinese firms. They conclude that the effects of both domestic and foreign technology transfer on firm productivity are largely conditional on their interactions with in-house R&D. However, FDI does not contribute to arms length technology transfer against royalty and technology fee payments. In fact, it could stand in the way of arms length transfer. This finding indicates that FDI and arms length transfer could be substitutes.

Thus, studies based on Chinese data show that spillovers from FDI are not automatic. They depend on the sources of FDI, the ownership pattern of firms and the resultant corporate governance, technological base of the local firm and its R&D intensity. By and large, FDI from OECD countries has a higher spillover effect on privately-owned firms with a good R&D base.

The Indian Experience

With regard to productivity spillovers, the issues facing Indian firms are in some respects different from those of the Chinese as the Indian environment is not quite the same. The dominance of the State-owned enterprises in India is less than that in China and overseas Indians have not been investing in India like the overseas Chinese have been investing in China. India also enjoys the presence of large Indian industrial houses. Many of them are also investing overseas and are in the process of emerging as MNEs in their own right. Consequently, in several industries, the productivity gap between Indian enterprises and FDI enterprises is not large. Some of the Indian firms also enjoy productivity advantages.

India began liberalizing its economy and, in particular, its manufacturing sector over a decade ago. One of the objectives of liberalization has been to make Indian industries more efficient and globally competitive. Towards this end, the Government of India has been pursuing three sets of reforms: one, disbanding the complex network of industrial controls, industrial licensing and permits system; two, liberalizing foreign trade and currency transactions and three, instituting several measures to facilitate FDI inflows. These measures were launched in 1991 and the liberalization process is still continuing. It was argued that the removal of entry and licensing barriers would expose Indian firms to international competition and compel them to improve their efficiency and productivity and introduce new processes and products. Trade reforms aimed at exposing Indian firms to global markets would compel them to produce better quality goods. Removal of import restrictions and currency transactions would enable them to import better quality materials, components and technology. FDI inflows would have technology and productivity spillover effects and would improve the productivity of Indian firms.

In the case of India, inter-firm and inter-industry studies show conflicting results. Single industry studies also report varying results. Here we concentrate on inter-firm studies as most inter-industry studies assume that firms in an industry behave alike. During the period of liberalization and policy change such an assumption is not valid, as all firms do not react to policy change in a similar manner. There are firms that would benefit while others would become victims of liberalization.

A study by Kathuria (2002) shows that Indian firms that invested in R&D benefited from FDI spillovers. Indian firms with low or nil R&D expenditures did not benefit from spillovers. Further, in the case of low R&D intensive industry groups the impact of import liberalization was found to be productivity depressing. Based on these results, Kathuria concludes that spillovers were not automatic and depended largely on the level of investment of the firm in R&D. In other words, only firms that had low productivity gaps benefited from spillovers.

One of the single industry studies for the Indian pharmaceutical sector showed that the MNEs' local R&D efforts did not benefit the local firms. Feinberg and Majumdar (2001) examine whether knowledge spillovers from MNEs' local R&D activities benefits domestic firms in the Indian pharmaceuticals industry during the period 1980–94. They estimate separate production functions for MNEs and domestic firms and their results show that while the MNEs gained from each other's R&D the domestic firms did not benefit. They attribute this to the intellectual property regime prevalent in India during the sample period. Now that the current Indian intellectual property regime is in conformity with the WTO regime the results could change if the model is tested for a more recent period.

The rest of the section will deal with inter-firm analysis. Ray (2004) analyses the impact of liberalization measures and the consequent technological changes on the efficiency of firms. The paper argues that the impact would depend on whether the technological changes are incremental or *paradigmatic*. It considers incremental changes as movements along the trajectories and paradigmatic changes as those involving changes in the frontier itself. Paradigmatic changes would lead to an increase in efficiency of the firms adopting the same but could raise the distance between the frontier and the average firms.

The results show that for the Indian manufacturing sector taken as a whole the average efficiency levels had declined over the period 1991–96, a result similar to earlier studies that used a different methodology. However, after 1996, there has been an improvement in the average efficiency though it has not reached the 1991 levels. On the other hand, there were inter-industry differences. In the second part of the paper, the efficiency estimates discussed in the first part are used as the dependent variable in the regression exercise. For each of the years 1991 to 2001, separate regressions have been run to explain the factors affecting these efficiency estimates. The results show that foreign ownership or MNE affiliation was significant in explaining efficiency and that the value of its coefficient increased over the years. Furthermore, among the domestic firms, that is, firms that are not affiliates of MNEs, non-equity strategic alliances—a variable captured through royalty payments in foreign currency for technology imports—emerged important. This variable was not important in the early 1990s but emerged as being significant in the later half of the 1990s. In addition, capital intensity was also important. In sum, MNE affiliates, domestic firms that imported technology through royalty payments and used capital intensive methods emerged as more efficient than the rest.

The paper by Goldar, Ranganathan and Banga (2004) analyses the effect of ownership on the efficiency of engineering firms in India in the 1990s. The technical efficiency of firms is estimated with the help of a stochastic frontier production function using parametric techniques. A comparison of technical efficiency is made among three groups of firms in Indian engineering: (i) firms with foreign ownership, (ii) domestically owned private sector firms, and (iii) public sector firms. In particular, the paper poses the following two questions: Was the technical efficiency of foreign owned firms generally higher than that of domestically owned private sector firms and public sector firms? How far could the domestically owned firms catch up with foreign firms in terms of technical efficiency during the 1990s?

Their study shows the mean technical efficiency of foreign firms to be higher than that of domestic firms—both private and public sector enterprises. Further, their results indicate that there has been a process of convergence in technical efficiency among Indian engineering firms during the 1990s—the domestically-owned firms tending to catch up with the foreign firms. However, this process of convergence weakened in the second half of the 1990s. Thus this study reconfirms the higher efficiency levels enjoyed by MNEs and their affiliates and at the same time shows the narrowing of the gap between the two groups over the years. The narrowing of the gap does indicate the existence of spillovers from MNEs to the domestic firms. Also, this study establishes a positive relationship between the trade orientation of a firm and the level of its efficiency. Trade liberalization seems to have contributed to the efficiency of the Indian enterprises.

In the liberalized environment, MNE affiliates seem to enjoy productivity and efficiency advantages. Nevertheless, this raises a further question, namely, do all MNEs behave alike or do home country specific characteristics influence their behaviour? Banga's (2004) paper concentrates on this issue. The paper analyses whether the source of FDI influences productivity growth. Productivity growth in the Indian manufacturing sector is separately estimated for Japanese-affiliated, US-affiliated and domestic firms in three broad industrial categories, where both Japanese and US firms are a significant presence, namely, automobiles, electrical and chemicals for the period 1993–94 to 1999–2000. Banga carries out the estimations at three levels. First, total factor productivity growth (TFPG) is estimated using 'time-variant firm specific' technical efficiency approach (parametric approach) and average TFPG in the Japanese-affiliated firms is compared to that in the US-affiliated and domestic firms. Second, the impact of the source of affiliation on TFPG of a firm is estimated using least square regressions on seven-year averages. Finally, to investigate to what extent inter-firm differences exist in explaining TFPG and to what extent TFPG in a firm is explained by technical progress and efficiency growth, Data Envelopment Analysis (DEA) (non-parametric approach) is carried out and Malmquist indices are estimated using panel data in the three industries.

Her results show that affiliation with foreign firms of different countries-of-origin would lead to differential impact on TFPG of a firm. She finds that Japanese affiliates enjoy higher productivity growth, after controlling for other firm-specific and industry-specific effects compared to the US affiliates. Total factor productivity growth can occur either due to technological progress, that is, due to shift in the production function or due to efficiency improvements in the firm. She deploys DEA analysis using the panel data set to further disaggregate the technical efficiency change indices and technological change indices. The results suggest that the major source of TFPG in all the three industries for Japanese-affiliated firms is increase in efficiency while for the US-affiliated firms it is mostly technological progress. This result is as anticipated in the literature as Japanese firms have managerial advantages like Japanese management techniques, just in time delivery, total quality management, and quality circles.

The paper by Siddharthan and Lal (2004) argues that in analysing the impact of liberalization on productivity spillovers, it is essential to take into account the entry of new enterprises and the exit of some older ones. Furthermore, the value of the spillover coefficients could change over time. Therefore, estimating an average coefficient (averaged over several years) may not reflect the changes in the spillover effects. In addition, labour productivity measures used by earlier studies do not take into account heterogeneity in the skill content of the workforce. In their study, therefore, they advocate another measure, namely, value added per unit cost of labour, which avoids the problem posed by skill diversities and the consequent wage differentials of the workers. Instead of combining cross-section and time-series data, they estimate separate equations for each year from 1993 to 2000. This procedure aids in studying the possible changes in the behaviour of the determinants over the years. In addition, they also used panel data techniques, combining time-series with cross-section, and estimate fixed effect models. The results of the balanced panel models are not very different but panel data methods can produce only an average coefficient (average for the whole period) for the respective variables and cannot show the changing trend in the coefficients. The balanced panel does not take into account the entry and exit of the firms. Therefore, the authors do not prefer this procedure.

They estimated the following equation:

$$VAL_{ijt} = \alpha_{0t} + \alpha_{1t}MS_{ijt} + \alpha_{2t}MSF_{jt} + \alpha_{3t}VALF_{jt} + \alpha_{4t}GAP_{jt} + \alpha_{5t}COR_{ijt} + \alpha_{6t}AD_{ijt} + \alpha_{7t}EXPORT_{ijt} + \alpha_{8t}IMPTECH_{ijt} + \alpha_{9t}IMPCAP_{ijt} + \mu$$

where the subscript i stands for the firm, j for the industry and t for time. VAL is value added divided by the wages and salaries bill of the locally owned Indian firms; VALF, the industry average of value added divided by the wages and salaries bill of MNE affiliates in India; GAP is equal to $VAL_{ijt}/VALF_{jt}$; MS, the market share, is sales turnover of the given Indian firm; MSF, the market share of MNE affiliates in the given industry; COR, the capital–output ratio of the Indian firm; AD, advertisement expenditures of the Indian firm as a ratio of sales turnover of the Indian firm; EXPORT, exports to sales ratio of the Indian firm; IMPTECH, technology imports, royalty and technical fee payments as a ratio of sales turnover of the Indian firm; and IMPCAP, import of capital goods as a ratio of sales turnover of the Indian firm (Table 3.7).

Table 3.7: Determinants of VAL

(White Heteroskedasticity-Consistent Estimates)

Ind. Variables	*1993*	*1994*	*1995*	*1996*	*1997*	*1998*	*1999*	*2000*
MS	–0.010	0.002	0.007	0.001	–0.002	–0.003	0.009	–0.002
t	–0.748	0.158	0.385	0.049	–0.207	–0.342	1.382	–0.179
MSF	–0.026*	0.038	0.024	–0.027	–0.040	–0.001	0.030	0.018
	–3.30	1.025	0.449	–0.690	–1.118	–0.025	1.249	1.116
VALF	0.654*	0.981*	1.073*	1.248*	1.391*	1.557*	1.548*	1.349*
	7.612	6.079	5.073	5.266	4.899	7.314	5.844	5.969
GAP	3.325*	2.992*	3.201*	3.455*	3.246*	2.952*	3.201*	3.644*
	16.393	13.232	15.655	16.401	21.427	16.617	13.461	18.089
COR	0.006	0.007	–0.029	–0.026	–0.038	–0.082*	–0.044	–0.041*
	0.862	1.216	–1.293	–1.777	–1.252	–3.109	–1.746	–2.961
AD	–6.895	–14.77+	–4.061	–0.432	–10.14	–2.569	–1.512	–2.262
	–0.960	–2.323	–0.605	–0.105	–1.395	–0.596	–0.493	–0.994
EXPORT	0.012	0.037	0.010	0.011	0.183	0.025	0.253	0.396
	0.227	1.084	0.058	0.061	0.629	0.136	0.996	1.079
IMPTECH	1.823	–22.26+	–20.88*	–3.222	–1.852	0.352	5.446	–2.519
	0.509	–2.250	–2.996	–0.626	–0.195	0.061	0.782	–0.559

(contd...)

Table 3.7 (contd...)

Ind. Variables	*1993*	*1994*	*1995*	*1996*	*1997*	*1998*	*1999*	*2000*
IMPCAP	0.043	0.480	0.337	–0.478	–1.596*	–0.997*	–1.589*	–0.745*
	0.110	0.912	0.944	–0.562	–2.822	–2.551	–3.034	–2.547
CONST	–2.147*	–3.564*	–3.816⁺	–4.199*	–3.759*	–4.406*	–5.262*	–4.914*
	–4.119	–2.842	–2.408	–3.246	–4.007	–4.774	–4.939	–5.974
D_AUTOAN	1.302*	–0.099	0.119	0.795	1.027	–0.167	–1.103	–0.673
	8.721	–0.121	0.099	0.924	1.213	–0.199	–1.162	–1.230
D_COMVEH	1.206*	–0.048	0.050	–0.047	–0.240	–1.126	–0.818	–0.437
	3.495	–0.103	0.066	–0.079	–0.403	–0.492	–1.658	–1.089
D_MCYCLE	2.506*	–1.236	–1.096	1.437	2.232	–1.126	–3.538	–2.626
	6.829	–0.602	–0.363	0.609	1.004	–0.492	–1.597	–1.614
D_CAR	–6.002*	–14.00*	–19.31*	–31.83*	–24.11*	–21.48*	–19.92*	–17.66*
	–5.468	–3.524	2.793	–4.006	–3.886	–4.419	–3.958	–4.258
D_CHEM	2.152*	1.336*	1.735⁺	0.458	0.417	–1.362	–1.029	–0.281
	7.192	2.821	2.100	0.414	0.334	–1.272	–0.959	–0.374
D_DOME-	1.905*	1.928	–2.509*	–0.714	0.131	–2.553*	–0.719	0.079
APPLS	4.665	1.551	–2.790	–1.134	0.222	–2.552	–0.645	0.131
D_DRY-	–0.637	–3.805*	–3.906⁺	–2.893	–2.826⁺	–4.400*	–3.970*	–3.008*
CELLS	–1.085	–2.769	–2.015	–1.771	–2.399	–3.633	–2.683	–2.969
D_ELE-	–1.979*	0.809*	–0.964*	–0.147	–0.432	–0.562	–0.711	–0.514
CTRIC	–4,025	–2.794	–3.087	–1.151	–1.401	–1.810	–1.768	–1.609
D_ELECT-	–1.606*	–1.897*	–1.589	0.028	–1.932	–0.955⁺	–1.569*	–1.252*
RONICCOM	–3.588	–4.782	–1.811	0.049	–1.716	1.964	–3.088	–3.309
D_CONEL-	–2.120*	0.765	–0.948	–1.151	–2.569⁺	–0.477	–0.899	–5.036*
ECTRONIC	–2.755	1.190	–1.234	–1.893	–2.233	–1.074	–1.834	–3.712
D_ENGINES	2.103*	0.546	–0.509	0.561	1.406	0.171	–0.858	–0.603
	8.475	–0.419	–0.334	0.503	0.934	0.126	0.843	–1.233
D_PAINT	1.477*	–0.196	–1.143	–1.747	–1.135	–1.894⁺	–2.198⁺	–2.043⁺
	2.675	–0.232	–1.067	–1.419	–1.196	–2.176	–2.095	–2.189
D_PERCARE	4.690	0.488	0.669	0.801	2.031	–1.751	–3.222	–1.744
	1.729	0.204	0.221	0.274	0.751	–0.655	–1.626	–1.398
D_PEST	0.692*	–0.135	–0.969	0.364	0.538	–0.051	–0.719	–0.525
	5.469	–1.626	–1.276	0.692	1.154	–0.075	–1.023	–1.607
D_PHAR	0.361	–0.748	–0.114	–0.113	0.459	0.175	–0.307	–0.414
	1.564	–1.225	–0.153	–0.363	1.109	0.477	–0.678	–1.526
NOBS	499	599	694	726	680	635	603	535
R^2	0.905	0.907	0.871	0.903	0.874	0.844	0.882	0.927

Note: D relates to industry dummy.
Source: Siddharthan and Lal (2004).

Their results show a rapid increase in the values of the spillover coefficients over the years. It is also evident that spillovers are more likely to occur in cases where the technology-gap between the MNE and the domestic firm is small. The results also show that value added per unit cost of labour of local firms is high wherever the corresponding values of the foreign firms are also high. This result holds good even after the introduction of industry dummies in the unbalanced panel. By and large, firms with higher labour productivities gained by spillovers while those with lower productivities (larger gaps) did not benefit by spillovers. In other words, spillovers are possible only if the firms are in a comparable technological paradigm.

The survey of Indian literature shows that successful Indian firms did not wait for spillovers to take place. They had a positive strategy to tackle the entry of foreign firms with advanced technology. Some Indian firms entered into a series of non-equity strategic alliances with several MNEs and Indian firms (Siddharthan and Nollen 2004). Such strategic alliances seem to have enabled these Indian firms to enhance their productivity and emerge competitive in several sectors like IT, automobiles, electronics, drugs and pharmaceuticals.

The studies surveyed in this chapter show that technology and productivity spillovers from MNEs to local firms are not automatic. Spillovers depend on the nature of the investing MNE and the technological base, ownership and managerial practices of the domestic firms. In the case of China, FDI from developed countries resulted in technology and productivity spillovers to non-State owned Chinese firms. State-owned firms did not benefit from spillovers nor did investments from overseas Chinese result in productivity spillovers (Buckley et al. 2002).

Studies done for India (Siddharthan and Lal 2004; Kathuria 2002), and for Latin American countries (Aitken and Harrison 1999; Kokko et al. 1996), show that firms that already enjoyed a good technological base, had a smaller productivity gap with regard to MNEs, and spent on in-house R&D captured spillovers. The rest did not. Further, in several industries, local firms also enjoyed higher productivity levels than the MNEs and, therefore, the assumption that MNEs always demonstrate higher productivity levels is not valid. Some studies also reported negative spillovers indicating a market stealing effect by MNEs. Some studies (Kokko et al. 2001) also show a higher presence of spillovers in the import substitution regime than in the liberalized regime. In the liberalized regime, the quantity of FDI inflows could be more but in the regulated regime, the quality of FDI in terms of spillovers and domestic sourcing of components was higher (Kumar 2002). Given this finding the spillovers from FDI could decline in the current WTO regime, which aims at elimination of regulations. Under these conditions, firms from developing countries should develop positive strategies such as non-equity strategic alliances and networking with other firms to compete successfully with MNEs than passively wait for spillovers to occur.

References

Aitken, Brian J. and Ann E. Harrison (1999), 'Do Domestic Firms Benefit from Direct Foreign Investment? Evidence from Venezuela', *American Economic Review*, Vol. 89, No.3, pp. 605–18.

Audretsch, David B. and Erik E. Lehmann (2005), 'Does the Knowledge Spillover Theory of Entrepreneurship Hold for Regions?', *Research Policy*, Vol. 34, No. 8, pp. 1191–202.

Banga, Rashmi (2004), 'Impact of Japanese and U.S. FDI on Productivity Growth: A Firm Level Analysis', *Economic and Political Weekly, Review of Industry and Management*, 31 January, Vol. 39, No. 5, pp. 453–60.

Belderbos, Rene and Martin Carree (2002), 'The Location of Japanese Investments in China: Agglomeration Effects, Keiretsu, and Firm Heterogeneity', *Journal of the Japanese and International Economies*, Vol. 16, No. 2, pp. 194–211.

Breschi, Stefano and Franco Malerba (2001), 'The Geography of Innovation and Economic Clustering: Some Introductory Notes', *Industrial and Corporate Change*, Vol. 10, No. 4, pp. 817–33.

Broadman, Harry G. and Xiaolun Sun (1997), 'The Distribution of Foreign Direct Investment in China', *World Economy*, Vol. 20, Issue 3, pp. 339–61.

Buckley, Peter J., Jeremy Clegg and Chenjqi Wang (2002), 'The Impact of Inward FDI on the Performance of Chinese Manufacturing Firms', *Journal of International Business Studies*, Vol. 33, No. 4, pp. 637–55.

Cooke, Philip (2001), 'Regional Innovation Systems, Clusters, and the Knowledge Economy', *Industrial and Corporate Change*, Vol. 10, No. 4, pp. 945–74.

Cuervo-Cazurra, Alvaro (2006), 'Who cares about corruption?', *Journal of International Business Studies*, Vol. 37, No. 6, pp. 807–22.

Dougherty, Sean, Richard Herd and Ping He (2007), 'Has a Private Sector Emerged in China's Industry? Evidence from a Quarter of a Million Chinese Firms', *China Economic Review*, Vol. 18, No.3, pp. 309–34.

Eaton, Curtis B., Richard G. Lipsey and A. Edward Safarian (1994), 'The

Theory of Multinational Plant Location: Agglomeration and Disagglomerations', Economic Growth and Policy Program, Canada Institute of Advanced Research, Canada.

Fan, C. Simon and Yifan Hu (2007), 'Foreign Direct Investment and Indigenous Technological Efforts: Evidence from China' *Economics Letters*, Vol. 96, Issue 2, August, pp. 253–8; also available at *www.ln.edu.hk/econ/staff/fansimon/Hu-letters.pdf*.

Feinberg, Susan E. and Sumit K. Majumdar (2001), 'Technology Spillovers from Foreign Direct Investment in the Indian Pharmaceutical Industry', *Journal of International Business Studies*, Vol. 33, No.3, pp. 421–37.

Globerman, Steven (2002), 'Global Foreign Direct Investment Flows: The Role of Governance Infrastructure', *World Development*, Vol. 30, No. 11, pp. 1899–919.

Globerman, Steven and Daniel Shapiro (2003), 'Governance Infrastructure and US Foreign Direct Investment', *Journal of International Business Studies*', Vol. 34, No. 1, pp. 19–39.

Goldar, B., V.S. Renganathan and Rashmi Banga (2004), 'Ownership and Efficiency in Engineering Firms: 1990–91 to 1999–2000', *Economic and Political Weekly*, *Review of Industry and Management*, 31 January, Vol. 39, No. 5, pp. 441–7.

Guo, Hongjun and Reinhilde Veugelers (2006), 'MNEs, Internationalization of R&D and the Impact on Local Firms: Evidence from China's High-tech Industries', AIB Annual Conference, Beijing, China, June.

Habib, Mohsin and Leon Zurawicki (2002), 'Corruption and Foreign Direct Investment', *Journal of International Business Studies*, Vol. 33, No. 2, pp. 291–307.

He, Canfei (2002), 'Information Costs, Agglomeration Economies and the Location of Foreign Direct Investment in China', *Regional Studies*, December, Vol. 36, No. 9, pp. 1029–36.

Hu, Albert G.Z., Gary H. Jefferson, and Qian Jinchang (2005), 'R&D and Technology Transfer: Firm-level Evidence from Chinese Industry', *The Review of Economics and Statistics*, November, Vol. 87, No. 4, pp. 780–6.

Jianping, Ding (1999), 'Agglomeration Effects in Manufacturing Location—Are There Any Country's Preferences?', *Economia Internazionale*, Vol. 52, No. 1, pp. 59–78.

Kathuria, Vinish (2000), 'Productivity Spillovers from Technology Transfer to Indian Manufacturing Firms', *Journal of International Development*, Vol. 12, pp. 343–69.

______ (2002), 'Liberalisation, FDI and Productivity Spillovers—An Analysis of Indian Manufacturing Firms', *Oxford Economic Papers*, Vol. 54, pp. 688–718.

Kokko, Ari, Ruben Tansini and Mario C. Zejan (1996), 'Local Technological Capability and Productivity Spillovers from FDI in the Uruguayan

Manufacturing Sector', *Journal of Development Studies*, Vol. 32, No. 4, pp. 602–11.

Kokko, Ari, Mario Zejan and Ruben Tansini (2001), 'Trade Regimes and Spillover Effects of FDI: Evidence from Uruguay', *Weltwirtschaftliches Archiv*, Vol. 137, No. 1, pp. 124–49.

Kumar, Nagesh (2002), *Globalisation and the Quality of Foreign Direct Investment*, Oxford University Press, New Delhi, p. 274.

Motohashi, Kazuyuki (2006), 'R&D of Multinationals in China: Structure, Motivations and Regional Difference', Research Institute of Economy, Trade and Industry (RIETI) Discussion Paper Series 06-E-005.

Ray, Saon (2004), 'MNEs, Strategic Alliances and Efficiency of Firms: Emerging Trends', *Economic and Political Weekly, Review of Industry and Management*, 31 January, Vol. 39, No. 5, pp. 434–40.

Ronde, Patrick and Caroline Hussler (2005), 'Innovation in Regions: What does Really Matter?', *Research Policy*, Vol. 34, No. 8, pp. 1150–72.

Siddharthan, N.S. and K. Lal (2004), 'Liberalisation, MNE and Productivity of Indian Enterprises', *Economic and Political Weekly, Review of Industry and Management*, January 31, 2004, Vol. 39, No. 5, pp. 448–52.

Siddharthan, N.S. and Stanley Nollen (2004), 'International Growth by Networking but not M&A: The Counter Example of the Indian Software Industry', in Michael A. Trick (ed.), *Global Corporate Evolution: Looking Inward or Looking Outward?*, International Management Series, Vol. 4, Carnegie Mellon University Press, Pittsburgh, pp. 53–60.

Siddharthan, N.S. and Y. Rajan (2002), *Global Business, Technology and Knowledge Sharing: Lessons for Developing Country Enterprises*, Macmillan, New Delhi, pp. i–xvii, 1–217.

Todo, Yasuyki, Weiying Zhang and Li-An Zhou (2006), 'Knowledge Spillovers from Foreign Direct Investment in R&D: Evidence from a Chinese Science Park', Social Science Research Network (SSRN) Working Paper, October.

Tuan, Chyau, Ng, and F.Y. Linda (2003), 'FDI Facilitated by Agglomeration Economies: Evidence from Manufacturing and Services Joint Ventures in China', *Journal of Asian Economics*, January, Vol. 13, No. 6, pp. 749–65.

Wei, Shang-jin (1999), 'Can China and India double their inward foreign direct investment?', Paper presented at the NBER Conference on India, Neemrana, December, *www.nber.org/~confer/99/indiaf99/India-China-FDI.PDF*

Wei, Shang-jin (2000), 'How Taxing is Corruption on International Investors?', *The Review of Economics and Statistics*, Vol. 82, No. 1, pp. 1–11.

Wei, Yingqi (1999), 'The Regional Distribution of Foreign Direct Investment in China', *Regional Studies*, Vol. 33, No. 9, pp. 857–67.

Wei, Yingqi Annie (2004), 'Foreign Direct Investment in China', in Yingqi

Annie Wei and V.N. Balasubramanyam (eds), *Foreign Direct Investment: Six Country Case Studies*, Edward Elgar, Cheltenham, UK, pp. 9–46.

Wei, Yingqi Annie and V.N. Balasubramanyam (eds) (2004), *Foreign Direct Investment: Six Country Case Studies*, Edward Elgar, Cheltenham, UK.

Yao, Shujie and Zongyi Zhang (2001), 'Regional Growth in China under Economic Reform', *The Journal of Development Studies*, Vol. 38, No. 2, pp. 167–86.

Zucker, Lynne G., Michael R. Derby and Marilynn B. Brewer (1998), 'Intellectual and the Birth of US Biotechnology Enterprises', *American Economic Review*, Vol. 88, No. 1, pp. 290–306.

4

Agricultural Development Policies and the Growth of Indian Agriculture

RAMESH CHAND

Introduction

Agriculture was the predominant sector of the Indian economy at the time of independence. The share of agriculture in total gross domestic product (GDP) at that time was more than 55 per cent, and about 70 per cent of workforce was engaged in the sector. Since the urban industrial and tertiary sectors were very small, and absorbed only 26 per cent of the labour force, the vast majority of the Indian population, about 83 per cent, lived in rural areas (according to the 1951 Census). Although agriculture was the predominant sector, its productivity was very low and output growth during the period 1901–46 was less than half that of population growth. As a consequence, the per capita income of the rural population was extremely low.

Predominance of agriculture in the national economy, low productivity resulting in low level of per capita income of the rural population and pathetic condition of rural areas where the vast majority of population resided, gave rise to the idea that agricultural development was the key to economic development, improvement in living standards and living conditions of the people as well as eradication of widespread poverty and malnutrition prevalent in the country. It was thus imperative to follow a development strategy which favoured high growth rates of agriculture. In light of this,

this chapter reviews the policies followed in the country since independence for agricultural development. Growth rates achieved in agriculture and non-agriculture sectors and in various sub-sectors of agriculture in different phases of policies are discussed in-depth. Challenges to agricultural growth in recent years and the strategy to sustain high growth are also discussed.

Broad Characteristics of Indian Agriculture

Agriculture in India is in the hands of millions of peasant households which follow mixed crop and livestock farming. The bulk of these units comprise tiny land holdings with a preponderance of owner cultivation. The number of operational holdings has been increasing at a fast rate due to population pressure and lack of adequate employment opportunities outside the agriculture sector. During the three decades between 1960–61 and 1990–91, the net area available for cultivation increased by only 7.5 per cent but the number of holdings during the same period increased by about 218 per cent. Because of this, the average size of land holding declined from 2.69

Table 4.1: Major Characteristics of Indian Agriculture

(million hectare)

Particulars	*1950–51*	*1970–71*	*1990–91*	*2000–01*
Geographic area	328.7	328.7	328.7	328.7
Reporting area	284.3	303.8	304.9	306.2
Net sown area	118.8	140.3	143.0	141.1
	41.8	*46.2*	*46.9*	*46.1*
Number of holdings (million)		70.49	106.6	120.8
Average farm size (ha.)		2.30	1.55	1.32
Net irrigated area	20.8	31.1	47.8	54.6
	(17.5)	(22.2)	(33.4)	(38.7)
Area sown more than once	13.1	25.5	42.7	46.8
	(11.0)	(18.2)	(29.9)	(33.2)

Note: Figures in italics are per cent of reporting area and figures in parentheses are per cent of NSA.

Source: *Agricultural Statistics at a Glance*, various issues, Ministry of Agriculture, GOI, New Delhi.

hectares during 1960–61 to 1.55 hectares during 1990–91. During the next decade, net sown area (NSA) in the country showed a small decline, whereas the number of land holdings increased by 13 per cent to reach a level of 120.822 million. Consequently, the proportion of marginal holdings of (size below 1 hectare) reached 63 per cent of the total holdings during 2000–01 while 82 per cent holdings are of the size below 2 hectares (Table 4.1).

The second important characteristic of Indian agriculture is that despite tremendous expansion in major, medium and minor irrigation, 60 per cent of cultivated area does not have any access to irrigation and is still dependent on rainfall. The third important feature is that on most of the area only one crop is cultivated. More than one crop is raised only on 35 per cent of the cultivated area. The fourth feature of India's agriculture is that it is crowded due to heavy population pressure. Availability of cultivated land per worker has remained low and declined from 1.22 hectare during 1950–51 to 0.77 hectare in 1990–91 and further to 0.60 hectare during 2000–01. Thus, the development policies for the sector had to be tailored to suit the characteristics and needs of smallholder agriculture that was largely rain-fed.

Production Profile of Agriculture

India is a vast country that produces a wide range of food and non-food commodities. The highest importance is attached to cereals which are our staple food and the main source for meeting calorie (energy) requirements. Indian farmers have adjusted the production profile according to emerging opportunities which can be seen from the changes in composition of output of agriculture sector between crops and livestock and share of different crops/crop groups in the value of total crop output (Table 4.2).

Agricultural output has witnessed an increase in the share of livestock output and decline in the share of crop sector between 1970–71 and 2005–06. Livestock constituted less than 15 per cent of total agricultural output in 1970–71 and in the next three decades its share increased to about 27 per cent.

Significant changes have also been experienced in the composition of crop output. Cereals continue to dominate crop output though their share showed a sharp decline from close to 44 per cent during 1970–71 to 29 per cent during 2005–06. Share of fruits and

Table 4.2: Changing Profile of Agriculture Production in India

Group/Commodity	*1970–71*	*1980–81*	*1990–91*	*2000–01*	*2005–06*
Share in total agriculture output (per cent)					
Crop sector	85.14	82.65	76.93	73.30	73.26
Livestock sector	14.86	17.35	23.07	26.70	26.74
Share in crop output (per cent)					
Cereals	43.90	37.86	34.92	31.94	28.86
Rice	24.08	19.39	18.86	16.81	14.84
Wheat	10.06	10.53	10.71	11.09	10.12
Pulses	5.30	6.34	6.69	4.41	4.16
Chickpea	2.12	2.64	2.44	1.60	1.63
Oilseeds	9.88	8.70	13.27	7.02	10.54
Groundnut	4.92	3.29	4.77	2.17	2.41
Sugarcane	5.51	8.00	6.73	6.88	4.88
Cotton	3.68	3.28	3.35	2.47	3.79
Fruit and vegetables	15.55	16.89	18.04	25.58	25.61

Source: *National Accounts Statistics*, Central Statistical Organization (CSO), Government of India, New Delhi, various issues.

vegetables in total value of crop sector increased from 15.55 per cent to 25.61 per cent in the same period.

Paddy or rice is the most important crop of the country, which alone accounts for more than 20 per cent of the value of all crops produced in the country. Since 1970–71, the importance of rice has declined. Wheat is the second most important crop produced in India. Its share in total crop output has remained stable at around 10.5 per cent.

Production of pulses in India remained either stagnant or showed very small growth in some years. Due to supply constraints, the prices of pulses have been rising at a faster rate compared to other crops. This resulted in an increase in the share of pulses in the value of crop output between 1970–71 and 1990–91. Chickpea is the most important pulse crop of the country but its share like other pulses witnessed a decline after 1990–91.

The share of oilseeds showed an increase from 8.7 per cent in 1980–81 to 13.27 per cent in 1990–91 as this decade experienced almost a doubling of oilseed production in the country. This may have occurred due to several measures undertaken by the government to improve oilseed production and to make India self-sufficient in oilseeds during the mid- and late-1980s. These include measures like the Technology Mission on Oilseeds and National Oilseed Development Project. As the policy protection to the oilseed sector was withdrawn during the 1990s, growth in production slowed down and their share plummeted to less than 7 per cent of value of crop output by 2000–01. A similar trend is observed in groundnut, which is the most important oilseed produced in the country.

Among individual crops, sugarcane occupies the third position after rice and wheat, in terms of output contribution in value terms. The importance of sugarcane witnessed a huge increase during the period 1970–71 to 1980–81 after which its production could not keep pace with the growth in the crop sector. Cotton is another important cash crop of India, which contributed more than three per cent of crop output. Its contribution suffered a serious setback around 2000–01 but it has again recovered lost ground in recent years.

The share of fruits and vegetables, which constitute a very large number of commodities, has shown an improvement throughout. The highest gains were recorded during 1990–91 to 2000–01 with the contribution of fruit and vegetable to crop output witnessing an increase from 18.04 per cent to 25.58 per cent.

Phases in Agriculture Policy

The main task facing the country at the time of independence was to bring about rapid economic growth and to achieve several challenging development goals. To achieve this, the country embarked upon the strategy of Five Year Plans for the formulation and execution of development programmes; and the government started playing an important role in the creation of infrastructure for long-run growth as well as the development of the agriculture sector. At the same time, strong policy and institutional interventions were undertaken to achieve a transformation of the agricultural and rural economy. This led to the involvement of the State in diverse activities such as procurement of large agricultural output, supply of inputs and credit, provision of subsidies of different kinds, promotion of agronomic research for adaptation of exotic varieties and development of infrastructural facilities (Krishnaji 1990). According to Krishnaji (1990), the agricultural price policy which evolved subsequently must then be seen as an essential part of a large package of policies designed to promote rapid growth in a few regions well endowed with irrigation facilities and to encourage private investment in the necessary means (modern inputs, tube-wells, farm machinery etc.) for the production of new varieties.

Agricultural policy and development strategy followed in the country during the last five and half decades can be broadly divided into three phases. A detailed discussion on some of the policy measures in each phase is presented in Rao (1994).

Pre-green Revolution Period

This phase refers to the period 1950–51 to the mid-1960s which is also called the pre-Green Revolution period. This period witnessed tremendous agrarian reforms, institutional changes and development of major irrigation projects. The Indian National Congress, which assumed power after independence, had promised the peasantry freedom from semi-feudal exploitation by the landlords. In pursuance of this, legislations for the abolition of *zamindari* were enacted by all the states and the whole process was completed within the decade 1950–60 (Dandekar 1994). Under this, 20 million tillers got control over the land that they were cultivating. The tenancy reforms also provided for regulation of rent and security of tenure, beside conferring ownership rights on tenants.

Another measure under land reforms was legislation to impose ceilings on the maximum land that a household could own. Apart from these, efforts were made to minimize the exploitation of cultivators by money lenders and traders by expanding the co-operative credit system (Rao 1996).

On the production and technology side, the Intensive Agricultural District Programme was adopted with the main thrust to demonstrate potentialities of increase in food production through a package of improved agricultural practices and assistance to cultivators in the form of inputs and credit in favourable areas (Dantwala 1986).

About 8 million hectares of additional area was brought under irrigation during this period which increased coverage of irrigation from 17 per cent during 1950–51 to 20.8 per cent during 1965–66. Fertilizer use during the same period increased from less than 1 kg of NPK per hectare of NSA to about 6 kg.

In terms of achievement, output of all crops taken together increased at the rate of 2.42 per cent per annum. Expansion in area was the main source of output growth (see Table 4.3). Reliance on food imports could not be reduced during this period mainly because of violent fluctuations in the output of food grains, high growth in population and severe droughts during the mid-1960s.

While radical measures such as land reforms were widely acclaimed, Indian policy makers were accused of deliberately keeping food prices low, motivated alleged by an urban bias. It was alleged that food prices were suppressed by the policy of large scale imports which did not let Indian agriculture exploit its full potential.

The Green Revolution Phase

The country faced severe shortage of food during the early 1960s and the government imported 4.6 million tonnes of food grains in 1963 and 10.6 million tonnes in 1966 to meet the demands of the public distribution system. It was then felt that continuing reliance on food imports and aid would impose heavy costs in terms of political pressure and economic instability (Rao 1996); and India started looking desperately for a quick breakthrough in food production. One choice before the country was to go in for the spread of new seeds of high yielding varieties (HYVs) of wheat and rice which had been recently evolved by the Consultative Group on International Agricultural Research (CGIAR) institutes like the Centro Internacional de Mejoramiento de MaizYTrigo (CIMMYT) in Mexico and International Rice Institute (IRRI) in Philippines. Amidst serious differences, the government took the bold decision to go for the import and spread of HYV seeds of wheat and paddy. Along with this, a far more important policy decision was taken on agricultural prices (Bhatia 1988) to create a favourable price climate for agricultural products. To achieve this, the Agricultural Prices Commission was set up almost simultaneously to advise the government on agricultural price policy.

The adoption of HYV technology yielded such spectacular results that the phenomenon was hailed with euphoria as the 'Green Revolution' (Dantwala 1986). In a short span of less than five years following adoption of HYV technology, wheat production doubled in the country. Food grain production jumped from 83 million tonnes during the five years preceding the Green Revolution to 100 million tonnes in the five years, 1967–68 to 1971–72, which marked the beginning of the Green Revolution in India.

Food grain output during the period 1966–67 to 1980–81 moved on a trend growth rate of 2.66 per cent, exceeding population growth rate. The major gains in this came from productivity (Table 4.3).

Table 4.3: Growth Rates in Agriculture Output during Different Periods

(per cent per annum)

Period	*Food grains*			*Non-food grains*			*All crops*			*Population growth rate*
	Area	*Production*	*Yield*	*Area*	*Production*	*Yield*	*Area*	*Production*	*Yield*	
1949–50 to 1966–67	1.09	1.97	0.78	1.98	3.18	0.56	1.33	2.42	0.72	2.06
1966–67 to 1980–81	0.49	2.66	1.72	0.86	2.46	1.41	0.58	2.58	1.6	2.27
1980–81 to 1990–91	–0.13	2.99	2.78	1.45	4.07	2.39	0.25	3.39	2.61	2.12

Note: Growth rates based on semi-log trend equation fitted to index numbers of area, production and yield with base 1980–81.

Source: *Agricultural Statistics at a Glance*, various issues, Ministry of Agriculture, GOI, New Delhi; *National Accounts Statistics*, various issues, CSO, GOI, New Delhi; *Economic Survey*, various issues, Ministry of Finance, GOI, New Delhi.

The biggest achievement of the new agricultural strategy has been the attainment of self-sufficiency in food grains. Since the Green Revolution technology involved the use of modern inputs, its spread led to fast growth in the agro-input industry. Similarly, improvement in agricultural income increased the demand for industrial goods in rural areas. Agrarian reforms during this period took a back seat while research, extension, input supply, credit, marketing, price support and spread of technology were the prime concerns of policy makers.

Adoption of new farm technology followed by increased commercialization of agriculture, raised the demand for working capital to buy modern inputs and to make investments in irrigation structure, land improvement and farm implements and machinery. Since co-operatives were not able to cater to the credit requirements of the farm sector, the government took a decision on the nationalization of scheduled commercial banks which were then asked to open their branches in rural areas and charged with the responsibility to apportion 34 per cent of their advances to the priority sector which included agriculture and small-scale industry (Bhatia 1988).

The production-cum-technology approach supplemented by price and market support paid rich dividends, especially in food grain production during the late 1960s to 1980s. Agricultural growth witnessed acceleration during the decade of the 1980s for both food grains and non-food grains. An impressive feature of growth during this period has been that it happened due to acceleration in yield growth rate (see Table 4.3). The main factors underlying this growth rate have been:

(a) Output growth picked up in many less developed areas in the central and eastern regions where growth had been sluggish in the early days of the Green Revolution (Sawant and Achutan 1995);
(b) Diversification of crop pattern and activities.

Attainment of self-sufficiency in food during this period opened up opportunities for human development (Rao 1996). However, some grey spots remained. One, the new technology favoured well-endowed regions. While Punjab, Haryana, Western Uttar Pradesh, the deltaic region of Tamil Nadu and parts of Andhra Pradesh witnessed spectacular growth in food grains, output in rain-fed and dry land areas remained stagnant or crept on a low-growth path. This intensified regional disparities in income in the country.

Agricultural Policy During the Economic Reforms Period

Because of a serious fiscal crisis that developed during the 1980s in the country, the Government of India embraced the New Economic Policy in 1991 which consisted of two components: (i) the short-term stabilization measures which included reduction of fiscal deficit, devaluation of its currency (Rupee), and dismantling of the barriers to the free flow of foreign capital; (ii) the medium-term structural programmes involving reforms in fiscal policy, exchange rate policy, trade and industrial policy and policies on financial sector reform and capital market reforms. Further, thorough changes were made in the foreign trade policy in 1991 to make the trade policy consistent with the new economic policy and economic reforms. There was a shift in focus from an inward looking-policy towards an outward-looking policy. A series of reforms was introduced to provide competitive stimulus to the domestic industry and a New Industrial Policy was announced on 24 July 1991. The policy aimed at simplification and transparency. The procedures were reduced to the minimum. Further action planned in the area of trade included the eventual elimination of all restrictions on imports; removal of export licensing and minimum export prices; decanalizing and allowing private participation in the export of major agricultural and mineral products; reducing the role of State monopoly agencies in foreign trade; and, step-by-step reduction in peak ad-valorem tariff rates, leading to further simplification of the tariff regime.

Initially, the reforms focused mainly on the industrial and financial sectors and agriculture was mostly kept outside the scope of reforms. However, the agriculture sector benefited indirectly from reforms due to the exchange rate policy and improvement in terms of trade (TOT) (Dholakia 1997; Singh 1995). On the trade front, India followed highly protective trade policies for agriculture till early 1990s. Except for a few traditional commercial commodities, agricultural trade was subjected to measures like quantitative restrictions, canalization, licences, quotas and high tariff rates. However, this scenario witnessed significant changes in the era of economic reforms initiated in 1991 and with the implementation of the World Trade Organization (WTO) Agreement on Agriculture in 1995. As international prices were high during the initial years of formation of WTO, trade liberalization helped in improving TOT for agriculture. However, this turned out to be a short-term phenomenon, and, as international prices of agricultural commodities started falling around 1998, liberal trade started showing an adverse impact on domestic producers' prices.

Though external trade in agriculture was liberalized to a large extent, reforms in domestic agricultural trade and markets were rather slow. Domestic trade continued to be regulated by various provisions that were adversely affecting the efficiency of domestic markets, private trade and growers and the producers. Government intervention in the prices of some commodities was discouraging private sector investment and participation in agricultural trade (Chand 2003). Towards the year 2000, a realization started taking place that lack of reforms in domestic markets was putting domestic production in a disadvantageous position in competing with imports facilitated by the liberalization of external trade (Chand et al. 2003). Domestic trade in most of the agricultural commodities was regulated by the Essential Commodities Act (ECA) which put a number of restrictions on private trade to operate in agricultural market. Some of these restrictions were licensing requirements, stock limits, levy, and restrictions on inter-state and interregional movement of produce. Most of these controls were relaxed and gradually phased out through various amendments to the ECA during 2002, 2003 and 2004 except the levy component. Similarly, the Milk and Milk Product Order was amended during 2002 to relax restrictions on private investments in the dairy sector.

Other important restrictions on the private sector have been on direct purchase of farm produce from farmers, contract farming and setting up of private markets for agricultural produce. These vary from state to state and are governed by state level 'APMC' (Agriculture Produce Marketing Committee) Acts. In September 2003, the Central Government prepared a Model APMC Act and states were asked to change their APMC acts on the basis of the Model APMC Act to allow and encourage private sector to go for: (i) contract farming, (ii) direct purchase from farmers and (iii) establishment of private markets. Most of the states have reformed their APMC Acts as suggested by the Model Act, and others are in the process of making changes. Thus, reforms in the agriculture sector started very late, towards 2002. Following these reforms, the private sector has shown a lot of interest in entering agricultural marketing and trade and its full impact on agriculture sector and farmers will be realized after some time.

Agricultural Growth Rate during the Post-reforms Period

GDP of agriculture increased at more than 3 per cent per annum during 1980–81 to 1989–90 which was considered a reasonably satisfactory performance for the sector. The country started on a new economic path with far-reaching reforms in 1991 but the agriculture sector was not targeted directly by the reforms for a couple of years. However, this sector was affected indirectly through changes in the exchange rate, export liberalization, and improvement in TOT for some years resulting from reduced protection to industry. Another factor which contributed positively to agriculture growth during the initial years of reform was a substantial hike in minimum support prices of cereal crops given by the government, mainly to reduce the gap between domestic and international prices (Chand 2005a), that resulted largely from a devaluation of the overvalued exchange rate. The impact of these changes and various other factors was a small acceleration in the growth rate of agriculture during the first six years of reforms (Table 4.4). The growth rate of GDP in agriculture and allied sector was 3.64 per cent during the period 1990–91 to

Table 4.4: Growth Rate in GDP Agriculture and Non-agriculture Before and After Reforms

Period	*GDP Total*	*GDP agri. and allied*	*GDP agri.*	*GDP fishery*	*GDP non-agri.*
1980–81 to 1989–90*	5.52	3.12	3.29	5.93	6.88
1990–91 to 1996–97*	6.01	3.64	3.69	7.41	7.04
1996–97 to 2004–05*	5.72	1.66	1.65	4.30	7.06
2000–01 to 2005–06#	6.34	1.97			7.65

Note: * At 1993–94 prices

At 1999–2000 prices

Source of basic data: National Accounts Statistics, CSO, Government of India, New Delhi, various issues.

1996–87, which was 0.5 percentage points higher than the previous decade. In fact, during the early years of reforms, the gap in growth rates between agriculture and non-agriculture slightly narrowed.

Disaggregation of the agriculture sector into sub-sectors shows that fisheries and horticulture—which account for 4.6 per cent and 19.0 per cent of the value of output of agriculture and allied sectors—were the main source for acceleration in the growth rate of agricultural output in the initial years of reforms (Table 4.5). However, the situation for agriculture turned adverse after 1996–97 and this covered all the sub-sectors of agriculture. The growth rate in output of fruits and vegetables decelerated from 5.92 per cent to 3.28 per cent, while fisheries witnessed a decline from 7.41 per cent to 4.30 per cent. The deceleration is also seen in the case of livestock sector. Output of non-horticulture crops and cereal groups experienced nil growth after 1996–97. Output of the total crop sector showed an annual growth rate of a mere 0.79 per cent while agriculture sector excluding fisheries showed a growth rate of 1.65 per cent per annum. These growth rates are lower than the growth rates in rural population and workforce employed in agriculture. A clear implication of this growth trend is that per capita or per worker income in agriculture is declining. This seems to be one of the factors for rising rural and agricultural distress in the country.

Table 4.5: Growth Rate in Output of Various Sub-sectors of Agriculture at 1993–94 Prices

Period	*Crop sector*	*Livestock*	*Fruits and vegetables*	*Non-horticulture crops*	*Cereals*
1980–81 to 1989–90	2.71	4.84	2.42	2.77	3.15
1990–91 to 1996–97	3.22	4.12	5.92	2.59	2.23
1996–97 to 2004–05	0.79	3.67	3.28	0.05	0.02

Source of basic data: *National Accounts Statistics*, CSO, GOI, New Delhi, various issues.

In contrast to the slowdown in agriculture, GDP of the non-agriculture sector shows a robust and rising growth rate. Using the new base (1999–2000) of National Accounts Statistics, for which some of the data are available, annual growth rate in non-agriculture GDP after 2000–01 is 7.6 per cent, whereas growth rate in agriculture is hardly 2 per cent.

Causes for Slowdown in Agriculture Growth

The major causes for slowdown in agricultural growth are identified as: (i) decline in area under cultivation due to expanding urbanization and industrialization; (ii) deterioration in TOT for agriculture; (iii) stagnant crop intensity; (iv) poor progress of irrigation and fertilizers; (v) decline in supply of electricity to agriculture and (vi) slowdown in diversification (Chand et al. 2007). Besides these factors, regulation, price policy, institutional factors and technology are also quite important for the present state of agriculture. Progress and changes in these factors during the 1980s and during the initial and later years of reforms are presented in Table 4.6. The table shows that as compared to the 1980s there was a sharp increase in TOT for agriculture during the initial years of reforms. Agriculture prices relative to non-agriculture prices increased annually by 0.95 per cent. There was also some improvement in the growth of irrigation during the early years of reforms. Public sector investments did not grow during these years and consequently the growth in stock of public sector capital formation declined from 3.94 per cent to 1.87

per cent. However, private sector investments in the years 1990–91 to 1996–97 showed more than three times growth as compared to the period 1980–81 to 1990–91. This resulted in the same growth rate in total capital stock in agriculture during the period 1990–91 to 1996–97 as was seen during the decade of the 1980s. The pace of expansion in gross cropped area and the pace of diversification were also as strong as during the 1980s. There was a sharp decline in the growth of fertilizer use and electricity (power supply) used in agriculture but this was more than compensated by the expansion in area, irrigation, diversification, and movement of TOT in favour of agriculture. After 1996–97, almost all the factors except credit, turned unfavorable

Table 4.6: Growth Rate in Area, Input Use, Credit and Capital Formation in Agriculture Before and After Reforms

per cent/year

Variable	*1980–81 to 1990–91*	*1990–91 to 1996–97*	*1996–97 to 2004–05*
Gross cropped area	0.430	0.430	–0.480
Net sown area	–0.080	0.040	–0.550
Cropping Intensity	0.510	0.390	0.070
Gross irrigated area	2.280	2.620	0.510
NPK Use/ha NSA	8.255	2.401	2.044
Electricity consumed in agriculture/ha NSA	14.162	9.390	–0.159
Area witnessed crop shift per cent	5.600	5.600	4.800
TOT	0.189	0.947	–1.630
Public sector net fixed capital stock/ha NSA	3.939	1.872	1.976
Private sector net fixed capital stock/ha NSA	0.642	2.134	1.721
Total net fixed capital stock/ha NSA	2.085	2.010	1.838
Credit supply/ha NSA	3.810	7.466	15.336

Note: Growth rates in area and crop intensity are up to the year 2003–04; NSA: net sown area.

Sources of basic data:

National Accounts Statistics, CSO, GOI, New Delhi, various issues;
Agricultural Statistics at Glance, Ministry of Agriculture, GOI, New Delhi;
Economic Survey, Ministry of Finance, GOI, New Delhi.

for the growth of agriculture output. The NSA witnessed a decline at the rate of 0.55 per cent which was not compensated by any increase in cropping intensity. Gross cropped area also declined. The biggest setback to the output of the crop sector came from the decline in TOT for agriculture and slowdown in expansion of irrigation. Since 1996–97, TOT for agriculture have declined by 1.63 per cent per annum. Liberalization of trade has led to increased integration of the domestic market with the international market. Accordingly, the downward trend in international prices of agricultural commodities since 1997–98 has been transmitted to domestic prices resulting in deterioration in TOT for agriculture.

As compared to 2.62 per cent annual growth in irrigated area during the period 1990–91 to 1996–97, the later period shows an annual expansion in irrigation of just 0.51 per cent. The main causes of slowdown in irrigation are: (i) deceleration in public and private sector capital formation after 1996–97; (ii) decline in electric power to agriculture most of which is used for tube-wells and (iii) increased stress on water resources. The pace of diversification has also slowed down in recent years. Thus, the main factors which led to a slowdown in agriculture at the national level after 1996–97 are: (i) decline in area under cultivation, which seems to be the result of expanding urbanization and industrialization, (ii) deterioration in TOT for agriculture, (iii) stagnant crop intensity, (iv) poor progress of irrigation and fertilizers, (v) decline in supply of electricity to agriculture and (vi) slowdown in diversification.

Role of Agriculture in the Growth of the Economy

Agriculture is often considered the backbone of the Indian economy and until recently it was believed that the growth rate of the economy is determined by the performance of agriculture. The reason underlying this assertion was that among the nine major sectors, agriculture remained the largest sector of the economy. Its contribution to total GDP during 1950–51 was more than 50 per cent. Over time, as happens in a developing economy, the share of agriculture in national output started declining. Between 1980–81 and 2000–01, share of agriculture in national income declined from 35.7 per cent to 23.3 per cent. The workforce engaged in agriculture in the same period, however, witnessed a very small decline, from 60.5 per cent to 58.4 per cent (Table 4.7). This is in sharp contrast

Table 4.7: Share of Agriculture in Output and Employment in Indian Economy

Year	*Share of agriculture in GDP*	*Share of agriculture in employment*
1980–81	35.7	60.5
1990–91	29.2	59.0
2000–01	23.3	58.4
2006–07	19.0	

Source of basic data:
National Accounts Statistics, Central Statistical Organisation, GOI, New Delhi, Various Issues.
Agricultural Statistics at Glance, Ministry of Agriculture, GOI, New Delhi.
Note: Agriculture includes crops, livestock, fishery and forestry.

to the experience of developed countries where share of agriculture in employment declined much more sharply with the decline in agriculture's share in GDP.

Faster growth in output of the non-agriculture sector in India did not help much in shifting workforce from agriculture to non-agriculture sector. As a consequence, disparity in per worker income in agriculture and non-agriculture sectors has increased considerably. Recent estimates show that one worker in the non-agriculture sector earns more than the income of five workers in agriculture. This disparity is causing a great deal of concern in the country and is reflected in widespread agrarian distress, which in a large number of cases is culminating in suicides by farmers in some parts of the country.

The growth experience of India since 1950–51 shows that till 1990–91, the agriculture sector had a determining influence on the growth rate of the overall economy and both moved in the same direction. In recent years, particularly since 1996–97, the two types of growth rates have moved on disparate paths with the non-agriculture sector showing acceleration and agriculture sector showing deceleration (Table 4.4 and Figure 4.1). The gap is becoming more pronounced with the passage of time.

It is interesting to analyse the implications of a slowdown in agricultural growth on the growth rate of the total economy. Based on its share in the total output of the economy, a 1 per cent increase in agriculture output pushes up the growth rate of the economy by about 0.19 per cent. Conversely, a 1 per cent decline in agriculture

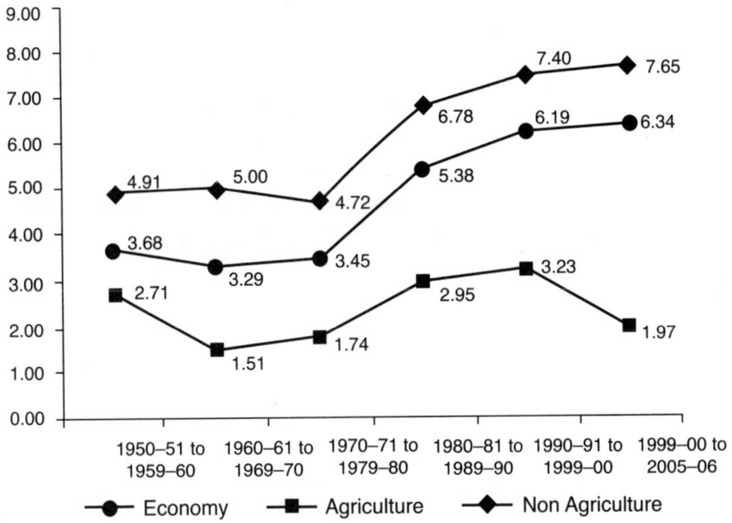

Figure 4.1: Growth in Indian Economy and Agriculture and Non-agriculture Sectors since 1950–51

output pulls down the growth rate of total economy by 0.19 per cent. Apart from the direct contribution, agriculture sector also affects the non-agriculture sector through backward and forward linkages. Recent empirical evidence suggests that a 1 per cent change in agriculture growth results in a 0.38 per cent change in the growth rate of industrial output (Bhanumurthy and Sinha 2004). However, slowdown in the growth rate of agriculture in recent years does not seem to have put a demand side constraint on the growth of industry and other non-agriculture sectors. One of the reasons for this seems to be that the rural (agriculture) sector used large-scale borrowings from private as well as institutional sources to meet its demand for non-agricultural goods. There is a lot of evidence of growing indebtedness among farm households in the country. This debt-ridden demand from the agriculture sector cannot continue for a long time. Therefore, if the growth rate of agriculture is not revived it would make it very difficult to sustain the high growth rate in the economy. Thus, growth rate of the agriculture sector is very important for meeting India's quest to raise the growth rate of the economy to the 10 per cent level.

Reviving and Sustaining High Growth in Agriculture

The present state of Indian agriculture is a matter of serious concern and there is a need to ponder over its future. It is widely acknowledged that there is lot of potential to raise agricultural output in the country. The present level of productivity of most crops in a large number of states is extremely low as compared to the productivity attainable with already available technology, and as compared to that in other countries of comparable level. The average yield of paddy in India is more than 25 per cent lower than the world average and less than half of the yield level in China (Table 4.8). Similarly, productivity of wheat in India is two-thirds that in China. The difference is much larger in the cases of maize and groundnut.

Table 4.8: Productivity of Selected Crops in India, China and the World, 2001–03

(kg/hectare)

Crop	*India*	*China*	*World*
Paddy	2862	6074	3837
Wheat	2693	3907	2665
Maize	1834	4854	4472
Groundnut (in shell)	933	2624	1347
Sugarcane	66,508	69,556	65,293

Source: Agricultural Statistics at a Glance, Ministry of Agriculture, GOI, New Delhi.

A comparison of agricultural productivity across various states within the country also indicates that there is tremendous scope to raise agricultural output by raising productivity. This potential is believed to be very large in the eastern and central regions of the country. The future prospects of agriculture depend upon how the domestic potential is exploited and how we adjust to global changes. The prospects remain bleak if appropriate measures are not taken. Next we discuss some measures which can help in improving the growth and profitability of agriculture and also address the other issues.

Infrastructure Development

The State has played a leading role in creating hardcore infrastructure such as major and medium irrigation projects, rural roads, rural

Table 4.9: Trend in Public Investments in Agriculture since 1976

Period	*Billion Rupees at 1993–94 prices*	*Share in GDP agriculture (per cent)*
1976–1980	59.86	3.39
1981–1985	70.33	3.51
1986–1990	56.78	2.96
1991–1995	48.44	2.09
1996–2000	47.90	1.91
2001–2003	48.97	1.89

Source of basic data: *Agricultural Statistics at A Glance*, various issues, Ministry of Agriculture, GOI, New Delhi.

electrification and setting up of agricultural markets. However, the start of the 1980s witnessed a very significant change in the policy of resource allocation to agriculture. It marked the beginning of a decline in public investment in agriculture. After 1979–80 public investments in agriculture not only failed to keep pace with the growth of GDP of the agriculture sector but their level also declined (Table 4.9). In the early 1980s more than 3.5 per cent of GDP of agriculture was used as public investment. In recent years this has fallen below 2 per cent. This decline in public investment in agriculture is an important factor in the slowdown of agricultural growth (Chand et al. 2007).

Increase in public investments in agriculture is considered a major source for the growth of agricultural output. It is estimated that raising the level of public investment to 4 per cent of sectoral GDP would alone infuse output growth of 2 percentage points (Planning Commission 2007).

Input Use

Irrigation, fertilizers and improved varieties of seed are the main ingredients for increasing agricultural production. Among other things, stagnation in public investment has adversely affected the development of medium and major irrigation. India has the potential to raise the level of irrigation from 40 per cent at present to 73 per cent. As the productivity of irrigated agriculture is double that of unirrigated agriculture, the development of irrigation could prove to be an important source for future growth of agriculture in India.

The present level of fertilizer use in the country is 93 kg, which is lower than that in the neighbouring countries like Bangladesh, Pakistan and Sri Lanka. It may sound incredible that 25 per cent farmers in kharif season and 46 per cent in rabi season do not use any fertilizers (Table 4.10). More than half of the farmers in kharif and about two-third in rabi season do not use improved seeds and pesticides. Veterinary services are availed by less than one-third of the farmers in the country. Spreading and ensuring the use of modern inputs would provide a big boost to agricultural production.

Table 4.10: Percentage of Farmers using Modern Inputs

Input	*Kharif*	*Rabi*
Fertilizer	75.7	54.2
Improved seed	46.3	34.3
Pesticides	46.4	30.8
Veterinary service	30.3	22.3

Source: Some Aspects of Farming, NSS 59th Round, July 2005, National Sample Survey Organization, Ministry of Statistics and Programme Implementation, GOI, New Delhi.

Elasticity of crop output with respect to fertilizers is estimated to vary between 0.17 and 0.70 in different states of the country (Chand 2005b). This shows the scope for raising agricultural output by promoting the use of fertilizers.

Input–Output Markets and Regulation

As shown in Table 4.6, TOT for agriculture have witnessed a sharp decline in recent years and have caused an adverse impact on output growth. Improvement in TOT for farmers and fetching remunerative prices to them require high competition and efficiency in output markets. This can be achieved through increased participation of the private sector at different layers of agriculture markets, by linking farmers to markets, eliminating unnecessary intermediaries, direct marketing from farmers to consumers and contract farming. Several changes have recently been introduced in the regulatory and legal environment for increased involvement of the private sector in agricultural markets, which are expected to provide incentives for raising production.

A major challenge facing the reform process in the country is to find the appropriate balance between the role of private and public sectors in the input delivery system and output marketing. In recent times, para-statal organizations involved in these activities have come under attack because of the high inefficiency in their operation. At the same time, attracted by the potential profits, a larger number of private national and international companies have entered the agricultural input market, particularly the seed and pesticide industry. It is generally believed that in a more liberalized market, the role of the private sector is bound to expand but during the transition phase the role of the public sector can in no way be underestimated as it ensures the shaping the legal environment, promoting transparency and building infrastructure.

In a country with diverse agro-climatic, socio-economic and institutional circumstances, the need, nature and impact of input–output market reforms would differ across regions. For instance, in some states, private trade may be involved in efficient marketing, helping the agriculture sector to adjust to the changing economic environment and needs. In another situation, private trade may not be forthcoming and there may be a need for group action through co-operatives and non-governmental organizations (NGOs) for efficient input provisioning and profitable output marketing.

Growth of agriculture is critically dependent on the use of modern inputs such as fertilizers, seeds, plant propagation material, agricultural chemicals and the availability of credit to purchase these and other inputs. There is a need to ensure adequate and timely supply of all these inputs. Out of these, the supply of seed needs urgent attention as the quality of seed is the basic determinant of productivity. Most of the farmers in India do not distinguish between grain and seed, either because of ignorance or due to lack of ready availability of seed. There is a need to revamp the seed production and distribution system by strengthening the public sector seed agencies and by involving private trade in the seed multiplication and distribution system. Quality checks on inputs are becoming more and more important as cases of unscrupulous traders fleecing farmers—by selling spurious seeds, fertilizers and chemicals—are on the rise.

Technology Policy

India has a large network of research and technology that covers all agro-ecological pockets of the country. This public research system in India has responded reasonably well to the challenges and opportunities and has shown a remarkable response to a need-based approach. Institutes under the Indian Council of Agricultural Research, and State Agricultural Universities have developed varieties and technologies which are demonstrated to be capable of giving high output per unit of resources. However, this has not helped in bridging a large gap between what is attainable through these technologies and what is actually attained in farmers' fields in most of the crops and across states. This is a clear pointer to the large potential for raising output through effective dissemination of technology. But this is not happening because of the absence of, or weak, research–extension–farmer linkages. There is an immediate need for a vibrant, dynamic and innovative approach for agricultural extension. It is evident that public extension by itself can no longer respond to the multifarious demands of the farming community. Therefore, public–private partnership needs to be promoted for sharing of resources and convergence. To promote private investment in agricultural extension, it is essential to provide fiscal incentives.

The extension system has to employ a variety of approaches spanning Rural Knowledge Centres (RKCs), ICT (Information and Communications Technology) based extension, farmer to farmer extension, involvement of PRI (Panchayati Raj Institutions), NGOs and private sector. Access of knowledge to women farmers should be ensured through women extension workers, especially in the remote, hilly and tribal areas where women farmers predominate.

India has also been very slow and cautious in accepting genetically modified crops even those which are cultivated on a very large scale globally. Though due precautions are necessary in such cases, long delays have caused major production losses. Recent experience with cotton has shown the potential of such crops in raising output and farm income in the country. Adoption of transgenics and hybrid varieties of cotton has resulted in doubling of cotton yield in a short span of five years (cotton yield was below 200kg/hectare during 2000–02 and it increased to 392 kg during 2006–07). This resulted in the doubling of cotton output in the country from 1.7 million tonnes to 3.57 million tonnes. Such choices are also available in some other crops which can help in raising agricultural growth in the country.

Diversification

Value of output and income from horticultural crops is much higher as compared to other crops in the country. At present, cultivation of fruits and vegetables is undertaken only on 4.75 per cent of total cropped area. According to the National Accounts Statistics prepared by CSO, value of fruits and vegetables from one unit of land was 7.25 times the average of other crops during 2005–06. As the demand for fruits and vegetables in the country is rising rapidly, this offers lot of scope for raising farm output through diversification.

Conclusion

The active role played by government and supportive policies for technology had played vital role in addressing many formidable challenges in agriculture and food sectors in India. However, after initiation of economic reforms in early 1990s, several adverse trends have emerged in Indian agriculture. The growth rate of GDP agriculture has decelerated sharply after mid-1990s whereas population dependent on agriculture has been rising at almost the same pace. As a result, per capita income for the population dependent on agriculture is not growing. This is considered a major factor for the large scale rural distress and a large number of suicidal deaths by farmers in various parts of the country. On the other hand, non-agriculture sector has witnessed sharp acceleration in growth. Domestic produce is finding it hard to compete with import and for export; and terms of trade for agriculture have turned adverse under the influence of international prices. An important reason for the present state of agriculture is that agriculture sector was largely left out of the ambit of domestic reforms which could help this sector to take advantage of liberalized domestic and global environment. The main reasons for deceleration and stagnation in agricultural output after 1995–96 are a slowdown in growth of fertiliser use, irrigation, and energy (electric power). The terms of trade for agriculture have also shown a deterioration. The agriculture sector is also experiencing effect of strain on natural resources like land and water.

However, large parts of the country operate at low productivity and they have large unexploited potential for increase in productivity. India can meet the challenges faced by the agriculture sector by stepping up investments and putting in place suitable institutional mechanisms to exploit irrigation potential that exists in most of the states; increasing power supply to the sector; promoting fertilizer use by expanding the distribution network and improving credit facilities for farmers; establishing competitive seed markets and ensuring attractive prices for seeds; improvement in terms of trade for agriculture; clear policy on new technology; and by promoting competitive markets for agricultural produce.

References

Bhanumurthy, N.R. and Sapna Sinha (2004), 'Industrial Recovery: Can It Be Sustained', *Economic and Political Weekly*, Vol. 39, No. 5, 31 January–6 February.

Bhatia, B.M. (1988), *Indian Agriculture: A Policy Perspective*, Sage Publications, New Delhi.

Chand, Ramesh (2003), 'Government Intervention in Foodgrain Markets in the Changing Context', Policy Paper 19, National Centre for Agricultural Economics and Policy Research, New Delhi.

——— (2005a), 'India's National Agricultural Policy: A Critique', in Ramesh Chand (ed.) *India's Agricultural Challenges, Reflections on Policy, Technology and other Issues*, Centre for Trade and Development, New Delhi, pp. 19–46.

——— (2005b), 'Demand for Urea Towards 2011', Research Report 1/2005, National Centre for Agricultural Economics and Policy Research, New Delhi.

Chand, Ramesh, P. Kumar and Sapna Sinha (2003), 'Impact of Agricultural Trade and Related Reforms on Domestic Food Security in India', Report of the Study done for FAO, Rome, Institute of Economic Growth, Delhi, November.

Chand, Ramesh, S.S. Raju and L.M. Pandey (2007), 'Growth Crisis in Agriculture Severity and Options at National and State Levels', *Economic and Political Weekly*, Vol.42, No. 26, pp. 2528–33.

Dandekar, V.M. (1994), *The Indian Economy 1947–92, Volume 1, Agriculture*, Chapter 6, Sage Publications, New Delhi.

Dantwala, M.L. (1986), 'Strategy of Agricultural Development Since Independence', in M.L. Dantwala and Others (eds) *Indian Agricultural Development Since Independence: a Collection of Essays*, Oxford and IBH Publishing Company, New Delhi.

Dholakia, Bakul H. (1997), 'Impact of Economic Liberalisation on the Growth of Indian Agriculture', in Bhupat M. Desai (ed.) *Agricultural Development Paradigm for the Ninth Plan under New Economic Environment*, Oxford and IBH Publishing Company, New Delhi.

Krishnaji, N. (1990), 'Agricultural Price Policy: A Survey with Reference to Indian Foodgrain Economy', *Economic and Political Weekly*, Vol. 25, No. 26, 30 June.

Sawant, S.D. and C.V. Achutan (1995), 'Agricultural Growth Across Crops and Regions', *Economic and Political Weekly*, Vol. 30, No. 12, 25 May.

Singh, Manmohan (1995), 'Inaugural Address delivered at the 54th Annual Conference of the Indian Society of Agricultural Economics', *Indian Journal of Agricultural Economics*, Vol. 50, No. 1, January–March.

Planning Commission (2007), *Report of the Steering Committee on Agriculture for the Eleventh Five Year Plan (2007–2012)*, Government of India, New Delhi.

Rao, V.M. (1994), 'Agriculture and Liberalisation: Some Implications for Development Policies', *Economic and Political Weekly*, Vol. 29, Nos 16–17, 16–23 April.

——— (1996), 'Agricultural Development with a Human Face: Experience and Prospects', *Economic and Political Weekly*, Vol. 29, Nos 16–17, 16–23 April.

PART II

Education

5

School Education
A Constraint to the Sustainability of High Growth Rate in India

MUCHKUND DUBEY

Contribution of Education to Development

It is fairly well established that among various categories of capital, human capital, in the form of education (particularly primary education),[1] makes the most important contribution to the growth of an economy, to an increase in per capita incomes and to the creation, adaptation, application and diffusion of knowledge and technologies which further accelerate and sustain growth. This proposition has been demonstrated through theoretical reasoning and empirical studies carried out over the last 40 years, covering a vast number of countries at different stages of development and based on data relating to periods ranging between a decade to 100 years or more. In addition to its

[1]The term 'primary education' is used internationally to cover Classes I to V. In India, schools providing education from Classes I to V are called 'lower primary' schools. Above lower primary schools are 'upper primary' or 'middle' schools consisting of Classes VI–VIII. Lower primary and upper primary together make up 'elementary education' which is synonymous with the term 'basic education' as used internationally. Most countries provide eight to nine years of education at the elementary level. In India, basic education has a very different meaning. It does not connote levels or grades of teaching, but method of teaching. It goes back to the Gandhian concepts of *Nai Talim* (new education) and *Buniyadi Vidyalayas* (basic schools) of the mid-1930s.

impact on growth and per capita incomes, education makes several other tangible and intangible contributions to development. For example, in the social field, it contributes to the improvement of children's health and nutrition, increase in life expectancy and reduction of infant mortality rates (IMRs), maternal mortality rates (MMRs) and fertility. Beyond its human capital dimension, education is a powerful tool for the empowerment of human capability. It promotes adaptability to change, widens choices and creates space for the exercise of fundamental freedoms. It forges national unity and social cohesion by bringing together children of different castes, classes and economic and social status, and by teaching common values, norms, ideologies and languages. In mid-nineteenth century Europe and United States, nation-building and promotion of social cohesion were seen as the principal purposes of public-funded schools. Education is the most potent defence against social vulnerability and marginalization. Returns from education 'are the very substance of what development is all about that is, the quality of life in its totality, including individual dignity and self-respect and command over ones own life which are the true hallmark of individual freedom' (Patel 2003). Education also improves income distribution and encourages more rational consumption patterns which can have a decisive influence on the preservation of the environment.

Both theoretical work and empirical studies over the last 40 years have demonstrated that education, particularly school education, by expanding human capital, increases individual incomes and the growth rate of the economy, and helps in creating and facilitating the application of knowledge and technology which are indispensable for sustained growth. All studies find very high private returns to education. Social returns are even higher as education leads to improved health and nutrition and encourages participatory democracy. The well-known shortcomings in defining human capital merely in terms of literacy or years of schooling are overcome in the broader concept of human capability. Unfortunately, school education in India has not received the priority it deserves. Consequently, 30 to 50 per cent of the children are still out of school, drop-out rates from Classes I to X average between 60 and 90 per cent, facilities available in the schools are extremely poor and the quality of teaching is very low. Moreover, school education in India is characterized by the grossest and the most widespread discrimination and inequality practised anywhere in the world.

These shortcomings are illustrated with detailed data from Bihar. These deficiencies cannot be removed without making school education universal, compulsory and free. Provision of such education is now universally accepted as a basic human right. In India, it has recently been recognized as a fundamental right. The establishment of a Common School System is an indispensable condition for the exercise of this right. The essential elements of a Common School System have existed in all countries which have succeeded in universalizing school education of a high and equitable quality. But in India, they are nowhere in sight. This is going to prove to be the single most important constraint to the sustainability of the current dynamism of the Indian economy, and combining high growth with equality. Universal school education has not been achieved partly because of lack of government financing. If the government had implement its promise of devoting 6 per cent of GDP to education, school education could have been made universal.

Education as Human Capital

The importance of human capital in development was first brought out by Theodore Schultz, in his Presidential Address to the American Economic Association in 1960; and in his further work on the subject. Prior to this, in the mainstream economic theory, physical capital—in the form of land, and producers' goods—and labour hour[2] were regarded as the instrument for accelerating and sustaining growth and per capita incomes. These assets were subject to diminishing returns which made the future of mankind bleak until the human capital theory came as a resurrection. It also solved the many puzzles that had surfaced in the realm of development thinking by the end of the 1950s. The most glaring among the puzzles was that the growth in national incomes in advanced countries had far exceeded the value of the physical capital deployed during the commensurate period.

Schultz (1961) argued and demonstrated by his analysis of facts and figures that:

(a) Human skills and know-how are a form of capital;
(b) This capital has grown in Western societies at a much faster rate than conventional capital;
(c) People invest in themselves and these investments are very large;

[2]In traditional economic theory, all labour was regarded as of equal quality and as being a commodity.

(d) This phenomenon explains the widely-observed trend that the increase in national output has been larger than the increase in land, man-hours and physical reproducible capital.

He regarded education as the most important form of human capital and estimated that the stock of education in the labour force in the US increased by about eight and a half times between 1900 and 1956 whereas the stock of reproducible capital rose by only four and a half times, both in 1956 prices. He also estimated that between 36 and 70 per cent of the hitherto unexplained rise in the earnings of labour could be explained by returns to the additional education of workers. He stated: 'It is simply not possible to have the fruits of a modern agriculture and the abundance of modern industry without making large investments in human beings.' He added that it was because of the increase in the stock in education that the US had become a leader in economic growth in the world (Schultz 1961). Subsequent to Schultz's pioneering work on the human capital theory, hundreds of statistical studies were carried out demonstrating the validity of his central thesis. Based on the human capital theory, a new theory of economic growth known as the endogenous growth theory was developed the 1980s (Romer 1986; Lucas 1988).

The human capital theory, while retaining its essential validity, was widened and enriched by the concept of human capability. Amartya Sen played a key role in the articulation and development of this concept. The proponents of the human capability concept argued that human capital was only 'a means to an end'. It no doubt contributed to the growth in production but it did not explain why increased production was 'good'. The answer to this question can be found in the human capability perspective. Amartya Sen defined development as an expansion of human capability by widening the range of choice and enlarging the space for exercising fundamental freedoms. As a matter of fact, Schultz himself had envisaged this potentiality of human development. In the *American Economic Review* article referred to earlier, he had written: 'By investing in themselves people can enlarge the range of choice available to them. It is one way free men can enhance their welfare.'

Contrasting the human capital perspective from the human capability perspective, Amartya Sen points out that human capital can be typically defined as the human quality that can be employed as capital in production in the way physical capital is. On the other hand, human capability enables an individual to do certain things that she has reasons to value (Sen 1997). Explaining the difference further, he points out that education in the form of human capital makes a person more efficient in production and thereby enhances his income. But even with the same level of income, a person may benefit from education in reading, communicating, arguing and in being able to choose in an informed manner. The broader human capability perspective would record these additional roles (Sen 1977). The human capability perspective does not replace the human capital perspective, but simply broadens it. There is also a virtuous circle between the two. The enhancement of growth and per capita incomes through the utilization of human capital leads to the expansion of human capability and the latter is itself instrumental in accelerating growth.

Returns to Education

In the early stage of statistical studies on the value of education as human capital, attention was focused mainly on the economic returns to education for individuals. The average years of schooling, and later, adult literacy rates and school enrolment ratios were used as proxies for education. These studies were pioneered by Jacob Mincer (1970, 1974). Subsequently, hundreds of such studies were carried out around the world. Some other prominent scholars who made notable contributions in this realm were Psacharopoulos (1973) and Barro (1991). Their studies have shown that more years of schooling is associated with higher individual earnings. In the case of low income countries, returns appear higher for investment in school education at lower levels of schooling than higher levels,[3] and are often responsible for bringing an increasing number of women to schools.

These estimates of increase in individual earnings may be regarded as private returns to schooling. Besides, there are social returns which come in the form of the positive effects on child health, fertility, improved participation by citizens' as well as on growth and productivity of the economy as a whole. There are a variety of reasons to believe that these social returns are noticeably higher than private returns.

[3]Returns for primary education are higher than for secondary education and for secondary education, compared to tertiary education.

There are three ways in which education increases the overall growth of the economy. First, education increases the human capital inherent in the labour force, which in turn, increases labour productivity. Second, education increases the overall efficiency and the innovative capacity of the economy which helps in creating and adapting new knowledge and new technology, and promoting processes and arrangements which promote growth. Finally, it facilitates the diffusion and transmission of knowledge and technology. Solow (1957) brought out the fact that nearly ninth-tenths of the growth of the per capita income in the US over the four decades up to 1949 was due to technological progress. This was confirmed by Kuznets (1966) who said that the direct contribution of man-hours and physical capital would hardly account for more than a tenth of the growth in per capita products. The remaining came from what he called 'improved quality of resources', 'effects of changing arrangements' and 'impact of technological change'. Patel (1985) has called these three elements put together as 'social technology' which is 'the most powerful and liberating instrument for economic and social progress'. And education is a key factor in accelerating the development of, and improvement in, social technology.

As in the case of private returns to education, there are a large number of studies on the contribution of education to the growth of an economy and to per capita incomes. One of the first scholars who undertook such a study was Psacharopoulos (1973). He examined the relationship between the growth in primary school enrolment and per capita gross national product (GNP) over a 110-year period (1850–1960) for 34 more advanced countries, and found that none of them had achieved significant economic growth prior to achieving universal primary education. The findings of the study by Psacharopoulos are as follows:

(a) Education has both private and social monetary pay-offs and these pay-offs are substantially higher in less developed countries than in advanced ones;
(b) The most profitable educational level in most countries is the primary one, while higher education shows a modest pay-off, particularly in advanced countries. This suggests that the argument for universal primary education based on human rights is also supported by good economic sense;

(c) Returns to investment in human capital are well above the returns to physical capital in less developed countries, while the two types of returns are of almost equal magnitude in advanced countries.

In the 1990s, important studies of social returns to schooling in economic terms, were carried out by Barro (1991), Benhabib and Spiegel (1994) and Sala-i-Martin (1997). All these found schooling to be positively co-related to the growth rate of per capita gross domestic product (GDP) across countries, both developed and developing. Virtually all the newly industrialized economies with dramatic growth in the past 25 years such as Hong Kong, Israel, Japan, Korea and Singapore had achieved universal or almost universal primary enrolment by 1965 (Lockheed, Verspoor and associates 1991).

Calculations of economic returns to education in India have also been attempted by a number of economists from both within and outside India. The most prominent among them are Psacharopoulos (1973), Dholakia (1974) and Tilak (2003). The findings of all these studies are that economic returns to education in India are also reasonably high and are comparable to the rates of return to investment in physical capital on the one hand, and to the returns to education in other developed and developing countries of the world on the other. Moreover, they are found to be increasing (Tilak 2003). The relative contribution of education to increase in per capita productivity in India was estimated to be as high as 14 per cent during 1948–49 and 1968–69. Education was responsible for 36 per cent of the improvement in the quality of the labour force (Dholakia 1974). According to Psacharopoulos (1973), the contribution of education to economic growth in India was as high as 34.4 per cent. Using 1971–81 data, Loh (1995) estimated this contribution to be 27 per cent.

Some of the studies on returns to education have established a positive co-relationship between investment in education and improvement in productivity and earnings in particular sectors. For example, Lockheed, Jamison and Lau (1980) have summarized the findings of 18 studies from 13 developing countries and concluded that four years of primary education increased the productivity of farmers by 8.7 per cent on an average. This improvement was brought about mainly by the contribution of education to enhancing their ability to: (i) allocate resources efficiently and (ii) improve their choice of inputs. Earlier studies done in the US had brought out a similar co-relationship between education and increased returns from agriculture.

Several studies have shown that education contributes to a higher level of earnings not only in the organized manufacturing sector where there is a large-scale infusion of capital but also in informal sectors. These studies have shown that the entrepreneurs in small and informal enterprises require at least some years of schooling to resolve technological and business problems and increase profitability. Thus, productivity in both agriculture and informal sectors was higher when those making decisions in farming and small enterprise had access to at least primary schooling.

Contribution of Education to Social Development

Empirical studies have demonstrated that schooling has a positive influence on child care, health and nutrition, on reducing IMR, MMR and fertility rates, and on increasing life expectancy. Among others, greater knowledge about child care and health practices has a powerful impact on children's health and nutrition. Much of this knowledge comes from the basic education of the parents.

Studies have shown that IMR is lower where parents' education is higher. One additional year of mother's schooling is associated with a reduction in IMR of 9 per 1000 (Cochrane, O'Hara and Leslie 1980). By increasing the mother's education by 6 years, that is, from 3 years of schooling to 9 years, it is possible to reduce an IMR of 100 by more than 50 percentage points (Carnoy 1992). This is possible because education increases the mother's understanding of modern health practices and gives her the power to make decisions concerning her child's health. Even with comparable incomes, households with educated mothers may spend proportionately more on food or health services or may use their resources more effectively and distribute them more equitably, thus promoting the child's nutritional status (Chen 1983).

Reduced fertility depends heavily on women's education (Cochrane 1979, 1983; Lockwood and Collier 1998). Although the size of the effect varies across countries, there is a general decline in the desired as well as actual size once a woman's education increases beyond the primary level (Pullum 1983).

Education and Inequality

Gross and pervasive inequality is built into the Indian school education system. Some one-third to half of the school-going children in different states of India are out of school. A very large proportion of those enrolled in schools drop out before completing their education. Most of the out-of-school and drop-out children belong to the marginalized sections that is, Scheduled Castes (SCs), Scheduled Tribes (STs), Muslims and girls in each category, of the population. Education is the most significant among the myriad ways in which these groups are excluded from both the development process as well as the fruits of development.

Educational exclusion has the effect of excluding these sections of the population from most of other activities in society. Besides, educational exclusion perpetuates itself from generation to generation. Moreover, if children are excluded from education then they are excluded not only from the job market but also from engaging in a variety of social interactions with a measure of confidence.

The most obvious constraint that inequality imposes on growth is that it narrows down the market and thereby makes it difficult to reap optimum benefits from the economies of scale. This, in turn, adversely affects the competitiveness of the economy and introduces distortions in the patterns of production, consumption and deployment of labour.

Moreover, inequality can be costly and destructive in several other ways. It creates resentment, discontent and social tension. If ignored over a long period of time, it can degenerate into large-scale violence and armed rebellion as is the case with the Naxalite violence in India. To a very great extent, what goes by the name of 'terrorism' in today's world is due to the perpetuation of gross inequality. Inequality has also an important bearing on governance. Extreme forms of inequality can undermine the legitimacy of the political regime and weaken the rule of law. They can thus make the society ungovernable and cause serious disruptions in the economy. On the other hand, measures to reduce inequality contribute to faster growth. This has been demonstrated by several studies particularly those on the benefits of re-distributive land reform.

Empirical studies have demonstrated that investment in education, particularly in school education is a highly effective way of reducing inequality in the distribution of income as well as in other forms. The experience of development in the South East Asian countries is a testimony to the fact that there is no easier way than large public investment in education to combine equality with rapid growth. The case study of investment in school education of the blacks in the US in 1939–49 and a recent study in Kenya have demonstrated that expansion of basic education reduces inequality in income distribution (Carnoy, 1992, p. 51).

Education and Sustainability of Growth

Education is an essential and perhaps the most important precondition for sustaining growth. The educated population can adapt to changes, absorb new technologies, develop new organization of work and create new products and services which are essential for sustaining growth. Schultz (1989) argues that greater flexibility of response associated with knowledge acquired through education is the key to long-term economic growth. Another reason why education sustains growth is that educated parents or families invest more in their children's education which creates the next and succeeding generations of children who can be expected to be capable of not only improving their own lot but contributing better to the sustained growth of the economy. In India, where a large proportion of the children are still deprived of school education, universalization and improvement in the quality of such education is essential for sustaining the dynamism witnessed in recent years of the Indian economy.

Complementary Role of Primary and Secondary Education

Most of the studies establishing a co-relationship between school education and returns of various kinds from it have shown that primary education yields higher returns than secondary or higher education. Moreover, since primary education is the foundation for subsequent phases of education, both the access to and quality of primary education go a long way towards determining the value of secondary and higher education. If the access to primary education is limited and its quality poor, then it cannot produce students who are really prepared to take full advantage of secondary and tertiary education. Statistical studies have also brought out the fact that primary education is specially needed in the early stage of development. Therefore, low income countries need primary education as a prerequisite for development. In view of these findings and reasonings, it is not surprising that in the realm of policy making, the main concentration of effort both at the national and international levels has been on primary education. This is reflected, among others, in the Millenium Development Goals (MDGs) and the World Bank's (WB's) Poverty Reduction Strategy Papers (PRSPs).

These findings have, however, been contested, or more appropriately supplemented, by scholars who have demonstrated that post-elementary education is also important for growth and reduction of poverty, and for realizing such social objectives as reductions in IMR, MMR and fertility rates (Tilak 2007). Tilak (2007) has argued that primary education rarely provides the skills necessary for students to get employment which can ensure a reasonable level of earning. Moreover, with the conditions prevailing in several developing societies including India, primary education does not impart skills that are sustainable and the relapse of literates to illiteracy is not uncommon. He has also argued that primary education can take people just above the poverty line but not much above it; for that secondary and tertiary education are necessary. Secondary education consolidates the gains of primary education and provides skills which are useful in the labour market. Tilak's study—based on state-wise data on stock of the population with secondary and higher secondary education in 1955–1996 and development indicators relating to the year 1999–2000, and the application of simple regression equations—comes to the conclusion that post-elementary education enhances the level of earning of the individual and also contributes to economic development. It significantly reduces absolute as well as relative poverty; negatively influences IMR and MMR and positively influences life expectancy.

The truth is that both elementary and post-elementary schooling should be expanded and their quality improved in order for school education to have an optimum positive impact on development. The relative importance of these two levels of education will vary according to the stage of development of the economy and of the spread of primary education itself. Martin Carnoy states that when primary school education expands to include almost all the children in the society, its value begins to fall and secondary education becomes much more important for future development. And when education through lower secondary school is widely available and is of good quality, then the most important level of education is higher secondary schooling and university education (Carnoy 1992, pp. 31–2).

Deficiencies of the Human Capital Theory

Several scholars, while recognizing the validity of the human capital theory, have pointed out the deficiencies in the methodology of co-relating educational achievements with development parameters. The first problem that arises is that education is not the only means of enhancing the stock of human capital. Other areas of social development, particularly health, also play an important role in the formation of human capital. Recently, several studies have been carried out relating health conditions to development outcomes.

Second, the methods employed in calculating returns to education have until recently been mainly in terms of average years of schooling, literacy rates, enrolment ratios etc. In this process, non-school factors, which contribute to the creation of human capital, have been ignored. These include skills and knowledge acquired in the family or from peers and in the workplace through on-the-job training. These factors have been excluded mainly because of the difficulty in quantifying them and in spite of all the limitations and qualifications, formal education has remained the most important and most measurable indicator of the progress in building human capital in a country.

Third, some of the broader cultural and sociological factors and structural features of the economy which have an important role in capital formation are not included in the calculation of returns to education. These include gender, race, the social milieu, capital intensity, the degree of monopolization in the economy etc. (Mehrotra, 2005 p. 39).

Finally, it has been pointed out that the influence of education depends not only on the period of schooling or other such quantitative measurements but also on its quality. More specifically, it has been pointed out that the quantitative method renders it difficult to make cross-country comparisons. It assumes that schooling delivers the same knowledge and skills regardless of the educational system.

There is, therefore, no doubt that the returns to quality of school education are as important, and in certain conditions even more important than returns to quantity. This has been borne out by various studies in recent years on the return to quality of education. The proxy taken for education here is cognitive skills, particularly in science and mathematics, for which international standards of measurement, in terms of scores in these skills, have been established (Hanushek and Woesmann 2007).

Condition of, and Policies for, School Education in India

If education is the means—through the expansion of human capital and the development of human capability—to increase individual incomes, enhance the rate of the growth of the economy, create knowledge and technology and facilitate their application; then school education is the indispensable first step towards realizing these objectives. Moreover, higher education will remain narrowly based and flawed without laying the widest possible and solid foundation of school education.

Unfortunately, throughout the period since independence, policy makers in India have not accorded school education the priority that it deserves. As a matter of fact, there is no area of the economy where there has been a larger gap between promises and performance and between goals announced and the resources applied for achieving the same, than in the field of education. If we consider elementary education, the objective of providing free and compulsory education within a period of 10 years, to children up to the age of 14 years, was included in Article 45 of the Indian Constitution in the Chapter on the Directive Principles of State Policy. In the 1986 National Policy on Education (NPE) and in the revised NPE (1992), this objective was reiterated and datelines were set for realizing it. In spite of these policy pronouncements, education continued to receive one of the lowest priorities in the allocation of resources in successive Five Year Plans for India's development.

This predicament of school education has been very well articulated by Jean Dreze and Amartya Sen (2003): 'There is something puzzling in the fact that the promotion of education has received so little attention from social and political leaders in the post-independence period. One aspect of this neglect is the flagrant inadequacy of government policy in the field of elementary education. But the lack of attention to education has not been confined to government circles. There has been much neglect of it on the part of the political parties, trade unions, revolutionary organizations and other social movements.' Giving the reason for this neglect they have pointed out that 'the fact that government was able to get away with so much in the field of elementary education relates to the lack of political power of the illiterate masses'.

Access and Quality

During the first three decades after independence, there was unprecedented growth in school education in India. The rate of growth was the highest during the 1950s but continued till the mid-1970s. However, this growth was mainly in quantitative terms—number of schools built, teachers appointed and trained, and in enrolment ratios and in bridging the gender gap in enrolment (for illustration, see Bihar Report 2007,[4] pp. 7–10). Very little improvement, however, took place in terms of quality. The infrastructure and facilities as well as the quality of teaching in schools continued to remain poor.

In 1986–87, when the NPE was promulgated, nearly half of all rural children in the age group 6 to 18 years had never been enrolled in any school. Today, 42 million children in the age group 6 to 14 years do not go to school. In a speech delivered under the auspices of the Federation of Indian Chambers of Commerce and Industry on 1 October 2007, the famous industrialist, Lord Swaraj Paul quoted a figure of 30 to 35 per cent as the percentage of children still deprived of primary school education. In rural India, 16.64 per cent of the villages are still without a primary school. In Bihar, 50 per cent of the school-going children, totalling 15 million, are today out of school (Bihar Report 2007, p. 180).

Literacy is not a good measure of educational attainment. A large number of those who are literate cannot be regarded as educated. Besides, with the prevailing conditions in a developing society like India, there is a large possibility of the literate relapsing into illiteracy. Nevertheless, the level of literacy has become a widely accepted measure of educational attainment; and numeracy and literacy do contribute to enhancing the incomes of workers and the enjoyment of wider freedom and exercise of wider choices. The latest available data, for the year 2005, indicate that more than one-third of the Indian population (33.7 per cent) is still illiterate, while female illiteracy is at a much higher level of 43.4 per cent (Government of India 2006b). In Bihar, at the time of the 2001 Census, more than half the population (53 per cent) was illiterate, whereas female literacy

[4]Throughout this section, data from the Report of the CSS Commission, Bihar (2007), have been given along with the national data, in order to juxtapose with the national situation, the prevailing picture in the worst performing state in the country, which is also the third largest in terms of population.

was at the abysmally low level of 33.1 per cent—the lowest in the country. Female literacy in some of the backward districts of Bihar was in the range of 18.49 per cent to 24.03 per cent (Bihar Report 2007, p. 43).

Taking the figures for the general educational level for 2004–05, only 36.1 per cent of rural male population in India was educated up to the primary level, 14 per cent up to the middle level and 13.4 per cent up to the secondary and senior secondary level. The corresponding figures for the rural female population were 29.3 per cent, 8.9 per cent and 6.7 per cent, respectively (Government of India 2006a).

Enrolment among the children studying in Classes I to V in 2003–04 was 73.9 per cent and by 2004–05, it had improved to 81.9 per cent. Though the enrolment levels have improved, there were still 18.1 per cent children in the age group 6 to 11 years who were not enrolled (NIEPA 2006). In Bihar, the Gross Enrolment Ratio (GER) at the primary stage for the year 2006 was 70.9 per cent, at the upper primary stage 48.7 per cent and at the secondary and senior secondary stages 12.2 and 11.5 per cent, respectively. Among underprivileged sections of the population, the GERs for the Muslims were the lowest at the primary and upper primary stages for which data are available. The ratios were 51.3 per cent and 36.4 per cent, respectively (Bihar Report 2007, p. 43).

Enrolment data are highly unreliable. They are deliberately inflated and bear little resemblance to actual school attendance. According to the data in the Report of the 61st Round of the National Sample Survey Organization (NSSO), the attendance rate of children belonging to the STs in the age group 6 to 14 years, was 84.2, 72.6 per cent in general, 67.8 per cent for females and 76.7 per cent for males and for SCs 77.5 per cent, 80.9 per cent and 73.7 per cent, respectively. The above figures are for schools in the rural areas. The attendance was higher in the urban areas, 86.5 per cent for STs and 82.2 per cent for SCs. The position regarding attendance was much worse in Bihar. In most of the schools visited by the Common School System (CSS) Commission, the presence of students was less than 50 per cent of those enrolled. In some schools, the presence was as low as 25 per cent (Bihar Report 2007, p. 54).

The picture that emerges from the data relating to enrolment and attendance of children, has to be seen in the light of the data for drop-out rates in order to get an idea of the proportion of children who are able to complete school education. At the all India level, the figures for the year 2003–04 indicate that drop-out rates were 31.36 per cent from Classes I to V, 52.2 per cent from Classes I to VIII and 62.68 per cent from Classes I to X. The drop-out rates for girls were a little lower in the first two categories of classes but somewhat higher at 64.92 per cent for Classes I to X. The drop-out rates for the SC children were appreciably higher from Classes I to V and from Classes I to VIII but quite high (at 73.13 per cent) from Classes I to X. The drop-out rates for the ST children were the highest in all three types of schools, the highest being 79.25 per cent in Classes I to X. The drop-out rate of ST girls was 81.16 per cent from Classes I to X. This shows that a relatively small percentage of children complete Class X and an even smaller percentage among SCs and STs and girls in all categories, do so. From Classes I to VIII, 62.9 per cent of SC, 71.43 percentage of ST and 52.48 per cent of the general category girls drop-out before completing Class VIII (MHRD 2006, pp. 91–2).

In Bihar, the drop-out rates are much higher, the highest among all the states in India. For the year 2003, the rates were 59 per cent for Classes I to V, 78.03 per cent for Classes I to VIII and 82.58 per cent for Classes I to X. Drop-out rates for SCs were 46.36 per cent, 83.85 per cent and 90.02 per cent, respectively for these categories and for STs, they were 61.22 per cent, 82.84 per cent and 89.09 per cent, respectively. The drop-out rate for children in the general population from Classes I to V is nearly double the national figure (Bihar Report 2007, pp. 47–48).

Various reasons have been put forth to explain the high drop-out rates in Indian schools. Among them the poor condition of the facilities available, the general environment in the schools and the low quality of teaching are perhaps the most important reasons. The factors which make for poor quality include lack of teachers, teachers' absenteeism, irregular classes, over-crowded classrooms and rote learning.

Deployment of the required number of teachers who are well trained is a precondition for ensuring the quality of education. The condition of Indian schools in this regard is far from satisfactory. In 2005, the average number of teachers in all schools was 4.02, in rural areas 3.61 and in urban areas 7.25. At the primary level, that is, Classes I to V the average number was 2.74 in all areas, 2.56 in rural areas and 4.63 in urban areas (NIEPA 2006). The utter inadequacy of these numbers becomes clear when we compare them with the norm of 8 teachers for each primary school, 17 teachers for a middle school and 20 teachers for a senior secondary school, as prescribed by the CSS Commission, Bihar. In India, 59.48 per cent of the primary schools have two or less teachers. The comparative figure for Bihar is 83.01 per cent (Bihar Report 2007, Table 4.7, p. 50).

The pupil–teacher ratio is a good index of the inadequacy or otherwise of the availability of teachers in schools. In 2005, the pupil–teacher ratio in India was 38 for all schools and 42 for primary schools. The ratios were a little higher in rural areas at 40 and 44, respectively (NIEPA 2006). In Bihar, in 2002, the ratio was 83 for primary schools, 73 for upper primary schools and 48 for secondary schools (Bihar Report 2007, Table 4.7, p. 50).

As regards the other elements contributing to quality, such as infrastructure and other facilities available in schools, in 2005 there were still 11.3 per cent schools in rural areas and 10.39 per cent in all areas which had only one classroom (NIEPA 2006). Also, 20 per cent of the schools were without drinking water facilities (NIEPA 2006). A fairly good percentage of schools either do not have or have inadequate toilet facilities. According to the observation of the CSS Commission, Bihar, on the schools visited by it, 'the infrastructure of most of them is in a dilapidated condition and most of the facilities one would associate with a good school are conspicuous by their absence—none of the secondary schools had a functioning laboratory and the library facilities in these schools were either non-existent or utterly inadequate' (Bihar Report 2007, p. 54).

Teacher education is a key determinant of quality. In most states in India, teacher education institutions are in a run down condition and the quality of teaching is much below the mark. The Education Commission (1964–66) showed a major concern regarding teacher education institutions 'remaining isolated from the mainstream of the academic life of the university as well as from the daily problems of the schools'. It further noted 'mediocre or poor' quality of teacher education institutions, their inability to attract competent staff, the lack of 'vitality and realism' in the curriculum and programmes and their pursuing 'set patterns and rigid techniques' in practice teaching. The Commission made a number of recommendations to improve these conditions. The NPE (1986) (as modified in 1992) recommended, among others, the launching of a Centre-sponsored scheme to establish district institutes of education and training (DIETs) as nodal institutions in every district of the country for the purpose of organizing pre-service and in-service teacher training, undertaking educational research and surveys and taking initiatives for quality improvement with respect to elementary education. Some states took advantage of this scheme whereas others, for a variety of reasons, lost this opportunity. Today training facilities for school teachers, particularly for primary school teaching, are utterly inadequate and of low quality. State Centres for Educational Research and Training (SCERT), the nodal agencies at the state level for training and research, are either non-functional or are functioning at a much lower than optimal level. The conceptual framework for teachers' education that has prevailed in India suffers from many flaws:

(a) the socio-political character of knowledge in the curriculum is pre-determined by the dominant social classes;
(b) the learner is seen as a passive recipient of knowledge and the teacher its sole source;
(c) diversity among children is ignored;
(d) a narrower view of intelligence is taken which is mono-dimensional and linear; and
(e) learning is viewed without its social context.

In Bihar, the SCERT is in a decrepit condition. The pre-service and in-service education that it provided earlier was stopped from 1992–93 onwards. It never undertook research activities because no budgetary provision was ever made for this purpose. A large number of posts in this institution are vacant and barely 10 per cent of its capacity is used. Following the state government's decision in the early 1990s that training was no longer a requirement for appointment as teachers, training for teachers in Bihar was stopped. The ongoing process of the conversion of Primary Teachers' Education Centres (PTECs) into DIETs and the establishment of new DIETs came to a standstill. B.Ed. training in universities as well as in stand-alone colleges, suffered a decline. Thus, the entire infrastructure of training in the state suffered a setback. As a result of the prolonged neglect it lies in shambles today.

The Indian school education system is characterized by the grossest and the most widespread discrimination and inequality in school education, practised anywhere in the world. The desegregated data on enrolment, attendance and drop-out, relating to SCs, STs and girls given in this paper, reveal this inequality and discrimination. We have seen that illiteracy among these categories is higher, enrolment ratios are lower and drop-out rates are higher than among the children in the general category. The discrimination and inequality in the school system that were inherited from the colonial past and continued for more than three decades after independence, were made worse by the new policy of school education that came to be practised on an institutionalized basis from the mid-1980s. The basis for the accentuation of discrimination was laid in the NPE in 1986 through its provision for non-formal education (NFE) or 'low cost schooling' as Dreze and Sen (2003) call it. This method of education acquired new dimensions in the early 1990s with the entry of international institutions, like the United Nations Children's Fund (UNICEF), United Nations Educational, Scientific and Cultural Organization (UNESCO) and the WB into the field of school education in developing countries, including India. They added to NFE such devices as alternative schools, education guarantee scheme centres and multi-grade teaching. Also, the regular teacher was replaced by the para-teacher who is unqualified and untrained and appointed on a short-term contract basis. The justification given for introducing these parallel streams of teaching was the supreme necessity of expanding literacy, particularly the reach of primary education, in spite of the ubiquitous budget crisis at the state level in India and the extremely difficult budgetary position at that time of the Central Government. This, in effect, turned out to be a device by the State, in collaboration with these international agencies, to evade the responsibility of providing equitable and quality education to all children at least up to the elementary stage in proper schools. This was also the period when under the influence of the Structural Adjustment Programmes of the WB, there were sizeable reductions in public expenditure in the social sector, including school education, in almost all developing countries, including India.

Dreze and Sen in their review of the NFE stream have raised objections to this on the grounds of quality, equality and sustainability. The NFE has affected quality because teachers' qualifications and infrastructural facilities are often poorer in second track schooling facilities than in regular schools. The NFE raises the equity issue because 'it dilutes the right of the under-privileged children to quality education. It perpetuates the deep inequities in India's schooling system, whereby children of different social backgrounds have vastly different educational opportunities not only in terms of the divide between the government and private schools but also within the framework of government schools'. The NFE raises the question of sustainability because the arrangements under it tend to be somewhat *ad hoc* and essentially fragile' (Dreze and Sen 2003, pp. 20–1). It is important to underline that all these innovations in effect apply only to the children of the deprived sections of the society. Relatively well-off families send their children to private schools and public schools established specifically to cater to the educational needs of such families.

It is not possible to eliminate discrimination and provide equality of opportunity in school education without instituting a system of free, compulsory and universalized education. The logic of this proposition was enunciated in very clear terms in the Sargent Commission Report submitted as early as in 1944. The Commission said 'If there is anything to be like equality of opportunity, it is impossible to justify providing facilities for some of the nations' children and not for others. In the first place, therefore, a national system can hardly be other than universal. Second, it must also be compulsory, if the grave wastage which exists today under a voluntary system is not to be perpetuated and even aggravated. And third, if education is to be universal and compulsory, equity requires that it should be free. ...' (Government of India 1944).

The provision of free and compulsory education is all the more necessary for bringing equality of opportunity in a country like India which harbours the largest population of poor and extremely poor persons in the world. A majority of the children in this country, particularly those belonging to the SCs and STs and the Muslim minority, cannot afford to go to the fee-charging private schools and are obliged to drop out of even government schools which, while providing education free of fees, levy charges of different kinds which the parents of these children cannot afford to pay.

That is the reason why the State—in almost all developed countries and most of the more advanced among developing countries—provides free and compulsory education to all the children up to the secondary level, and in any case up to the elementary level. The Universal Declaration on Human Rights 1948 and the subsequent UN Conventions on Civil and Political Rights; Economic, Social and Cultural Rights; and the Rights of the Child also include such a provision. In India, the right to free and compulsory education has been an issue of public debate since the late nineteenth and early twentieth centuries. An account is given in the section that follows, of the progress, or lack of progress, in translating the right to education into reality in the post-independence period.

Right to Education

The right to free and compulsory education was provided in Article 45 of the Indian Constitution. The Article stated: 'The State shall endeavour to provide, within a period of ten years from the commencement of the Constitution, free and compulsory education for all children until they complete the age of 14 years.' However, as this right was not included in Chapter III on Fundamental Rights, but inserted in Part IV of the Constitution, which lays down Directive Principles of State Policy, it was not justiciable. The State did not pay much heed to this Article on the plea of paucity of financial resources. The target of providing free and compulsory education to children below the age of 14 within a period of 10 years was not met, and up to this date, it remains unredeemed. In 1986 when the first NPE was announced, more than half of the children and two-thirds of the girls in this age group were out of school.

The 1980s and the 1990s saw a very liberal interpretation of Article 21 of the Indian Constitution relating to the fundamental right to life. As a part of this process, in 1993, the Supreme Court of India, in its famous Unnikrishnan Judgement, ruled that Article 45 must be read in harmonious conjunction with Article 21, since right to life loses its meaning if a child is deprived of elementary education. After this, the Central Government came increasingly under pressure to amend the Constitution to bring it in line with the Unnikrishnan Judgement. Ultimately, nine years after the judgement, the Indian Parliament enacted a Constitutional Amendment Bill in December 2002 which elevated the right to education to the status of a fundamental right. The amendment became the new Article 21A of the Constitution which reads: 'The State shall provide free and compulsory education to all children of the age 6 to 14 years in such a manner as the State may by law determine.'

The amendment, though representing some progress, was widely criticized mainly for three reasons. First, unlike the original Article 45 and the Unnikrishnan Judgement, the amendment left out of the scope of right to education, children below the age of 6 years, thus depriving some 170 million children of the fundamental right to education. Second, both the Unnikrishnan Judgement and the Constitutional Amendment based on it, did not include within the scope of right to education, children in secondary schools. The Supreme Court judgement stated that after the age of 14 years, the fundamental right to education continued to exist but was 'subject to limits of economic capacity and development of the State'. Third, the implementation of this new provision on fundamental rights was made conditional on the State passing a law. The law is yet to be passed and has a chequered history.

Since the passage of the Amendment Bill in 2002, the Central Government considered various draft Bills on the right to education, but could not settle on any of them till 2004 when it constituted a Committee of the Central Advisory Board on Education (CABE), the highest advisory body on education in the country, to draft a Bill. The CABE approved with certain modifications the draft recommended by the Committee. However, the Central Government, instead of introducing the Bill in the Parliament, circulated a diluted version of it among the states of India on 16 June 2006 and asked them to use it as a model for enacting or amending their own legislations on school education. The unstated but widely publicized and believed reason for transferring the onus to the state governments was the so-called financial constraint of the Central Government. As the state governments are even more tightly strapped for resources, it is learnt that most of them have turned down the Central Government's suggestion and have instead demanded a Central legislation on the right to education.

Equal Opportunity for School Education

International instruments on the right to education invariably call for equal opportunity for school education for all children, with a specific focus on minorities, the disabled and the disadvantaged. The objective of equal opportunity is also unequivocally enunciated in the Preamble and Articles 14, 15 and 16 of the Indian Constitution. However, like the right to education, the question of equality of opportunity in education has so far not been effectively addressed in India. Several scholars, particularly Scrase (1993) and Haq (1989) have brought out the stark educational inequality in India. Most of the commissions and expert groups set up by the Government of India on education have also underlined the phenomenon of inequality of opportunity in education in the country and have made recommendations for overcoming it. In spite of this, equal opportunity and social justice have not received much space in the educational politics and policy making in the country. In fact, the discrimination and inequality in school education inherited from the colonial past, has been intensified (as has been brought out in the earlier part of this paper). Developments during the past two decades have reinforced this trend. Some of these developments are as follows:

(a) emergence of NFE for the poor and the disadvantaged, parallel to the formal schools;
(b) growth of fee-charging private schools which can be afforded only by the upper middle and privileged classes, at the cost of government schools to which the children of the underprivileged castes and classes go; and
(b) promotion of segregated schools in a non-inclusive environment for SCs and STs, minorities, child labour and children with disabilities.

Common School System

What is needed is a complete restructuring of the present school education system in the country. A mere tinkering with the present system, which has been the story since independence, will not do. Suggestions such as concentrating on only government schools or primary schools first and other half measures like NFE, various campaign modes of raising levels of literacy like the National Literacy Mission (NLM) or sending children to schools like the Sarva Shiksha Abhiyan (SSA), though useful, are unlikely to enable the nation to deal adequately and within a time-bound framework with the problems besetting the school education system. In fact, they will further complicate the task of restructuring the school system. Moreover, the Constitutional obligation to provide free and compulsory education to children at the elementary level can be discharged only if school education of an equitable quality can be provided to all the children in the relevant age group. The establishment of a CSS in India is an indispensable precondition for ensuring the exercise of the fundamental right to education by the children of India. Historical experience shows that in an overwhelming number of cases, this goal has been realized only by those states which have established and run primarily a state-funded CSS.

A CSS can be defined as a system of schools providing education of an equitable quality to all children, irrespective of their caste, creed, community, language, gender, economic condition, social status and physical or mental ability. The commonness of the CSS derives from the application of common minimum norms and standards of quality education by all schools in the system. The common minimum norms and standards ensure both the quality and equality of the system. In the Indian context, the most fundamental among the minimum norms is the adherence by all schools in the system to the principles of secularism, equality and social justice which alone can hold the Indian society together and which are enshrined in the Indian Constitution. In addition, the system must provide for the following:

(a) minimum infrastructure consisting of land and buildings; minimum number, size, design and furnishing of classrooms; drinking water and toilets, playgrounds and sports facilities; libraries, laboratories and teaching aids; and easy access and other required facilities to students suffering from disabilities;
(b) well-qualified trained teachers and optimal pupil–teacher ratios;
(c) a minimum curriculum framework with a core component with comparable syllabi applicable to all schools, but with adequate flexibility in relation to textbooks, teaching aids, teaching–learning process and evaluation parameters;
(d) a pedagogy which is holistic and child-friendly and which has a liberating influence;
(e) a decentralized school management with adequate autonomy and representation of parents; and
(f) a common language policy in a multi-lingual society, of which India is a quintessential example.

Moreover, the CSS should be based on the concept of neighbourhood schools according to which a school must admit all the children living in the neighbourhood which is to be specified and delineated for each school.

The basic rationale of CSS is that it promotes equality and social justice; helps in nation-building and the creation of social capital and is most conducive to providing good education. In the nineteenth century, when the philosophical foundation of public education was being laid in Europe and the US, the CSS was introduced principally for nation-building in countries having different classes, religions and languages. The objective was to forge and maintain social cohesion and thereby ensure the security of the State (Bushnell 1847; Datton 1848; Stuurman 1983; Heyneman 2000).

Recent empirical studies have shown that if children with different caste and class backgrounds are mixed, their overall performance improves (Kehelnberg 2001; Tomlinson 2004; Skrtic 1991). Skrtic (1991) has stated that it can be empirically demonstrated that 'the successful schools in the post-industrial era will be the ones that achieve excellence and equity simultaneously—indeed one(s) that recognize equity as the way to excellence'.

There is hardly any developed or developing country which has achieved universalization of elementary or secondary education without a State-funded and well functioning CSS. In India, the adoption of CSS was first recommended by the Kothari Commission in 1966. The idea was subsequently endorsed by other commissions and committees on education set up by the government, and twice approved unanimously by the Indian Parliament. However, all this support has been confined to the realm of rhetoric. In practice, there has been a constant and continuing attempt to dilute and sidetrack the idea (Bihar Report 2007, p. 35). The cumulative neglect of the school education system, that resulted from the failure of the nation to build the CSS, has now made the task of establishing such a system much more difficult than it was when the proposal was first mooted. The three formidable obstacles to building a CSS today are (i) its very large financial implications, due in no small measure to the cumulative neglect, (ii) the emergence in the country of a whole hierarchy of schools catering to the needs of different groups of children, and (iii) the vested interest of the elitist class of the society to maintain the present, grossly unequal and discriminatory system.

In this context, a development of considerable significance was the announcement by the Chief Minister of Bihar in July 2006 of his government's intention to establish a CSS in the state and to constitute a commission to advise the government on how to go about it. The government promptly established the commission which submitted its report in June 2007. In carrying out its mandate, it set before it the following objectives:

(a) the goal of free and compulsory education for children in the age group 5–14 years will be reached in five years starting from April 2008;

(b) the goal of universalizing secondary education up to Class X will be reached in eight years; and,
(c) the goal of providing facilities for senior secondary level education to 70 per cent of the children completing Class X will be achieved in 9 years.

The commission established a set of norms and standards for ensuring education of an equitable quality. Among these, the following may be highlighted:

> (a) A primary school will be provided within 1 kilometre from habitation; a middle school within 3 kilometres and a senior secondary school within 5 kilometres;
> (b) A primary school will have a capacity of 210 students; a middle school, 440 students; and a senior secondary school, 420 students;
> (c) Each class or section in a primary and middle school will have 40 students; at the secondary level, 40 students; and at the senior secondary level, 30 students;
> (d) Norms relating to school land and total floor area calculated on the basis of square metres per child, have been prescribed for each category of school;
> (e) In each primary and middle school, there will be a hall for pre-elementary children, measuring 50 square metres;
> (f) Norms have been laid down for school furniture, which includes desks, benches, computers, library books, utensils for mid-day meals (for primary and middle schools only), equipment for games and sports, office equipment, teaching–learning equipment, etc;
> (g) There will be eight teachers in each primary school, 17 in each middle school and 20 in each senior secondary school. The derived pupil–teacher ratio in these schools will be 35:1, 30:1, and 22:1 respectively; and
> (h) All teachers will be trained and otherwise qualified according to the norms of the National Council for Teachers' Education (NCTE).
>
> (Bihar Report 2007, pp. 174–9).

The commission then estimated the total number of children at different levels of education, that is, primary, middle and secondary and senior secondary, who have to be enrolled and for whom education of equitable quality has to be provided. By applying the norms set by it, the commission calculated the number of schools to be built, and the number of teachers to be recruited and those to be trained. Next the commission established the unit cost of building a new school and repairing and renovating an existing school, of teachers' salary and training, building of new and the renovation of the existing teachers' training institutions and the costs of other recurring and non-recurring expenditures which are required to be incurred in order to conform to the agreed objectives.

Some of the figures that the commission arrived at in the process of undertaking the above exercise bring out the present sad state of school education in Bihar and, by implication, in India. For example, the total number of school-going children estimated for the year 2007–08 is 30 million, out of which 15 million are out of school. The total number of additional primary schools to be built is 25,900; additional middle schools, 15,500; and additional senior secondary schools, 19,100. The total number of additional teachers to be recruited is 480800 for primary schools, 4,40,000 for middle schools and 4,42,000 for secondary schools. This will call for increasing the number of primary school teachers by 205 per cent, middle school teachers by 440 per cent and secondary school teachers by 14 times (Bihar Report 2007, pp. 180–2).

The commission estimated the aggregate expenditure required for building a CSS in Bihar by adding up the different components of non-recurring and recurring items of expenditure. It also prepared a complete year-wise plan for implementing the CSS within a period of nine years. The total expected expenditure came to Rs 1,99,512 crores or an average of Rs 22,168 crores per annum (at 2007–08 prices). After deducting the estimated public expenditure by the state government on school education for the year 2008–09, the first year of the implementation period, the commission estimated that the additional expenditure in 2008–09 would be Rs 9954.6 crores. This figure is 26 per cent of the total public expenditure estimated for that year and 61 per cent more than the public expenditure on school education in that year (Bihar Report 2007, pp. 185–6).

This figure may appear daunting but it is by no means surprising. Nor is it beyond the reach of the state government if the Central Government chips in with an appropriate contribution. Besides, given the magnitude of the task, the mobilization of resources on the scale indicated by this figure is absolutely essential. There has been a cumulative neglect of school education in the country as a whole, but the neglect has been the most rampant and on the largest scale in Bihar. Moreover, in assessing the feasibility of mobilizing additional resources of this magnitude, it is essential to bear in mind the significance of the CSS for the state of Bihar as well as the nation.

Most importantly, it would mark the beginning of the elimination of inequality and discrimination in the school education system in the country, which is the most important source of exclusion in Indian society. Moreover, the CSS will lay the most comprehensive foundation of human development in the state and pave the path for more rapid growth. Though the inadequacies of the school education system are most glaring in Bihar, the problem is present in varying degrees across all states in India. Therefore, the establishment of a CSS for the country as a whole is necessary for ensuring the sustainability of the current dynamism of the Indian economy.

Financing School Education

The Target for Expenditure on Education

Since the mid-1960s, India has been chasing what has now become a mirage of making 6 per cent of its GDP available for expenditure on education. Several committees and commissions have made recommendations to this effect. Almost all major political parties have included this goal in their election manifestos. The latest was the inclusion of this target in May 2004, in the Common Minimum Programme (CMP) of the ruling United Progressive Alliance.

If the 6 per cent target had been in operation today and if Bihar had spent an amount proportional to its share in the national population, which is 8 per cent, a major part of the resources gap estimated by the CSS Commission, Bihar, for establishing a CSS in the state, would have been bridged. The additional resources that the state would have been required to mobilize would have been a little over Rs 1500 crores per annum over the next nine years, which would have been well within its reach with some extra effort.

The target of devoting 6 per cent of the GDP to education was first mooted by the Kothari Commission in 1966. This was reiterated in the NPE which stated: 'The investment on education be gradually increased to reach a level of 6 per cent of national income as early as possible.' Subsequently, the NPE included the dateline of 2000 for attaining this target. Till now there has hardly been any progress in achieving this target.

Expenditure on education as a proportion of GDP has been steadily coming down since the closing years of the 1980s when it was approximately 4 per cent. In 2000–01, the proportion was 3.17 per cent. It further declined to the lowest level of 2.74 per cent in 2004–05. There is a slight increase in the ratios during the last two completed financial years that is, 2005–06 when it was 2.88 and 2006–07 when it was 2.87 per cent.[5] The reason for the decline during the 1990s was the cut-back in public expenditure in the social sector on account of the impact of the conditionalities imposed under the WB's Structural Adjustment Programmes. Towards the end of that decade, the WB started paying greater attention to education and increased its contribution to this sector in its aid programme. In the process, the Bank also imposed on the Government of India its own philosophy on education which has resulted in the introduction of serious distortions in the school education system in the country, as brought out in the earlier part of this paper. Today, the international financial agencies, mainly the WB, finance as much as 40 per cent of the resources for implementing the SSA, the flagship scheme of the Government of India for elementary education. In the process, the government has reduced its own expenditure for financing school education and has projected the SSA as the panacea for removing all the ills of elementary education and for its universalization. This has been a major factor accounting for a decline in the proportion of GDP devoted to the expenditure on education, witnessed since the year 2000–01.

Another device used by the government to distract public attention from the real problems of school education in India is the levy of a 2 per cent cess on income tax for financing education. This levy fetched about Rs 7000 crores in the year 2005–06 which is less than 10 per cent of the additional resources estimated by the expert group of the CABE Committee for giving effect to the fundamental right to education and which is also supposed to be spent for secondary, university and higher technical education. Besides, the cess is of an *ad hoc* nature subject to be withdrawn any time if the government finds itself under pressure. Surely, this cannot be a substitute for a planned effort to provide free and compulsory education to all children up to the elementary level and to universalize secondary education at least up to Class X, within a time-bound framework.

[5]*Source*: *Economic Survey* 2005–06 and 2006–07.

Cost of Providing Free and Compulsory Elementary Education

In 1998, the then United Front Government at the Centre set up an expert committee under the Chairmanship of Tapas Mazumdar, an eminent expert in education. The terms of reference of this committee were to assess the financial requirements for providing free and compulsory education to children at the elementary level and to suggest measures for mobilizing the required resources. In its report submitted in January 1999, the committee estimated expenditures of Rs 1,37,000 crores over a ten-year period, beginning from 1998–99, namely an average annual additional expenditure of Rs 13,700 crores. This was equivalent to 0.86 per cent of the GDP in 1998–99.

The committee felt that meeting this requirement was entirely within the realm of possibility if the government fulfilled the longstanding promise given to the nation of achieving the 6 per cent target. The committee was also of the view that after the Unnikrishnan Judgement, the right to free and compulsory education up to Class VIII had become justiciable. The government, therefore, was no longer in a position to shirk its responsibility on the plea of paucity of resources. It was essential for the government to mobilize additional resources and for this purpose to reprioritize its budget expenditure in order to make additional resources available for education at the cost of expenditures in other sectors except those which were required for ensuring the exercise of other fundamental rights.

Neither the United Front Government nor those which came to power at the Centre subsequently took any action to implement the recommendations of the Tapas Mazumdar Committee, on the ground of the so-called resources constraint. The issue of estimating the additional resources required for implementing the right to education was revisited by the CABE Committee set up by the Central Government in June 2005, to draft a Bill to give effect to the 86th Amendment of the Constitution on the Fundamental Right to Education. An expert group of this committee estimated the additional resources requirement for giving effect to the right to education under four scenarios. The estimate under the best scenario, based on the assumption of a pupil–teacher ratio of 35:1, average salary for a teacher at Rs 8000 per month, and a set of norms to be applied by all schools at the elementary level, came to Rs 4,36,500 crores over a period of six years from 2006–07 to 2011–2012. The annual average additional expenditure under this scenario worked out to be approximately Rs 72,500 crores. This was equivalent to 1.5 per cent of the GDP that year. This additional expenditure, like that suggested by the Tapas Mazumdar committee could have also been accommodated if the 6 per cent target had been met—in fact leaving a balance of 0.6 per cent of GDP available as additional resources to be spent in other sectors of education.

If the 6 per cent target recommended by the Kothari Commission and included in the NEP had been implemented by the end of the year 2000, it would not have been necessary to mobilize additional resources amounting to Rs 13,000 crores per annum for ten years as recommended by the Tapas Mazumdar Committee. This additional expenditure became necessary because of the cumulative gap in public expenditure that developed over a period of 35 years after the submission of the report of the Kothari Commission. Similarly, if the Tapas Mazumdar Committee's recommendations had been implemented, starting from the year 1998–99, the resources required by the year 2005, when the expert group under the CABE Committee made its estimates, would not have jumped to Rs 72,500 crores per annum. This was again because of the widening of the cumulative gap since the turn of the last century. The inference from this is that if we further delay the implementation of the right to free and compulsory education, the cumulative gap will be so wide as to put the goal beyond the reach of the nation. This could very well turn out to be the single biggest constraint to the continuation of the present dynamism in the growth of the Indian economy.

The estimate of additional resources made by the CABE Committee expert group appears to be daunting. But it is achievable if there is a reprioritization of public expenditure by the government in order to divert resources from expenditures in sectors or on events which are not intended to ensure the exercise of any fundamental rights under the Indian Constitution. One is tempted to cite a few examples in this regard. First, the total expenditure likely to be incurred for organizing the forthcoming Commonwealth Games, has been estimated to be between Rs 50,000 crores and Rs 100,000 crores. This is certainly dispensable for the sake of ensuring free and compulsory elementary education to Indian children. Second, an amount of Rs 40,000 crores was recently waived in favour of business houses which held non-performing assets with Indian banks. The total amount of such non-performing assets would be a multiple of the amount waived. If even a part of it is realized from those from whom it is due, it would go a long way towards meeting the additional expenditure required for school education. Third, government sources have estimated that the total amount of taxes waived and concessions given to enterprises for setting up special economic zones (SEZs) in India would amount to more than Rs 200,000 crores. This is nearly half the total additional resources estimated by the CABE Committee expert group. SEZs are at best highly controversial. In any case, they have nothing to do with the exercise of any fundamental rights. Public expenditure on them certainly cannot have priority over providing elementary education to children in India.

Besides, the additional resources required are only for a finite period, six years in the present case. After six years, additional resources will be required only for maintaining the infrastructure and further upgrading the quality of education. This should well be within the reach of the government without further raising the ratio of expenditure on education to GDP.

Cost of Building a CSS

Finally, it is naïve to believe that the present problems of school education in India will be solved and the widest possible basis for creating knowledge and developing technologies, commensurate with the country's potential, will be laid, only by universalizing free and compulsory education up to the elementary level. Let us consider what would happen if elementary education is universalized but the subsequent stages of school education are left as they are today. It is quite clear that once elementary education is universalized, there will be an inevitable pressure for universalizing secondary education. If secondary education, at least up to Class X, is not universalized by the time elementary education becomes available to all children, then the children completing 8 years of education will either drop out or opt for private schools, which is possible only for those who can afford it. The children who drop out would belong mostly to the marginalized groups. This would mean the perpetuation of inequality and discrimination in school education.

We have argued that the establishment of a CSS in India is an indispensable precondition for providing school education of an equitable quality to all the children in school-going age and for ensuring the exercise of the fundamental right to education. We have also given the figures for the additional expenditure required for establishing a CSS in Bihar as estimated by the CSS Commission, Bihar, in its report submitted on 8 June 2007. The additional resources required for building a CSS for the country as a whole will be several times more than the estimate for Bihar.

Conclusion

Education, particularly primary education, has been found theoretically and empirically to be a very significant contributor to economic growth. Unfortunately, school education in India has serious shortcomings both in terms of quantity and quality. Large numbers of children remain outside school and drop out rates for those who start school are high. Furthermore, there are serious shortcomings in the training of those who remain in school for some years. The curriculum is outdated. An important cause is the lack of adequate funding, and without funding it would be impossible to implement realistically the basic right to education which has been accepted. Funding for universal education is not beyond the capacity of the government. A serious shortcoming of the current structure of schools is the lack of a common school system, which has been so instrumental in making education available to all in other countries.

References

Barro, R. (1991), 'Economic Growth in a Cross Section of Countries', *Quarterly Journal of Economics*, Vol. 6, No. 2, pp. 404–44.

Benhabib, Jess and Mark M. Spiegel (1994), 'The Role of Human Capital in Economic Development; Evidences from Aggregate Cross Country Data', *Journal of Monetary Economics*, October, Vol. 34, No.2, pp. 143–74.

Bihar Report (2007), Report by CSS Commission on Common School System (CSS), submitted to Govt. of Bihar, 8 June.

Bushnel, H. (1847), *Discourses on Christian Nature*, Massachusetts Sabbath School Society, Boston.

Carnoy, Martin (1992), *The Case of Investing in Basic Education*, UNICEF, New York.

Chen, Lincoln (1983), 'Child Survival: Levels, Trends and Determinants', in R. Bulatao and R. Lee (eds) *Determinants of Fertility in Developing Countries*, Academic Press, New York, pp. 199–232.

Cochrane, Susan (1979), *Fertility and Education: What Do We Really Know?* Johns Hopkins University Press, Baltimore.

_____ (1983), 'Effect of Education and Urbanisation on Fertility', in *Determinants of Fertility: A Summary of the Knowledge*, National Academy of Sciences, Washington DC.

Cochrane, Susan, D.J.O'Hara and J. Leslie (1980), 'The Effect of Education on Health', World Bank Staff Working Paper, No. 405, World Bank, Washington, DC.

Datton, Rev. W.S. (1848), 'The Proposed Substitution of Secretarian for Public Schools', *Common School Journal*, Vol. 10, No. 11, pp. 166–8.

Dholakia, B.H. (1974), *The Sources of Economic Growth in India*, Good Companions, Baroda.

Dreze, Jean and Amartya Sen (2003), 'Basic Education as a Political Issues', in J.B.G. Tilak (ed.) *Education, Society and Development, National and International Perspective*, APH Publishing Corporation, NIEPA, New Delhi.

Government of India (1944), 'Post War Educational Development in India', Report by the Central Advisory Board of Education, Government of India Press, Shimla.

_____ (2006a), *Employment and Unemployment Situation in India, 2004–05*, Vol.I, Report No. 515, NSSO, Ministry of Statistics and Programme Implementation, New Delhi, September.

_____ (2006b), *Employment and Unemployment Situation Among Social Groups in India, 2004–05*, Report No. 516, NSSO, Ministry of Statistics and Programme Implementation, New Delhi, October.

Griffin, Keith (1997), *Culture, Human Development and Economic Growth*, UNRISD and UNESCO, Geneva.

Hanushek, Eric A. and Ludger Woessmann, (2007), 'The Role of School Improvement in Economic Development', National Bureau of Economic Research, Working paper No12832, National Bureau of Economic Research, Cambridge, Mass.

Haq, E. (1989), 'Open Education and Closed Society: A Study in Social and Educational Inequality in Contemporary India', in A. Yogev (ed.) *International Perspectives on Education and Society*, Jai Press, London.

Heyneman, Stephen P. (2000), 'From the Party/State to Multiethnic Democracy: Education and Social Cohesion in Europe and Central Asia', *Educational Evaluation and Policy Analysis*, Vol. 22, No. 2, pp. 173–91.

Kehelnberg, R.D. (2001), *All Together Now: Creating Middle-Class Schools through Public School Choice*, Brookings Institutions Press, Washington, DC.

Kuznets, S. (1966), 'Modern Economic Growth: Rate, Structure and Spread', Yale University Press, New Haven, pp. 80–1.

Lavin, Henery M. (1987), 'Improving Productivity through Education and Technology', in G. Burk and Russel Rumberger (eds) *The Future Impact of Technology on Work and Education*, Palmer Press, London.

Lockheed, Marlaine, T. Jamison and L. Lau (1980), 'Farmer Education and Farm Efficiency: A Survey', *Economic Development and Cultural Change*, Vol. 29, No. 1.

Lockheed, Marlaine E., and Adriaan M. Verspoor with Deborah Bloch et. al. (1991), *Improving Primary Education in Developing Countries*, Oxford University Press, New York.

Lockwood, Matthew and Paul Collier (1988), 'Maternal Education and the Vicious Cycle of High Fertility and Malnutrition', World Bank Policy Planning and Research Working Paper No. 130, World Bank, Washington, DC.

Loh, J. (1995), 'Education and Economic Growth in India: An Aggregate Production Function Approach', in *School Effectiveness and Learning Achievement of Primary Stage*, National Council of Educational Research and Training, New Delhi, pp. 509–27.

Lucas, Robert E. (1988), 'On the Mechanics of Economic Development', *Journal of Monetary Economics*, Vol. 22, No. 1, pp. 3–42.

Mehrotra, Santosh (2005), 'Human Capital or Human Development? In Search of a Knowledge Paradigm for Education and Development', *Economic and Political Weekly*, Vol. 40, No. 22, Jan 2005, pp. 300–6.

MHRD (Ministry of Human Resources Development) (2006), *Selected Educational Statistics 2003–2004*, Government of India, New Delhi and UNICEF.

Mincer, Jacob (1970), 'The Distribution of Labour Incomes: A Survey with Special Reference to the Human Capital Approach', *Journal of Economic Literature*, Vol. 8, No. 1, March, pp. 1–26.

——— (1974), *Schooling Experience and Earnings*, NBER, New York.

NIEPA (National Institute of Educational Planning and Administration) (2006), *Elementary Education in India*, Analytical Report 2004–05, NIEPA, New Delhi.

Patel, Surendra (1985), 'Educational Miracles in Third World, 1950–1981', *Economic and Political Weekly*, Vol. XX, No. 31.

Patel, I.G. (2003), 'Higher Education and Economic Development', in J.B.G. Tilak (ed.) *Education, Society and Development, National and International Perspectives*, APH Publishing Corporation, NIEPA, New Delhi.

Peaslee, Alexander L. (1965), 'Elementary Education as a Prerequisite for Economic Growth', *International Development Review*, Vol. 7, pp. 19–24.

Psacharopoulos, George (1973), *Returns to Education: An International Comparison*, Elsevier Scientific Publishing Company, Amsterdam.

Pullum, T. (1983), 'Correlates of Family–Size Desires', in R. Bulatao and R. Lee (eds) *Determinants of Fertility in Developing Countries*, Academic Press, New York. pp. 199–232.

Romer, Paul M. (1986), 'Increasing Returns and Long-run Growth', *Journal of Political Economy*, Vol. 94, No. 5, pp. 1002–36.

Sala-I-Martin, Xavier (1997), 'I Just Ran Four Million Regressions', National

Bureau of Economic Research Working Paper No. 6262, NBER, Cambridge, MA, November.

Schultz, Theodore (1961), 'Investment in Human Capital', *The American Economic Review*, Vol. L1, No. 1.

_____ (1989), 'Human Capital in Restoring Equilibrium', Paper presented at the Conference on Human Capital and Economic Growth, Institute for the Study of Free Enterprise Systems, State University of New York, Buffalo.

Scrase, T.J. (1993), *Image, Ideology and Inequality: Cultural Domination, Hegemony and Schooling in India*, Sage Publications, New Delhi.

Sen, Amartya (1997), 'Human Capital and Human Capability', Editorial in *World Development*, Vol. 25, No. 12, pp. 1959–61, Elsevier Science Ltd, Amsterdam.

Skrtic, T.M. (1991), *Behind Special Education: A Critical Analysis of Professional Culture and School Organization*, Love Publishing, Denver.

Solow, R. (1957), 'Technical Change and Aggregate Production Function', *Review of Economics and Statistics*, Cambridge, Mass., Vol. 39, pp. 312–20.

Tilak, J.B.G. (ed.) (2003), *Education, Society and Development, National and International Perspectives*; APH Publishing Corporation, NIEPA, New Delhi.

Tilak, Jandhyala B.G. (2007), 'Post Elementary Education, Poverty and Development in India', *International Journal of Educational Development*, Vol. 27, pp. 435–45.

Tomlinson, Sally (2004), The Third Caroline Benn Memorial Lecture 'Comprehensive Success and Bog-Standard Government', January, delivered at the Institute of Education, London reprinted in Benn M. and Chitty C. (eds), Education and Democracy—A Tribute to Caroline Benn, Continuum Press, London, pp. 59–75.

Uzawa, H. (1985), 'Optimal Technical Change in an Aggregate Model of Economic Growth', *International Economic Review*, Vol. 6, pp. 18–31.

6

Dream India
Is its Education Competitive Enough?

P.V. INDIRESAN

In 20 years time, only three people are guaranteed a place at the top table of world affairs—the presidents of the US and China and the prime minister of India.

Ken Livingstone, Mayor of London[1]

Introduction

During the first half of 2007, industry in India enjoyed double digit growth rate and modern services grew even faster. The stock market was at record levels while the inflation rate was at a modest 2.3 per cent. Later, the situation got reversed: inflation is in double digits, industry has all but stagnated and the stock market has lost 40 per cent of its peak value.

Not long ago, the Indian Institutes of Technology (IITs) were arguably the best-known Indian brand worldwide. The United States Congress went to the extent of passing a special resolution lauding the contribution made by IIT graduates to the US economy. Sherlock Holmes asked his best known question: 'Why did not the dog bark?' We might likewise ask why the Indian Parliament did not commend IIT graduates the same way.

[1] *TOI*, 2007.

The answer lies in recent developments. Apparently, India's politcians do not view IITs as a force for facing global competition but as a resource for political patronage. They have amended the Constitution and have passed orders enforcing 49.5 per cent reservation for backward caste candidates in admissions to IITs and for faculty selections. Of the 542 members of Parliament (MPs), only two opposed the move. In Tamil Nadu, where reservation for certain castes has operated for nearly 80 years, no more than 2.6 per cent of 'other communities' could gain admission to government medical colleges and 97.4 per cent of the seats have been captured by preferred groups.

It is possible that the economic downturn will be temporary and the Indian economy will recover. However, in the field of education with virtually 100 per cent political opposition to quality in higher education, and zero resistance from the academic community, it is difficult to be optimistic.

Will Gresham's Law apply and poor quality teachers and students drive away good ones, or will India take a turn towards better quality education? Will the future of higher education in India be a dream or will it be a nightmare? It is difficult to tell at present.

I first note that education and R&D have been found to be very important for economic growth as their contribution is much greater than that of physical capital. The Indian tertiary education system is vast in terms of numbers, but small in relation to the population. Furthermore its quality is poor particularly in terms of output of research papers and winning of patents. Lack of resources with the government is a major constraint to improving the quality of tertiary education. I discuss some innovative ways of raising money for tertiary education without having to depend on the government. Furthermore, if private institutions do not award degrees they can free themselves from government interference.

Productivity and GDP Growth

If the present rate of growth persists, India will overtake Germany in a few years in terms of gross domestic product (GDP), Japan in a decade and become a dozen times larger to surpass the US in another 30 years. That is a big 'if'. Extrapolation is ever an uncertain business. Yet, we can enquire how probable it is that India will maintain its current rate of GDP growth.

Table 6.1: Components of GNP Growth in the US, 1929–82

Component of Growth	*Share*
Labour input except education	–23
Education per worker	30
Capital	10
Advances in knowledge (R&D)	64
Better resource allocation (management)	19
Economies of scale	20
Land	–04
Other determinants	–20

Source: Denison (1985).

What makes an economy grow? In a longitudinal study, Denison[2] estimated the share of various factors that contributed to the growth of US economy for the period 1929–82 (see Table 6.1)

Two points in Denison's analysis are noteworthy. One, education is three times as important as capital is in a nation's development. Two, research and development (R&D) is six and a half times more valuable than capital. Then, the nation should invest more in educating workers (or recruiting educated workers) than on materials and machinery and spend more on research, design and development than on capital equipment. How this cost should be shared between the State and business is a matter of detail but the broad outline is clear.

In a more recent study by the Boston Consulting Group,[3] US productivity is estimated to have tripled in the past 50 years. Of this, a little over half has been attributed to innovation, about 10 per cent to labour and the remaining to financial capital. This difference between the current estimate and the earlier one by Denison is probably because the US economy has started to decline. For India, it would be wiser to model on Denison.

Mancur Olson[4] approached the same issue of growth from a different perspective. He raised the question as to why countries that are adjacent to each other and have similar natural endowments differ widely in their income and wealth. He considered pairs of countries such as South and North Korea, erstwhile West and East

[2]See Denison (1985).
[3]*Economist* (2007).
[4]See Olson (1996).

Germany as also Mexico and Southern US. The countries in each pair were geographically contiguous, their basic economic endowments were not very different; yet their material prosperity was miles apart. Olson came to the conclusion that these pairs of countries grew at widely different rates because of vital differences in their cultures, particularly political cultures—freedom for enterprise, rule of law, for example.

Paul Krugman[5] in a study of Singapore came to a conclusion not dissimilar to that of Denison. He argued that Singapore grew by increasing inputs (education and capital) quantitatively. He raised the question: Once Singapore produces as many Ph.Ds as it can, what next? He concluded that the East Asian Model is basically self limiting. In contrast, Western economies, based as they are on qualitative technology development rather than on quantitative increase of technology, will suffer no such limits to growth. Krugman's comments are now outdated—Singapore has been voted this year as the most competitive nation in the world. Nevertheless his basic argument that quality of innovation is more important than quantity of skill remains valid.

According to Mokyr,[6] the following three conditions should be satisfied before a culture will support innovation and development:

(a) a cadre of ingenious and resourceful innovators who are both willing and able to challenge their physical environment should be available;
(b) economic and social institutions have to encourage potential innovators by presenting them with the right incentive structure;
(c) diversity and tolerance should prevail in the society to enable technological creativity to overcome entrenched vested interests that might incur losses if innovations are introduced.

Thomas Kuhn[7] scientist, historian and philosopher, has explained that the West has been dominating science and technology (S&T) for the past 400 years whereas others have stagnated because of the prevalence of scientific temper which others do not have. That temper manifests itself by adopting the following processes for scientific research:

[5]Krugman (1994), 'Myth of Asian Miracle'.

[6]Mokyr (1990).

[7]Kuhn (1970), *Structure of Scientific Revolutions.*

(a) *continuously* devising newer puzzles to stretch the existing paradigm farther and farther—the puzzles are so chosen that theory will predict the result beforehand;
(b) checking the limits to the validity of the theory and paradigm by verifying the theoretical predictions with experimental results;
(c) as and when anomalies are noticed, searching for suitable explanations, without giving up the paradigm itself;
(d) when it becomes impossible to explain away the anomalies, looking for a new paradigm. That should not only explain the anomalies, it should also explain all earlier results, the way for example, semi-conductors have superseded vacuum tubes. Compare that with the way we have preserved the Ambassador car in India; and
(e) once the new paradigm is established, *discarding the old paradigm altogether. For that purpose writing new textbooks for students propagating the new paradigm only.*

Donald Christiansen[8] has written: 'A country that trains its engineers and technologists well, then rewards them with both real and psychic income, should have little trouble competing in a world economy that thrives on trading high quality, high tech products over international boundaries.'

In the light of these arguments, we may say, a nation will be globally competitive and enjoy sustained growth when it:
(a) values human capital above the financial;
(b) emphasizes quality over quantity;
(c) accepts change readily and allows a constant flux of new ideas;
(d) encourages innovators;
(e) enforces contracts through rule of law.

The question to be answered is how far India satisfies these conditions and thereby maintains high potential for rapid growth.

Status of India's Higher Education

By the year 2006, India had 355 universities including 20 Central, 216 state, 101 deemed universities, 5 institutions established under state legislation, 13 institutes of national importance and 18,064 colleges. During the year, as many as 439 new colleges were added.

[8]Christiansen (1987), *Engineering Excellence.*

At that rate, India probably has over 20,000 colleges. During the academic session 2005–06, the total enrolment in all courses and levels in the regular stream was 11 million including 4.5 million women students constituting 40.5 per cent of the total. Of these, 89 per cent were undergraduates, 10 per cent post-graduates and barely two-thirds of one per cent at the doctoral level.

College admissions for the tertiary level constitute barely 10 per cent of the relevant age cohort. At the same time, unemployment is the highest among graduates as compared to the less educated youth. Thus, even though higher education in India is relatively small in proportion to its population, it is large compared to economic demand.

Tamil Nadu is amongst the most progressive states in the country. Next to Maharashtra, it has the largest number (272) of engineering colleges in the country. Table 6.2 gives the current position of admission in those colleges. Table 6.3 shows that even in a progressive state like Tamil Nadu, a large numbers of seats in engineering remain unfilled, in spite of lowering of the admission criteria to rock bottom levels—to no more than 40 per cent marks in some cases—because most graduates are unemployable. It is understood that this year, 50 per cent of the students failed in Mathematics in the first year of the engineering course. There is a real risk that—Gresham's Law—a bad coin will drive away the good—will apply in this case too, to the detriment of quality in India's higher education (Tilak 2004).[9] That risk has already materialized in many universities, where, by the sheer force of their numbers, mediocre students have dumbed down quality.

Higher Education in India: Pace-setting Institutions

At the other end of the spectrum, India is fortunate to have a few pace-setting institutions such as the IITs, the Indian Institutes of Management (IIMs) and the All India Institute of Medical Sciences (AIIMS). They provide benchmarks for others to emulate. Till recently, the IITs also trained an overwhelming proportion of engineering college teachers, and provided the nation's engineering colleges with a steady supply of well-qualified teachers. Due to the extremely rapid expansion of engineering colleges—nearly 20 times in 20 years—the IITs are no longer able to supply teachers to these colleges.

[9]Tilak (2004), *Quality of Higher Education.*

Table 6.2: Trends in Higher Education in India

	1981–82	*1991–92*	*2001–02*
Total enrolment	3,000,000	5,270,000	8,821,000
Intake in Engineering	28,500	66,600	359, 723
No. of Engg colleges	158	337	1208
All colleges	4886	7592	13,150
Faculty Strength	199,904	264,000	351,000
Ph.Ds awarded	6080	8743	11,450
Ph.Ds in Engineering	139	299	739
Higher Education Expenditure (per cent GNP)	1.0	0.46	0.40

Source: University Grants Commission Annual Reports; Report of the Review Committee of the All India Council of Technical Education, New Delhi.

Table 6.3: Admission to Engineering Courses in Tamil Nadu, 2007–08

Branch	*No. of seats*	*No. admitted*	*No. unfilled*	*Per cent left unfilled*
Civil Engineering	4295	3115	1180	27.47
Mechanical Engineering	11,720	10,435	1285	11
Electronic and Electrical Engineering	16,025	12,721	3304	20
Computer Science	22,815	21,116	1699	7.44
Electronic Communication	24,509	22,532	1977	8.06
Information Technology	17,015	15,089	1926	11
Architecture	300	182	118	39.33
Electronic & Instrumentation	2610	2139	471	18.05
Automobile Engineering	2790	1968	822	29.46
Biotechnology	1855	1259	596	32.13
Chemical Engineering	795	462	333	41.89
Bio-medical Engineering	1020	576	444	43.53
Other branches*	4035	2752	1283	31.8
Total	109,784	94,346	15438	14.06

Source: Government of Tamil Nadu under the Right to Information Act.

In arts and humanities, there are truly no pace setting universities like we have in technology, management or medical education. At one time, the University of Calcutta played that role, but no longer. Jawaharlal Nehru University attempted to take on that role by embarking on a new form of university structure through inter-disciplinary centres. Unfortunately, Indian universities prefer the traditional department structure. Traditional universities are also hamstrung by outdated university managements and are held back by teacher–politicians.

Resistance to change has become a contagion in Indian universities. The situation is so bad that even such a prestigious institution as the Delhi School of Economics, where Amartya Sen, India's only Nobel Prize winner in economics, and the current Prime Minister Dr Manmohan Singh used to teach, could not update its syllabus for 25 years.

In July 2008, Delhi University, arguably amongst the most prestigious universities in the country, updated its syllabus in Mathematics after a lapse of 17 years. This evoked strong opposition among the faculty. If this is the case in Delhi, the situation elsewhere can be imagined. No-changers are powerful; they oppose any change on any available excuse.

The state of higher education in India has started ringing alarm bells. Delivering the P.V. Narasimha Rao Memorial Lecture, N. Narayana Murthy, one of the country's most reputed entrepreneurs said:[10]

> The country produces nearly 2.3 million English-speaking graduates, including nearly 300,000 engineering graduate(s)...But the quality of the engineering graduates varies, and only 25 per cent of them are employable as per the McKinsey report.
>
> ...the number of patents per one million people is one in India, 289 in the US and 779 in South Korea. The number of people engaged in research per 100,000 population is 149 in India and 3805 in the US.
>
> ...the industry faces the prospect of a severe shortage from 2012. ... In the Massachusetts Institute of Technology nearly 150 new companies come up each year through the efforts of its faculty and staff. There are nearly 4000 such companies in the US whose combined sales were worth $232 billion, which was nearly 40 per cent of India's

[10]Murthy (2006), P.V. Narasimha Rao Memorial Lecture.

> GDP. This means the productivity of every MIT graduate is equivalent to the productivity level of nearly one lakh Indians.
>
> N. Narayana Murthy (2006)

Prof. Altbach who has studied the Indian education system for several decades has written:[11]

> Its systematic disinvestment in higher education in recent years has yielded neither world-class researchers, nor very many highly trained scholars, scientists, nor managers to sustain high-tech development. ... India's colleges and universities, with just a few exceptions, have become large, under-funded, ungovernable institutions. At many of them, politics have intruded into campus life, influencing academic appointments, and decisions across levels. ... India's best universities require sustained state support...they also require effective management and an ethos of academic meritocracy. At present, the structures are not in place to permit building and sustaining top-quality programmes even if resources are provided.

That is a fair description of what ails the Indian education system. Though India has a number of good undergraduate colleges, once we go below the top two–three per cent institutions, quality deteriorates rapidly. Altbach's hopes, that strong State support and better management will lift India's colleges, can materialize only in a small fraction of the country's 18,000 colleges. For most of them, there is no hope of their ever reaching world standards; their faculties are so poor that they can only produce, as Mr. Narayanamurthy has complained, virtual illiterates who have to be content with low level jobs unworthy of university education. India will ignore these pessimistic assessments by two independent and knowledgeable observers of the Indian scene only at its own peril.

Status of Indian Research

It is usual to measure the quality of a research paper by the number of times it is cited by subsequent researchers. As a further filter, those that rank among the top one per cent of cited papers (selected on the basis of the number of citations) are considered to be papers of exceptional quality. Then, a country's share of such exceptional papers is an accepted indicator of the quality of its scientific output.

[11]Altbach (2005).

Table 6.4: Research Capability: International Comparison

Country	*Scientists per million population*	*Total R&D expenditure (billion US$)*	*Per capita R&D expenditure (US$)*	*Expenditue per scientist* (US$ 000s) (US$)*	*No. among top 1 per cent of cited papers*	*R&D expenditure per top cited paper (US$ million)#*
USA	4099	206	705	230	23,723	8.4
England	2666	27	450	172	4831	5.6
Japan	5095	120	978	192	2609	6.1
China		16	12	16	375	4.0
India	157	5.5	5.5	35	205	2.7
South Korea	2319	12	241	104	294	3.9
Brazil		9.5	56	36	188	5.1

Notes: *US national expenditure on R&D divided by number of R&D scientists;
#US national expenditure on R&D divided by number of cited papers published.
Source: Chidambram, R. (2005), 'Measure of Progress in Science and Technology', *Current Science*, Vol. 88, No. 6, pp. 856–60.

The figures for some selected countries are given in Table 6.4. The number of exceptional papers published by Indian scientists is less than 1 per cent of those published by US scientists and lag behind the numbers published by S. Korean and Chinese scientists.

Figure 6.1 gives a comparison of R&D spending across the world. India and China put together have a third of the world's population but less than a twentieth of R&D spending. As China's share is around twice India's, the situation in India can only be described as unsatisfactory.

The limited success of Indian R&D is partly due to financial and administrative constraints and largely due to a lack of scientific spirit. For a thousand years, India has been cast in a rigid mould impervious to change. Indian scientists and engineers tend to cling to myths even after they cease to be useful. The Ambassador car is the most glaring example of this weakness. This car was originally the 1958 model of Morris Oxford. In 50 years since its production began in India, the car has remained the same giving India the unenviable distinction of being the only country that still manufactures a vintage car. As this paper is being written, the

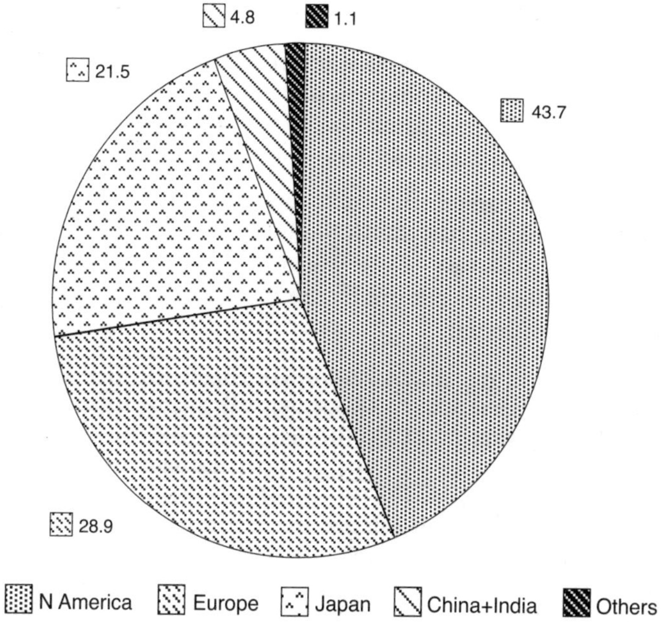

Figure 6.1: R&D Spending in Different Regions of the World

manufacturer has pressurized the government to place more orders for it (Times of India).[12] Furthermore, Indian businesses are reluctant to invest in R&D as the judicial system in India is so slow and convoluted that it is very difficult for any industry to enforce patent rights.

Essentially, in India, once a technology is inducted, it hardly benefits from further improvement. It becomes static. Once an innovation is introduced, the product (like the Ambassador car) becomes virtually immortal; its technology ceases to grow the day it produces a marketable product. Our respect for the past is much too great to give up outdated ideas. Fortunately, there are exceptions and the exceptions are growing. Yet, the country has far to go before it can be said to be receptive to innovation.

[12] *TOI*, (2008), 'Ambassador Gets a Fresh Lease of Life'.

Threats to Quality Education

In the introduction, five necessary conditions for quality higher education were listed. From the foregoing description of the state of affairs in India's higher education and R&D, India will have great difficulty in measuring up to those conditions.

1. *Value human capital above financial capital:* After 60 years of socialist rule, India has the dubious distinction of having more illiterates than the rest of the world. According to the Eleventh Plan Approach Paper put out by the Planning Commission of the Government of India:

> 38 per cent of the children who have completed four years of schooling cannot read a small paragraph with short sentences meant to be read by a student of Class II. About 55 per cent of such children cannot divide a three digit number by a one digit number. ...we should also note that just 28 per cent of our schools had electricity in 2005 and only about half had more than two teachers or two classrooms. Only 40 per cent of primary school teachers were graduates and 30 per cent had not even completed Higher Secondary. For a large proportion of our children, school is therefore an ill-lit classroom with more than one class being taught together by someone who may not have completed her own schooling.

Universal suffrage has had a debilitating effect on Indian education because the country's politicians have found that illiterate people can be cheaply organized as vote banks. Hence, they have a vested interest in *not* educating people. It is not an accident that unlike in the West, where academics are influential in policy decisions, in India, they have next to no voice in such matters—only money talks in India.

2. *Emphasize quality over quantity:* The Indian Government has just initiated 20 new universities and seven additional IITs even though the existing ones are short of faculty, are overcrowded and handicapped by meagre physical facilities. In the Indian milieu, starting new institutions is politically and financially advantageous. The country is still so poor that most people behave like Oliver Twist in the Charles Dickens novel of the same name—they ask for more, not for something better. Policy debate in India is about raising enrolment ratios, not improving quality, to produce more graduates and not quality graduates that are employable.

3. *Accept change readily:* This point has been laboured upon already. Neither universities nor industries are willing to accept change readily.

4. *Encourage innovators:* It is relatively easier in India than elsewhere for university teachers to get research grants from the government. That is good but the disposal of the grants is so rigidly controlled by the bureaucracy that researchers are frustrated all the time. The country also has a strong preference for imported technology. Therefore, there is next to no support for infant technology or any culture of rearing new ideas until they overcome their teething troubles. It is no accident that while Indians have been at the forefront in the Silicon Valley, within India, similarly educated persons almost never develop or produce new products. As Mr. Vittal, former Chairman of the Telecommunication Commission used to say, they often function as 'techno-coolies'. In fact, the most productive R&D laboratories in India are run by foreign multinational companies.

4. *Establish Rule of Law:* The Indian Constitution does pay homage to the principle of equality of all persons. However, the Constitution has been recently amended (for the 93rd time) as follows:

> In article 15 of the Constitution, after clause (4), the following clause shall be inserted, namely:-
>
> '(5) Nothing in this article or in sub-clause (g) of clause (1) of article 19 shall prevent the State from making any special provision, by law, for the advancement of any socially and educationally backward classes of citizens or for the Scheduled Castes or the Scheduled Tribes in so far as such special provisions relate to their admission to educational institutions including private educational institutions, whether aided or unaided by the State, other than the minority educational institutions referred to in clause (1) of article 30.'

On petition, the Supreme Court has upheld this amendment. Armed with this power, the government has ordered that in all educational institutions in the country, 49.5 per cent of the seats and a similar percentage of faculty positions (including professorial positions in non-science departments) will be reserved for backward castes.

This rule has rigidly been in operation for nearly 80 years in Tamil Nadu and a few other states. As candidates who qualify on merit are not included in the reservation quota, the actual number of backward caste candidates often goes as high as 97–98 per cent. In Indian law, upper caste persons are inferior citizens.

Interestingly, institutions run by minority communities enjoy special privileges. Even when they are entirely funded by the State, they are free to run their institutions anyway they desire. This freedom has been exploited by St Stephen's College, possibly the most prestigious Catholic institution in the country. It has now decided that 50 per cent of its faculty and 50 per cent of students must be Catholics. In one episode of the programme *Face the Nation* on CNN–IBN, the representative of the college vigorously argued why merit should be important for an educational institution, particularly when the Constitution does not mandate it. He asserted that welfare of the Catholic community is its main responsibility, not quality education.

Encouraged by the politicians, voices demanding rejection of considerations of merit, and according favours to select communities, have become strident. Even those institutions that prided themselves on their excellence have changed their tune. As the 93rd Constitution Amendment empowers the government to direct private institutions also, all institutions in the country, whether state-run or private, will have to fall in line with the government's reservation policy. Whatever hope people had that the Supreme Court would uphold the principle of equality of citizens has now been shattered as it has declared the amendment valid.

Scheduled Caste (SC) persons have a powerful legal power: any one who calls them by their caste name is liable to be sent to prison. For that reason, it is all but impossible to discipline them—at the slightest provocation, SC teachers can threaten to take their superiors to court.

Finally, there is a palpable atmosphere of fear. The 93rd Constitution Amendment was passed virtually unanimously by the Parliament with only two out of 542 members dissenting. It was fear and not conviction that made the MPs vote as they did. India has nearly 300 vice-chancellors, a similar number of top level heads of R&D institutions including a number of internationally reputed scholars and scientists who also hold important positions in the counsels of the government. They privately express concern at the dictatorial ways of the government. Not one of them has dared to express in public their concern on the consequences of the draconian orders on caste-based reservation. Virtual unanimity is based on dread of reprisal by the government. The fear is not physical, merely loss of administrative perks. Yet, the effect is the same. In the matter of intellectual freedom in Indian universities, the situation in India is not very different from what prevailed in the Soviet Union during the Stalin era.

Twenty-five years ago in my Convocation Report of IIT Madras, I said:

> Some members of the (Parliamentary) Committee have gone so far as to say that what we need is an Indian standard and not an international standard of education.
>
> Whether we need or need not be aware of the latest developments in technology, it is necessary to debate the fundamental question whether, just because a group of people cannot cope with a certain level of education, they should have the veto power to deny such an education to the rest; whether social justice should imply that there shall be no institution at all in the country where merit is the criterion and also while the socially deprived should have special privileges, the talented need have no right of their own.
>
> These are debatable issues about which much may be said on both sides. Unfortunately, a stand has been taken that these should not be debated in public—a typical instance of the conflict between the freedom of the intellectual and the authority of the commissar. A university needs to have three basic freedoms: the freedom to decide what to teach, whom to teach and who will teach. It is the corrosion of these freedoms that we are witnessing today.
>
> Unfortunately, a university...like a flower, is helpless; it can be easily destroyed and depends entirely on goodwill for its survival. Not so long ago, universities of Allahabad and Calcutta were the most prestigious in our country and honoured all over the world as the IITs are today. Looking at what has happened to them, we cannot but be concerned about our own future.

More than the attack on the IIT system, the manner in which it was done is a matter for concern. The directors of all the IITs were bullied, insulted and abused in unprintable language.

The situation today is not any different after 25 years.

Limited Finance

Apart from this social problem, Indian universities are very poor by world standards. Even the much-pampered IITs have an annual budget of about US$ 20 million (Rs 1 billion) each, about 4000 dollars (Rs 160,000) per student per year. Even after factoring in the much lower salaries in India, funds are a small fraction of what most world universities command. The endowments they possess are pitifully small and the government imposes onerous constraints on donors.

Since independence, faculty salaries have risen, in nominal terms, 40–50 times, and those of lower staff nearly a 100 times. Each time salaries were increased, the government economized by cutting down non-salary expenditure. As a result, in many colleges, salaries account for 95–98 per cent of the total budget leaving next to nothing for academic inputs such as library books or even routine maintenance. That is the reason why all government buildings are dilapidated, libraries are shorn of books and journals and laboratories are bereft of basic equipment and materials.

In this connection, it is important to note that, in the matter of books, journals and materials of consumption, India has to pay dollar prices. Often, Western firms provide substantial discounts to their universities as a promotional policy to familiarize future customers with their products. Such gestures are not available to Indian universities.

Costs of education are best valued in terms of per capita income. Table 6.5 makes a comparison between MIT, USA and a typical IIT in terms of per capita hourly income or *perchi*. As a matter of interest, IITs lag behind six times in R&D income, ten times in endowments but student fees and faculty salaries are 5–6 times higher.

In the West, it is common for industries to provide substantial research grants for in-depth studies on matters of practical interest. Such interaction makes teachers compete among themselves for grants, and forces them to take an interest in the practical problems of industry.

University–industry interaction is fruitful only when it relates to basic studies. In turn, only those industries that operate at the cutting edge of innovation encounter basic problems. Unfortunately, only few Indian industries operate at the cutting edge of technology. Once, a product becomes obsolete, they buy new machine know-how from

Table 6.5 University Financing: A Comparison

Item	*MIT, Cambridge, USA*	*IITs*
Salaries	5,000 perchis	30,000 perchis
R&D Income	60%	10%
Fees Income	13%	20%
Endowments	20%	2%
Fees Rate	600 perchis	3,000 perchis

Source: Compiled by the author from information collected from the web.

foreign manufacturers. For that reason, Indian industrialists expect Indian laboratories to provide machines for manufacture, not ideas for better manufacture. Also for the same reason, Indian universities are unable to interact with the world of work, and get blamed in the bargain for being 'ivory towers'.

Indian businessmen feel that they are too poor to support education and R&D. It is the other way around. They are poor because they do *not* support education and R&D. Likewise, Indian universities are as poor as they are because their R&D is of no use to commerce and industry.

In the US, there is a culture of transferring accumulated wealth to health services, educational and other similar institutions. Warren Buffet, often rated as the richest person in the world, has famously said: 'I want to leave enough for my children to feel that they can do anything and not so much they feel they need not do anything.' India does not yet have such a culture. Hence, it is doubtful whether Indian universities can earn much from endowments too.

With limited finances from R&D grants and from endowments, with student fee already very high in terms of purchasing power, Indian universities are critically dependent on government patronage. In turn, as political compulsions induce politicians to prefer quantity over quality, Indian universities face an uphill task in becoming world class.

At the same time, most new institutions, particularly in education, management and medicine are coming up in the private sector. Quite a few of them are outshining age-old government colleges. While that is reassuring, most such institutions are good only for undergraduate teaching. Even there they depend on the academic leadership provided by pacesetting institutions such as the IITs and the IIMs. Once these reputed institutions are burdened by faculty chosen on the basis of caste and not merit, their academic leadership is liable to fade away. Hence, the challenge before India's higher education is how to empower private colleges to graduate to cutting edge research that Indian industry can, and will, support.

World-class Research Universities for India

For lack of both human capital and financial capital, prospects of world-class universities emerging in India under the aegis of the government are dim.

The entire Parliament, with practically no exception, is committed to having 50 per cent faculty and students (over 95 per cent if the Tamil Nadu policy is adopted) reserved for backward castes. Past evidence suggests that, given an opportunity, backward caste youth will throw up as competent scholars as the forward castes. Unfortunately, as the Planning Commission has reported, government schools have mostly become defunct. Being poor, most backward caste students are not getting a reasonable foundation for studies later on. There are just not enough numbers to choose from.

When sub-standard students and teachers are given preference, Gresham's Law comes into operation with full force—really competent students and faculty avoid reservation-based institutions. Even those who hail from backward castes, and qualify on merit, often shy away as they do not want to be labelled backward. With denudation of talent all round, global quality is almost impossible.

The government is spreading its finances very thin. It made grand promises of increasing the higher education budget by ten times. With that promise, it forced the IITs to increase their enrolment and to mentor newer IITs. As of date, not one cent of the promised bonanza has been received. With inflation in double digits, government finances are under severe strain.

Suffering as they do from severe shortage of both human and financial capital, prospects of governments succeeding in developing and nurturing world-class universities are dim. Hence, there is no alternative but to induce private enterprise to take up the challenge. Admittedly, they are at present good only for undergraduate teaching. What is needed is a viable business plan to transform them into research universities.

Self-sustaining World Class Universities

Three approaches appear feasible for establishing world-class universities without State support.

IIT Delhi has received an offer of Rs 100 crores (about US$ 25 million) in return for setting up a branch on land owned by the donor. An even larger offer has been received by the Indian School of Business, Hyderabad. In both cases, real estate developers want to exploit the fact that the presence of global quality institutions multiplies land prices ten or even hundredfold. Instead of letting speculators enjoy that bonanza, the university itself may acquire land in its vicinity and use the resultant income to run its academic operations. Land for education has been a successful model in Land Grant universities in the US. The Indian Institute of Science too started with the income from properties donated by Jamshedji Tata.

Of late, industrial R&D is picking up in India. Mostly, multinational corporations are investing in R&D but Indian firms too have begun to show interest. For them, a world-class university is a form of backward integration. They may be willing to support such universities. However, universities need multiple disciplines to perform well. Hence, they will need the support of not one but a conglomeration of industries. Then, an S&T Park becomes a useful adjunct for a university. Such parks have proved successful in several parts of the world.

We can visualize an S&T Park sharing its research staff and research facilities with a neighbouring university and thereby subsidizing its costs. It is not impossible to visualize a model where the research scientists in the park are several times the number of teachers needed for the university. Then, a fraction of them offering part-time courses and research guidance can substantially reduce the cost of running the university and make it affordable even for poor students.

It is estimated that India spends between 5–10 billion dollars a year (enough to run a couple of hundred IITs) educating its youth abroad. Many of them go abroad because admissions have become very difficult in our prestigious institutions. If those students are good enough to be admitted to Harvard or Columbia, there is no reason why they should not be admitted to quality institutions here in India—and use their wealth to cross-subsidize brilliant but poor students.

By combining the above-mentioned sources of funding, it should be possible for a private visionary entrepreneur to establish and develop a world-class university with no help from the government, and therefore, be free from government restrictions and impositions.

The government may not permit such a university to grant degrees without insisting on debilitating controls. Fortunately, the Indian public is quite used to higher education without degrees. For over 50 years, the Indian Institute of Science did not confer degrees. The IIMs do not do so even now but they are hampered by the fact they received government grants. The Indian School of Business has so far kept itself from the impositions of the government by accepting no grants and by not offering degrees. Considering the political situation in India, any university which has ambitions to be world class has to accept both sacrifices.

There is a temptation to rely on private grants. Unfortunately, private funding too has its own drawbacks as Derek Bok, former President of Harvard University explains in the form of a colourful dream:[13]

> The first 'dream' began at a dinner in New York where I met the alumnus, an extravagantly successful investment banker. After listening to my troubles raising the money to meet Harvard's never-ending needs, he persuaded me to take the gigantic loan. ...The next and happiest 'dream' saw Harvard enter a wildly successful period. ... All too soon, however, my euphoria ended. From that night on, each successive 'dream' brought forth a more difficult, more controversial scheme to earn the money needed to meet the escalating payments required by the loan. ... Undaunted, I quickly changed course and offered interested companies exclusive rights to license the discoveries in our best life-science departments, a gambit that worked for a time but not well enough...he returned the following night with one final proposal to spare me the public disgrace of having to default on the loan. All I had to do, he said, was to agree to set aside the last one hundred places in every entering Harvard College class and auction them off to the highest bidders.

This imaginary dream describes in more minute detail than discussed here how commercialization can bring disaster to a university. David Brooks[14] describes the opposite scenario from his experience in China, albeit with a word of caution and tinge of scepticism.

> Imagine the Harvard Alumni Association with an army...This is a government of talents...The meritocratic corporocracy absorbs rival power bases. ... Once there were students lobbying for democracy, but now they are content with economic freedom and opportunity... The corporocracy doesn't stand still. Its members are quick to... embrace modernizing reforms...Most of all,...China is booming. Hundreds of millions rise out of poverty. There are malls in Shanghai richer than any American counterpart. ...You feel pride in what the corporocracy has achieved and now expect it to lead China's next stage of modernization—the transition from a manufacturing economy to a service economy. But in the back of your mind you

[13]Bok (2003), *Universities in the Market Place.*
[14]Brooks (2007).

> wonder: Perhaps it's simply impossible for a top–down memorization-based elite to organize a flexible, innovative information economy, no matter how brilliant its members are.

The moral is, though private funding is useful or even necessary, for their own good, universities should be cautious not to get into a trap. In particular, they should not get into debt; nor should they seek bargains from business houses or politicians. On worldly matters, when it comes to bargaining, universities are not as adept as businessmen and politicians are.

Creating a Talent Pool

Attracting talented students is the first charge on any university which has ambitions to sustain high quality. That is particularly true in India where school education is in poor shape. In this connection, UK's experience after it abolished Grammar Schools is illuminating. As late as the early 1960s, Britain had the Plus Eleven system by which at age 11, children were streamed academically: the good ones went to grammar schools and the rest to vocational ones. Streaming adversely affected children from poor families, who, it was felt, would not be able to compete with upper class students at the tender age of eleven; the separation of bright students into grammar schools was abandoned in the 1960s. According to the *Economist*:[15]

> The abolition of grammar schools is probably one reason why recent figures suggest that social mobility in Britain has slowed: Many of the best state-funded schools chose to go private as a result, so the gap between rich and poor people's education widened. ... Of the 100 schools that get the top A level grades now, only two are comprehensives: they rank 96th and 99th. Compared with children who grew up in the 1960s and 1970s, those who grew up in the 1980s had less chance of being more successful than their parents. ... The answer is not to tweak the system when people are 18, but to provide them with better education earlier on. The government needs to re-create something like the grammar schools, to let down for the next generation the ladder up which this generation of top people climbed.

Here is a lesson that India can learn, should learn. 'Catching them young and nurturing them well' is better than neglecting them

[15] *Economist* (2002).

when they are young and giving them the special privilege of reservation when it is too late.

For a private university, this issue poses a difficult, and hopefully, not an insolvable problem. It appears that it would be best for the university to recognize a selection of outstanding schools, which in addition to imparting quality education, also offer scholarships to brilliant but poor students. Once preference is given in university admissions to the students graduating from those schools, there will emerge a cascading effect: such schools will attract talented students and become the catchment from which the university can draw both outstanding students and wealthy ones.

Conclusion

In the prevailing political climate, with 50 per cent or more faculty and students to be compulsorily drawn from backward castes, it is all but impossible for any government or government-aided institution to attract high quality faculty or students. The government is also finding it impossible to honour the financial support that it had promised for the expansion of existing institutions. Hence, we may conclude, that in the foreseeable future, India cannot depend on the government or government-aided institutions to create or sustain global quality higher education. Sadly, it is not unlikely that existing quality institutions like the IITs will dwindle the way universities of Calcutta and Allahabad have done.

It is not wise either for a university to depend entirely on business support. A few altruistic donors may be of value but they are few. Under the circumstances, a quality university may organize its funding in three ways, as discussed earlier.

Universities may acquire land and earn rents from such land, set up commercially viable R&D laboratories or attract some of the moneys spent by Indian students on education abroad.

By combining all three of these resources, it may be possible for a high quality university to emerge which is completely independent of the State. If the university foregoes the right to offer degrees, it should be able to keep itself from the impositions of the government, the way the Indian School of Business is doing.

The deteriorating quality of government schools also remains a worry. The university would do well to concentrate on a few reputed schools for its student intake. If those schools have enough scholarships to let poor students to study there, the university can be assured of a reservoir of well-trained students to choose from.

The current year will be seen by historians as a watershed in the history of college education in India. On the one hand, it will be seen as a bold move for including backward caste students and teachers; on the other, it will be seen as the year when considerations of merit were given an unceremonious burial. Whether the country can sacrifice merit and yet remain globally competitive is a question that only the future can answer. As the entire academic community appears to be paralysed by the dread of reprisals by the government, there is no one to resist the dictates of the State.

For politicians intent on winning elections, economic growth and global competitiveness are not of paramount concern in a country where most people are poor. That is not so for Indian business, hemmed in as it is by increasing global competition. So far, it has complained but has felt no alarm at the increasing number of unemployable graduates that our colleges are turning out. It cannot hope that the system will correct itself because academics stand paralysed by fear of reprisals by the government. Hence, in its own self-interest, it will have to take steps own to establish world class research universities.

References

Altbach, Philip (2005), 'Higher Education in India', *The Hindu*, 12 April.

Bok, Derek (2003), *Universities in the Market Place: The Commercialisation of Higher Education*, Princeton University Press, pp. viii–ix, New Jersey.

Brooks, David (2007), 'The Dictatorship of Talent', Opinion, *The New York Times*, 4 December.

Denison, Edward F. (1985), *Trends in American Growth, 1929–1982*, Brookings Institution, p. 30.

Donald, Christiansen (1987), *Engineering Excellence: Cultural and Organisational Factors*, IEEE Press, New York.

Economist (2002), 'How Britain's Elite Has Changed', 5 December, London.

——— (2007), 'Investing in Ideas', 11 October, London.

Krugman, Paul (1994), 'Myth of Asian Miracle', *Foreign Affairs*, November–December.

Kuhn, Thomas S. (1970), *Structure of Scientific Revolutions*, University of Chicago Press.

Mancur, Olson Jr. (1996), 'Big Bills on the Sidewalk: Why Some Countries are Rich and Others are Poor', *The Journal of Economic Perspectives*, January.

Mokyr, Joel (1990), *The Lever of Riches: Technology, Creativity and Economic Progress*, Oxford University Press, New York, pp. 11–12.

Murthy, N. Narayana (2006), P.V. Narasimha Rao Memorial Lecture published in *The Hindu*, 4 January.

Tilak, Jandhyala B.G. (2004), *Quality of Higher Education*, NAAC Decennial Lectures, National Assessment and Accreditation Council, August.

TOI (2007), 'Britain as India's Colony', *Times of India*, 19 November, New Delhi.

TOI (2008), 'Ambassador Gets a Fresh Lease of Life', *Times of India*, 14 July, New Delhi.

7

Reservations and the Idea of Fairness
Quotas for OBCs in Higher Education

Gurpreet Mahajan

Over the past few years, the Indian economy has registered an annual growth rate of around 8 per cent.* This performance has attracted considerable attention, particularly since the more advanced economies are currently showing much lower growth rates, and the World Bank has declared India to be an 'Asian giant.' At a time when the market is buoyant and foreign investors are looking towards India, the Indian Government's decision (in 2006) to reserve 27 per cent of seats in institutions of higher learning for people from certain disadvantaged socio-economic groups called other backward classes (OBCs) met with considerable resistance from the students and alumni of these institutions as well as from industry and market watchers. Reservations or fixed quotas for weaker sections, the scheduled castes (SCs) and scheduled tribes (STs), have been in place for many years in higher education, and they have been criticized for promoting inefficiency, lowering standards, and sacrificing the 'well-being of institutions' (Béteille 1991, 2000). It is not surprising, therefore, that the recent extension of reservations to OBCs has been followed by a fresh articulation of old and by now familiar anxieties,

*An earlier version 'Higher Education Reservations and India's Economic Growth: An Examination' was published as CIGI Working Paper No. 36 in September 2008.

with the difference that this time they have been supplemented by the fear that such reservations will adversely affect India's economic growth.

Are these fears well grounded? Will reservations in higher education and the politics of identities curtail economic growth and limit India's emergence as a major economy? This paper attempts to assess these concerns, and begins by placing them in the context of existing debates about policies on reservations in India. Taking note of the apprehensions expressed by critics, the paper argues that the impact of the new policy is likely to be more complex than is suggested at present. While most detractors lament that merit will be sacrificed, the real danger is that it might vitiate the social environment that is required to nurture not just growth but also democracy.

As a society, India needs to make its institutions more reflective of diversity, but it is equally important to be mindful of the ways in which this agenda is pursued. Policies that are suitable for eliminating discrimination that stems from formal policies of exclusion and segregation have to be differentiated from those meant to minimize disadvantages that are the result of other social and economic processes. It is the failure to make this distinction (between discrimination and disadvantage) that is likely to have a long-term negative effect on India's ability to sustain growth.

The Issue in Context

Reservation Policies in Post-independence India

Reservation policies have a long history in India. In the late nineteenth century, the British prepared a list of 'depressed classes' or *shudras*, most of whom were victims of the practice of untouchability. For their betterment, the British set up scholarships, special schools and other programmes.[1] Subsequently, in 1925, with a view to assuaging the growing objections to the Brahmin domination of government and administration, the British introduced a form of reservation system. In Bombay (now Mumbai), seats were reserved for all groups except Brahmins, Prabhus, Marwaris, Parsis, Banias and Christians (Galanter 1984, p. 156). In 1927, the Communal Government Order in Madras Presidency reserved five of every twelve jobs for non-Brahmin Hindus,

[1]As early as 1858, the Government of Bombay Presidency, which included today's Maharashtra state, declared that 'all schools maintained at the sole cost of Government shall be open to all classes of its subjects without discrimination' (GoI, 1969, p. 4).

two each for Brahmins, Christians and Muslims, and one for 'others.'[2] In the Madras Council, 28 of 65 seats were reserved for non-Brahmins.[3] Following the British initiatives, a few princely states—most notably Baroda, Travancore and Kolhapur—also introduced similar provisions. In Kolhapur (now part of Maharashtra state), Shahu Maharaj reserved 50 per cent of the vacant seats in his administration for non-Brahmins. In time, the quantum and scope of reservations steadily increased, for example, in 1943 the British introduced reservations in services in addition to those in place for seats in legislative bodies (Jogdan 1991).

After independence, reservation policies continued, albeit in a form quite different from that of the colonial period. The Indian Constitution placed SCs (Scheduled Castes) and STs (Scheduled Tribes) in a separate category and reserved seats for them in legislative bodies, the reasoning being that these communities might remain excluded and segregated if special efforts were not made to include them. Although this was the only sphere in which certain percentage of seats were reserved for specific communities by the Constitution, nevertheless concern for marginalized communities led the framers of the Constitution to include an exception to the clause that guaranteed equality of opportunity in public employment. Instead of identifying any particular group, the exception referred to 'backward classes' (and not simply SCs or STs) and it permitted the State to reserve seats for classes that were not 'adequately represented in the services under the state'.[4] Till the 1990s,

[2]Demands for separate electorates were growing at this time. In fact, the All-India Depressed Classes Association had proposed separate electorates for each of what it termed the four major groups in India: Brahmins, Muslims, Depressed Classes, and Non-Brahmins. The Governments of Assam and Bombay supported similar concepts (see de Zwart 2000, p. 243).

[3]According to Jaffrelot (2003, p. 174), this allowed the Justice Party, which represented itself as the voice of the non-Brahmins, to win the 1920 regional elections. The government formed with the Justice party then introduced a 48 per cent quota for non-Brahmins in administration. See also Irschick (1969).

[4]Article 16 (4) of the Constitution stipulates that '[n]othing in this article shall prevent the state from making any provision for reservations, appointments or posts in favour of any *backward class of citizens* which in the opinion of the State is not adequately represented in the services under the state' (emphasis added). Just a year after the Constitution was formulated, the First Amendment added another exception—this time to Article 15, affirming the principle of non-discrimination on grounds of one's ascribed identity—allowing the state to make 'any special provision for the advancement of any *socially and educationally backward* class of citizens' (emphasis added).

subsequent governments at the Centre used this provision to reserve seats for SCs and STs in all Central Government posts and public institutions.[5] Similar arrangements, however, were not initiated for other backward castes (OBCs).

The first amendment to the Constitution, in 1951, vested an additional power upon the State. It allowed the State to initiate special policies for 'socially and educationally backward' class of citizens. Following this, individual states set up commissions to determine suitable criteria for identifying 'backward classes' in general and 'socially and educationally backward classes' in particular. As each state devised its own criteria for identifying eligible backward classes, policies for the backward classes differed across states. At times, even within a state, different commissions have applied different criteria to determine which groups should be granted reservations. As a consequence, the percentage of seats reserved for backward classes varies across political boundaries and even in the same state it has changed over time.

The Central Government also set up Backward Classes Commissions, but no seats were reserved for OBCs in All-India Civil Services and other public institutions until 1990. This changed when V.P. Singh became the Prime Minister and announced his decision to implement the recommendations of the Second National Backward Classes Commission (commonly referred to as the Mandal Commission)—a decision that was followed by protests and violent clashes between pro- and anti-Mandal groups. At this time, reservations for OBCs were introduced in Central Government posts but they were not extended to higher education. Singh subsequently resigned, but the sharp polarization of society yielded a new political arithmetic: as sections of identified OBCs came together in electoral politics, they formed a winning coalition that displaced the traditional political elite in many parts of North India (see Jaffrelot 2003, pp. 150–60).

A second change came in 1992, when the Supreme Court of India declared that 50 per cent of seats had to be left open and filled through open competition. Since 22.5 per cent of the seats were already reserved for SCs and STs, this meant that a maximum of 27 per cent could be reserved for OBCs, a cap that applied to both the Central Government and the states. In practice, this meant that almost

[5]While seats were initially reserved only at the entry level, subsequent amendments introduced in-service promotions also.

all the states had to revise their reservation policies significantly to meet the norms prescribed by the Court. The decision was important because, in many states, more than 50 per cent of the population had been identified as OBC, but now seats could not be reserved for them in proportion to their fraction of the total population. The Court, in effect, said that the right to equality must receive priority and that reservation policies could not entirely negate that right. Significantly, the Court also asked the Central Government to ensure that the 'creamy layer' (the elite) of the OBCs was excluded from the benefits of the reservations policy. In the past, the Court had ruled consistently against the use of *caste* as the *sole* basis of identifying beneficiaries of reservations; indeed, the Constitution speaks of backward *classes*, not *castes*. In its 1992 ruling, however, the Court accepted caste as the basis of identifying disadvantage but brought in considerations of class by eliminating the creamy layer from the benefits of reservations.

Almost a decade after this somewhat altered framework came into effect, the Indian Government announced, without any public debate, its decision to extend reservations for OBCs to all institutions of higher learning funded by the Central Government, including Indian Institutes of Technology (IITs), Indian Institutes of Management (IIMs) and medical colleges (but not minority institutions).[6] The government justified this policy change on the ground that it would ensure 'inclusive' growth by giving a fair share to the large majority of the population identified as belonging to the OBCs.[7]

Development and Inclusive Growth

The Indian Government has placed concern for inclusive growth in the foreground while continuing to pursue privatization, liberalization and globalization—policies that have been assessed in fairly contrary ways. If some analysts have associated these policies with economic growth, others have linked them to a growing disparity between the rich and the poor.

At the time of the general election in 2004, the Bharatiya Janata Party (BJP), the dominant partner in that coalition government,

[6]That is, institutions that are administered and run by a minority in the region, and that have claimed the status of a minority educational institution.

[7]It should noted that the list of OBCs includes not only Hindus but also some communities of Muslims and Christians, in sharp contrast to the case of SCs, since untouchability was a practice solely observed in Hinduism.

showcased economic growth, presenting a picture of 'India Shining'. In retrospect, it is evident that this slogan did not connect with the popular sentiment in much of India. The BJP and its allies secured just 185 seats, 113 less than in the previous election. The winner was the Congress Party, which spoke of 'globalization with a human face' and, with its allies, secured 217 seats, confounding the predictions of poll pundits and psephologists. The Congress Party accepted the larger framework of liberalization, privatization and globalization, but pledged to check the perceived effects of these policies, including unemployment and increasing inequalities in society. This language of political discourse was closer to the ordinary citizen's understanding of development, and it marked a shift from the rhetoric that had dominated the globalizing Indian economy. Previously, when the story of India's success and growing economy was told, the focus was primarily on the high rate of growth, measured most often in terms of gross domestic product (GDP). Although GDP is a useful measure in some respects, one that enables economists to predict the flow of money and other market trends, governments, particularly in decolonized democratic societies, are concerned with development rather than just growth.

It is often believed that high economic growth will yield perceptible development but it is becoming increasingly evident that growth, measured in terms of GDP, does not always translate into development that ensures better life conditions and opportunities for the large majority of the population. Indeed, scholars and multilateral agencies increasingly recognize the distinction between development and economic growth. As far back as 1975, the Dag Hammarskjold Foundation identified five pillars of development: basic needs (such as food, shelter, health and freedom), self-reliance, economic development (including the right of survival of people in different contexts), endogenous development and structural change to ensure that society corresponds to people's desire for equitable development (Trzyna 2000). This idea has since gained wide acceptance. Today, scholars and activists speak of human and ecological development, in addition to economic development. The United Nations, for example, invokes a Human Development Index (HDI) that combines GDP per head, life expectancy and educational attainment. By this measure, the United States had the highest GDP per person in 1998, but Canada ranked first on the HDI; likewise, the United Kingdom had a higher GDP per person than France, but the latter ranked higher on the HDI scale. In 2004, both Canada and Japan scored better on HDI than the United States, though their GDP per person was lower (World Bank 2006). These differences suggest that most citizens of democratic societies are concerned more with improvements in their life conditions than with statistics of economic growth.

To some extent, both the slogans 'inclusive growth' and 'globalization with a human face' register this difference between growth and development. While both speak of the need to rectify prevailing inequalities, the shift in phraseology has meant a subtle but important shift in emphasis. If 'globalization with a human face' identifies excluded and marginalized people, primarily along class lines, 'inclusive growth' pinpoints the beneficiaries and non-beneficiaries of growth in terms of their religion and caste. In the case of the former, it was farmers caught in a spiral of increasing debt, the poor and workers in areas that were being privatized who received primary attention. In the latter case, the community, rather than individuals, became the focal point, and the spotlight was turned on disadvantage *per se*, rather than disadvantage that might accrue from globalization and privatization.

Critical Voices

The idea that governments should help vulnerable groups and ensure that opportunities are available in equal measure to all sections of the population is an important and well-recognized principle of democratic life. Yet, the Indian Government's new policy of reservations faces resistance from even those who might agree with this principle of justice. There are at least three reasons for this: (i) a lingering discontent with the principle and practice of reservations; (ii) concern about identity politics; and (iii) specific problems related to reservations for OBCs and the extension of special consideration for these groups in the field of higher education.

First, although quotas have existed in some form or another in India for more than a century, one school of liberal scholars opposes them on the grounds that they mark an unacceptable deviation from the principle of equal and identical treatment for all. Even while they accept the need for some remedial measures to undo structures of past discrimination, such critics see reservations as a form of reverse discrimination that places unacceptable restrictions on the rights of individuals, setting aside merit, lowering standards and promoting inefficiency. This criticism is closely tied to the peculiar form that reservations take in India. Here, candidates from eligible communities who score well in entrance examinations (relative to candidates from non-reserved categories) are seen as part of the general category of students, and their presence is not counted towards filling the prescribed quota seats. Instead, reserved seats are filled by students who would otherwise not qualify in open competition. This has led critics to charge that reservations sacrifice merit and produce graduates with lower skills and weaker qualifications, a result that increasing the quantum of reserved seats only exacerbates. Moreover, the government intervenes to ensure that the quota of reserved seats is filled and that social prejudices alone do not hinder the entry of previously excluded populations, leading critics to maintain that reservations pose a threat to the autonomy of institutions and their ability to work efficiently.

A second concern is that reservations promote the politics of identity. Since caste was the basis on which some communities were segregated and discriminated against, caste identity was used to determine the beneficiaries of reservations and affirmative action programmes. It was assumed that reservations would provide social and economic mobility that would weaken caste-based distinctions, but this has not happened. Rather, critics maintain, the desire to be included in the list of beneficiaries and the equally compelling need to hold on to these benefits has reaffirmed caste identities (Bhambhri 1997, 2005). At the same time, political parties, in their quest for votes, have extended the promise of reservations to particular communities, further strengthening caste consciousness. The result has been, on the one hand, a steady fragmentation of Indian society and, on the other, the making of a context in which religious majoritarianism emerged and flourished as an alternative to caste-based politics. As caste configurations and alliances were region-specific, the Bhatiya Janata Party tried to retrieve the nation (the collective) by appealing to a pan-India identity in the form of a shared Hindu religious identity. The ensuing religious and cultural majoritarianism provided a new framework of political discourse where majority–minority distinctions became paramount, overriding caste-based distinctions.

Third, while there is still a reasonable degree of consensus around the need for reservations for SCs and STs, it is primarily the extension of reservations to OBCs in Central Government positions in the early 1990s that attracted strong opposition. Some of the resistance arose because the government's decision came without any prior discussion or attempt to bring different groups and parties together on this important issue. At a more substantive level, however, critics point out that the category of OBCs includes communities that might be low in ritual status and hierarchy but score well on other indicators, such as economic wealth and political power—aspects that make a crucial difference to the capacity of individuals from those communities to access opportunities (Chaudhury 2006, 2007; Gupta 2007a, 2007b; Radhakrishnan 1990, 2006). Hence, special treatment for such groups cannot be justified.

When, in 2006, the government announced its decision to extend reservations for OBCs to higher education, these criticisms became even sharper and were accompanied by the belief that the policy would adversely effect the country's economic growth. Once again, the decision was made without any discussion with other parties or the concerned institutions, reaffirming the view of critics that reservations have become a tool in identity politics. Indeed, the tendency to use group identity as a way of measuring and rectifying marginalization and the propensity to regard religious, linguistic and caste groups as homogeneous entities with a shared fate have reinforced this perception. While almost all political parties have pursued identity politics since at least the 1990s, this time, government policy is being subjected to severe criticism as it is seen as impeding the growth of the Indian economy.

The New Reservations Policy and Its Implications

The new legislation extending reservations for OBCs to higher education is not simply a continuation of past practices. It has two specific and different features of which we need to take note, as they are likely to have long-term implications for India's democracy. First, the enabling legislation exempts three kinds of institutions: minority educational institutions (including those receiving financial support from the government); Central Educational Institutions established in the tribal areas; and institutions of excellence, research institutions, and institutions of national and strategic importance specified in the legislation. Second, the law that the Parliament approved did not eliminate the 'creamy layer' from the benefits of reservations.[8]

While discussing the implications of reservations for OBCs in centrally funded educational institutions, it is important to recall that this initiative was preceded by a Constitutional Amendment that authorized reservations in private professional educational institutions even if they do not receive any financial assistance from the State. The Central Government has also been examining the possibility of introducing quotas in jobs in the private sector for identified minorities such as SCs and STs. In discussions with the business community, the government has said that it would not impose quotas on them, but might intervene if the private sector does not take appropriate steps voluntarily. The government is also considering special measures, including reservations and other forms of affirmative action, for other marginalized groups such as Muslims. Thus, there is a growing perception that the quantum and scope of reservations is likely to increase in the future.

It is against this setting that the current intense debate about reservations in higher education for OBCs has emerged. Along with other lingering objections to reservations for OBCs, this time the critics have questioned the policy on the grounds that it will affect the economic growth rate negatively. Their opposition rests upon two somewhat related arguments. They begin with the understanding that the knowledge industry—in particular, the information technology (IT) sector—is in large measure responsible for the current spurt in growth. This sector has registered enormous growth and is able to compete in the global market because it is driven by merit. What is assumed here is that India's human capital—its large pool of trained engineers and professionals—gives it a decisive advantage in the globalizing economy. Consequently, critics fear that the introduction of reservations in higher education and professional courses will shrink the pool of meritorious candidates and erode India's competitive edge, particularly in IT-enabled services (Ramachandran 2006). The second argument focuses on the increase in the quantum of reserved seats, which, its exponents suggest, will reduce the number of seats available to meritorious candidates. If

[8]This might change now, as the Supreme Court has recently ruled that seats may be reserved for OBCs in higher education but the 'creamy layer' must be excluded from this benefit.

these deserving students do not get seats, they are likely, in the globalizing world, to go to other countries.

Thus, the lowering of standards and dilution of human capital, coupled with a 'brain drain', will cause India's comparative edge in human capital-intensive activities to disappear. Employers are bound to turn increasingly to other countries that are rich in human capital. They are also likely to recruit 'fewer graduates from Indian institutions...[and] curtail their investments, at least in human capital-intensive production, in India' (Guha 2006).

Issues of Human Capital and Merit

Are the anxieties of the critics well founded? Will additional reservations for OBCs in 'elite' educational institutions erode India's edge in the IT industry and impede economic growth? These questions are exceedingly difficult to answer on the basis of available data. However, what is clear and unambiguous is that reservations are now being provided in institutions where admission is highly competitive; to give just one example, in 2006, approximately 300,000 students competed for 4078 seats in IITs. Entry into these institutions is highly sought after, because they have established a formidable reputation and their graduates obtain high-salary placements in well-known international and national companies. Moreover, although the number of Indian institutions catering to higher education and professional degrees has been steadily increasing, the number providing high-quality education is still very small.

In this scenario, those who are opposed to the extension of reservations for OBCs to higher education conclude that increasing the quantum of reservations in high-quality institutions will necessarily mean a decline in the number of available efficient, well-qualified personnel, and this will adversely affect India's economic growth prospects. This deduction is drawn from the fact that reservations will bring in candidates with lower entry marks. Students from communities that are now being given the benefit of reservations qualify for admission even under the present system, that is, without reservations. So it is not community identity that is the issue here. Rather, the concern is whether the presence of a sizeable group of students with lower entry marks will result in a lowering of efficiency and standards and, thereby, in the quality of trained professionals available in the country.

This is no doubt an important concern. And it might be significant if candidates who enter with a lower entry mark also graduate with a lower mark or, as some critics suggest, are unable to complete the degree programme successfully. Yet IITs, IIMs and medical colleges do not relax marks or give concessions at the exit point; all candidates, irrespective of the manner in which they gain admission, are required to have a minimum degree of competence when they graduate. So the situation created by increasing the number of reserved seats would raise serious concerns only if a sizeable percentage of admitted students fail to meet the minimum standards required to receive degrees.

It must be said, however, that this is a matter of conjecture. We cannot conclusively determine the effect of reservations since we do not have the caste profiles of the candidates who apply for admission to particular institutions of higher learning. We also do not know the caste profiles of those who are successful in obtaining admission to these institutions or of those who fail to gain entry by just a small margin. So it is exceedingly difficult to hazard a guess about the kind of students who will get in through the proposed quotas. We also do not know by how much the marks will have to be lowered at the entry level to fill the proposed quotas, and in many ways, this is crucial to assessing the effect of reservations.

Hence, it is exceedingly difficult to know with certainty what kinds of problems the new policy might eventually give rise to. The current experience of reservations is based on an assessment of candidates who come in with significantly lower grades but who are expected to make up the difference during the course of the degree programme. However, it is entirely possible that reservations for OBCs could yield a somewhat different outcome from what is currently anticipated. In South Indian states such as Tamil Nadu and Karnataka, reservations for OBCs have been in place for some time now, and a sizeable number of OBCs—particularly those categorized as backward castes (BCs), as distinct from most backward castes (MBCs)—qualify for admission under the general category. In other words, they manage to secure grades that are comparable to those of students who obtain entry through open competition. In Tamil Nadu, for instance, BCs secure almost 75 per cent of the seats in the open list, and the difference between the cut-off mark for the general category and that for the BCs is often as little as 1 to 2 per cent.[9] (This is, of

[9]For details of admission data, see *http://www.hindu.com/2005/07/20/stories/2005072011970100.htm*

course, not the case with MBCs and SCs.) It is entirely possible that many of the BCs who are competing through open competition in other states for professional and technical education will now come to the IITs, which might lower the cut-off mark but only by a small percentage; hence, even if the best are not admitted, these institutions will still obtain well-qualified students with merit.

The paradox, however, is that if the difference in the performance of those who enter through open competition and those who do so through reservations is only marginal, the reservations policy would appear to provide preferential treatment to some and would likely create a sharp polarization between those who receive reservations and those who do not. To put it in another way, additional reservations might not give rise to the problems that are currently anticipated, but instead might throw up a range of issues that could divide society and, in the process, vitiate the environment necessary to promote investment and economic growth. It is difficult to ascertain if standards will decline or if the availability of trained professionals will decrease, but the end result of a divided society might be the same.

For its part, the government has assured those who are concerned about a decline in the quality of human capital that the number of seats currently available for general category students will not be reduced; instead, it proposes to increase the total number of available seats in each institution to accommodate the quota that will be set aside for OBCs. The number of qualified personnel needed to teach might not be available to keep pace with the rising demand, but there is no reason to assume that students of merit would be pushed away to foreign lands due to reservations.

The debate on reservations for OBCs in higher education has centred on what might happen in professional courses such as engineering and medical sciences, which are perceived to be India's major comparative advantage. It should be noted, however, that the United States and China produce more engineering graduates each year than India does. So, it is not the availability of skilled professionals alone that gives India the decisive edge. This is not to say that human capital is not significant in the success of India's economy but, rather, that the reservations policy is likely to affect the social and economic life in ways that have not been sufficiently considered so far.

Attention has so far been focused on the fate of institutions that turn out engineers and doctors but the extension of reservations for

OBCs to higher education is likely to affect the teaching of the natural and social sciences far more severely. At present, the IITs, IIMs and medical colleges attract the most talented students, from all communities and castes. By comparison, the natural and social sciences face enormous difficulties in getting well-qualified and talented candidates, and this applies as much to candidates coming from the general category as it does to those coming with reservations. That is, since the pool of talented students is extremely small, filling the increased number of seats, along with the prescribed quota seats, is likely to pose a real challenge and could force institutions to lower entry marks significantly in these disciplines. The Indian educational system is facing a crisis, most acutely evident in the natural and social sciences, which the reservations policy will deepen even further. There are a number of ways in which the fate of the core disciplines, rather than applied sciences, can adversely affect the quality of social and political life, but even if we consider the story of economic growth, it is evident that the contribution of these courses and universities is crucial. India's growth has been nurtured not simply by innovations in engineering or IT, but also by the business process outsourcing sector and a range of other services. In these areas, it is not just the trained engineers but also graduates from social sciences and other disciplines who provide the necessary manpower. The issue is not that there are no people of merit in communities that will receive reservations—talent exists in all communities—but that the Indian school system fails to offer quality education to students. As a result, there is a remarkably small pool of well-trained candidates, and this is visible more sharply in some areas of learning than in others. This lacuna cannot be addressed merely by adding to the pool of reserved seats at the level of higher education. Besides, in the absence of a more egalitarian structure at the lower levels of education, reservations at the higher level tend to reproduce differences and inequalities. This is fairly well known and quite widely acknowledged, yet the government has paid little attention to this dimension, yielding the prevailing concerns about human capital and merit—concerns that have existed for some time now but have been accentuated by the proposal to increase the number of seats and reserve quotas for OBCs.

Building Institutional Capacities

The success of any policy depends crucially upon the manner in which it is implemented. The Indian Government asked all institutions of higher education to implement reservations for OBCs and to increase the number of seats available, beginning with the 2007–08 academic year.[10] Effectively, this meant that institutions were expected to prepare for the increase in seats—including infrastructure such as larger classrooms and more laboratories—in just a few months. This request, however, posed insurmountable difficulties, and almost everyone associated with the working of public institutions knew that the infrastructure could not be put in place in so short a time. Added to this was the need to hire fresh faculty to meet the increase in student intake; another task that was virtually impossible to accomplish in the given time. It is well known that most engineering colleges, including prestigious institutions such as IITs, find it difficult to retain even their existing faculty members, who are lured by the market with high pay packages, let alone attract substantial numbers of new ones. In any case, only a few graduates of these colleges go in for postgraduate studies and research and fewer still enter the academic profession. Moreover, these challenges confront not just engineering and medical colleges but all disciplines, including the natural and social sciences.

Until now, the government has responded by simply extending the retirement age of teachers, but that policy is not sufficient to meet the needs of these institutions. Not only will the increased number of students require a corresponding increase in the number of faculty members, but lower entry marks for students who fill the quota of reserved seats will mean that teachers will have to give more time and assistance to such students to enable them to perform well and eventually excel in their jobs. The quality of graduates depends critically on such provisions and planning, yet these matters have received little or no attention from policy makers thus far. This has renewed concerns about the capacity of these institutions to impart quality education and generated scepticism about the government's intentions in introducing a fresh set of quotas and reservations.

[10]This was deferred as the legality of the law introducing reservations for OBCs in higher education was challenged before the Supreme Court. While waiting for the Court's decision, most institutions did not prepare for the proposed increase in seats. In March 2008, the Court ruled in favour of an increase in quotas; this meant that the increase had to come into effect in the academic year 2008–09. Although some time had lapsed since the law was passed by Parliament, in effect the same difficulties confronted the institutions of higher education.

Another key issue is that of institutional autonomy. Policies might be framed by the government, but institutions still need to determine, given their needs, history and available resources, the best ways to pursue these policy goals. An element of autonomy is thus a critical variable not just for institutional well-being and democratic life but also for ensuring efficiency and quality of outcome.

Institutions have had some degree of freedom to devise ways of fulfilling the reservations that already exist for SCs and STs. Some institutions give concessions at the entry level alone and not at the time of exit; others reduce the entrance mark by a certain percentage—usually 10 to 15 per cent—a few lower the entry mark further but the admitted candidates take a one-year preparatory course to enable them to compete with the others. Some centrally funded institutions, such as the Jawaharlal Nehru University, already had a system in which OBCs received special consideration in the admissions process through a process of added weighting. Although no seats were separately reserved for OBCs, they received certain additional points, which were added to their examination marks; additional positive weighting was also given to women from these communities and to candidates who come from identified 'backward districts'. However, the government's decision to introduce quotas for OBCs meant that the university must set aside its prevailing system, which evolved against the background of its own history and experience, and had the merit of recognizing the difference between discrimination and disadvantage, addressing the concerns of the marginalized without overlooking the parallel concern of maintaining standards.

Thus, institutions have had some degree of flexibility in implementing reservations policy in the past, but it remains to be seen whether the new dispensation on reservations will erode this practice. Indeed, as things stand, institutions will not have the option of devising new frameworks to ensure that they have a more diverse group of students. In the United States, for example, where universities typically try to ensure that the student community is diverse, a great deal of attention is paid to the preparedness of the chosen applicants to meet the requirements of academic work. In India, however, where the system does not have space for such individual assessments, concerns about the maintenance of excellence have been met by innovating within the framework of prescribed reservations. The fear now is that the new reservations regimen could eliminate this flexibility and impose a rigid, standardized format on institutions of higher learning, reducing their capacity to offer quality education and to nurture India's human capital.

In brief, the challenges presented by the reservations policy for OBCs are many and far more complex in nature than has been anticipated. In the ongoing debate, only questions of human capital, merit and standards are being raised. Far more serious and imminent are concerns about institutional well-being. Will institutions be able to innovate and determine suitable ways of increasing opportunities for the disadvantaged? Will they have the autonomy and the space to set their schedules to meet the new demands presented by the increase in seats? Will the necessary changes be introduced in the schooling system to minimize differences at the higher level? If these questions are ignored or answered in the negative, then the proposed policy of reservations is bound to accentuate the existing crisis in the education system and further reduce the capacity of institutions to deliver quality education. This will undoubtedly affect India's ability to sustain economic growth and ensure development for all.

What is perhaps equally important, though relatively unattended, is that the new reservation policy is likely to have serious implications for the nature and functioning of India's democracy. The law extending reservations for OBCs in all centrally funded higher education institutions exempts minority educational institutions, including those that are funded by the government. India has a large number of religious and linguistic minority educational institutions, many of which offer degrees in professional courses such as medicine, engineering and business administration. Since the government institutions have not kept pace with the growing demand for such programmes of study, minority educational institutions have steadily increased. This trend is likely to be compounded if the quantum of reservations continues to increase in higher education. Already in Kerala more than half the medical and engineering colleges funded by the State are run by minorities, and in the neighbouring states of Karnataka and Tamil Nadu the situation is quite similar. Although many of these educational institutions operate as profit-making institutions and are open to people from different communities a certain percentage of seats is reserved for community members. As the competition for limited seats in IITs and IIMs becomes more intense, the middle class is likely to seek these coveted community quotas and seats in community-run institutions.

In every society the middle class plays a critical role in shaping the nature of democratic politics. If a significant portion of this class begins to rely on community resources and assiduously cultivates community networks to fulfil its material and development needs then community identities are likely to take on a more resilient and intense form—something that is only likely to deepen the divisions in society, and this cannot be encouraging either for India's democracy or for its economic growth.

Reservations and the Issue of Fairness

The idea that the opportunities and benefits of growth should not be monopolized by any one group but should reach all sections of the national community is an important and well-recognized principle of democratic life. Indeed, it constitutes a central norm of a just and fair society. For this principle to translate into fair and reasonable policies, however, it is equally important to identify *who* is being denied opportunities and *why* they are being excluded. Is the denial on the grounds of social prejudice and discrimination or is it the end result of other disadvantages? Corrective measures and policies have to be determined keeping these specifics in mind.

More importantly, we need to distinguish between systemic discrimination that is reinforced by formal rules and other circumstances that create disadvantages for certain groups. When formal rules discriminate against, and exclude, some groups, then strong interventionist policies, such as reserving seats, can be justified more readily since it is members of the society as a whole who are responsible for imposing such rules. But when groups find themselves disadvantaged for other reasons—such as the backwardness of the region from which they come, the occupations of their parents, low income, social networks, technological changes, market shifts and so on—members of the larger society are not similarly implicated. While it is in the collective interest to ensure that all available talent can develop and contribute to the well-being of society, it is difficult to hold other individuals responsible for the current predicament of these groups. For instance, several of India's agrarian communities have historically not valued professional jobs, and individuals from those groups have not pursued higher education or government careers. But this is not a predicament for which the rules of society or its individual members can be held responsible; in such cases, it is difficult to justify strong interventions of the sort that are considered necessary or appropriate for communities that have been discriminated against and excluded by the rules of the State and society.

We need to, therefore, devise a different set of policy measures to assist communities that face disadvantages on account of a range of circumstances. Moreover, if these policies are to meet the criterion of fairness, such communities cannot be bracketed with those that have been consciously discriminated against, such as the SCs and the STs. When differences between communities that are discriminated against, as distinct from those that face disadvantages of various kinds, are ignored or when community membership, rather than the availability of socially valued assets, becomes the basis of special treatment, reservations and other forms of strong affirmative action lose their justification and special treatment appears to be a privilege that undermines the need for fairness.

The government's reservation policy for OBCs in higher education, however, is inattentive to concerns about fairness. It fails to distinguish between groups that are actively discriminated against and those that are disadvantaged due to certain social processes and choices. Instead, the new policy looks only at end-result differentials and ignores the reasons for their existence. In addition, it operates under the assumption that reservations are the only viable way to remedy all forms of disadvantage. Instead of considering other ways in which disadvantages might be minimized, e.g better schooling and housing, it simply fixes quotas for different groups. It also ignores the fact that some communities of OBCs possess some socially valued assets, such as economic and political power, and that they cannot all be treated alike.

Moreover, since the reservations policy does not engage the issue of fairness, it risks being perceived as an instrument of the politics of identity, on which there can only be sharp polarization rather than a negotiated consensus. Will this polarization yield more social confrontation and conflict? It is difficult to predict the outcome, but one thing is clear: a sharp polarization has already occurred within Indian society and between politicians and sections of the society. This does not portend well for democratic politics.

In the long run, it is not simply the availability of India's skilled human resources but the capacity of the democratic system to negotiate and maintain harmony among groups that is likely to determine the country's future growth and stability. Increased polarization and social tension or conflict is likely to harm India's chances of becoming the 'dream destination' for capital.

Divergent Differences

Will the disadvantages of the reservations policy for OBCs in higher education be offset by the gains? Perhaps the policy's strongest defence is that it will make the institutions more diverse and representative of the wider society.

Diversity is certainly an important value and has much to commend it. Its presence suggests the absence of group monopoly and a narrow base of hegemonic power. In the economic sphere, it is said to be a positive resource that enables economic efficiency. Some scholars maintain that diversity offers competitive advantage and enhances performance (see Quigley 1998; Recascino and Tschirhart 2000). While these conclusions are contested by others, who point to the problems of communication and interpersonal relationships that diversity in the workplace brings (see, for example, Smelser and Alexander 1999), many entrepreneurs today acknowledge that diversity yields several positive results, and businesses flourish in cities that have a great degree of diversity. These claims, however, are made mostly with regard to ethnic and cultural diversity. The assumption is that different cultures nurture different skills and competences, and that having access to people from different cultures brings corresponding benefits, including easier ways of reaching out to diverse consumer populations.

Although diversity has been invoked in recent times in support of reservations for different groups, its application has certain limitations. In India, when one refers to the category of OBCs, one is not speaking of groups that have a distinct cultural identity or way of life—such groups share the language and culture of their region or religious community. The social, cultural and political institutions by which they are governed are, therefore, not distinct, and there is no conflict between their way of life and that of the larger society. Hence, in their case, the issue is not one of protecting or representing diversity. One could say that different castes have some cultural distinctiveness, but the category of OBCs consists of many different castes, each with its own ritual practices, histories and stories of origin. In any case, reservations are not expected to ensure that the distinct ways of life of these groups survive or are represented in the public arena. Rather, the rationale of the policy is to ensure that OBCs have access to jobs and opportunities in which they do not have adequate presence. Hence, the diversity defence sits uneasily with the policy of reservations for OBCs.

In the case of OBCs, then, the more relevant argument is that of under-representation rather than diversity. The two often tend to be conflated on the assumption that we are concerned about the inadequate presence of one community because we value diversity. Since the entry of OBCs into different walks of life is not expected to enhance cultural diversity, their under-representation is a stand-alone concern. It can be argued that it is desirable for all communities to have professionals such as doctors, engineers, lawyers and teachers, to act as positive role models and to serve the interests of their community. In some cases, particularly when we are dealing with extremely marginalized communities within the OBCs, this might well be an important consideration. But it does not justify extending reservations to the economically better-off among the OBCs—they might indeed want to have a presence in new areas of production, but other regional and linguistic communities might express the same desire, and there is no reason that caste communities should be privileged and considered the relevant unit of analysis. In other words, if the system is to attend to the desires and wants of people or groups, then the claims of other kinds of non-caste-based communities are equally compelling.

An even more serious problem is that the argument of under-representation invokes the notion of proportionality. It suggests that groups should be present in proportion to their size in the total population. The difficulty is that in a country like India, where diversities of various kinds exist, what should be the basis of identifying groups—religion, caste, language or gender? Is there any reason to privilege caste over the other forms of identity? Moreover, should identities be fixed and individuals be placed unambiguously in one community or another? This is not to deny that the absence of a group is a matter of concern and we need to be attentive to the possibility of informal processes of exclusion that might prevent a group from entering into certain spheres of public and social life. But the idea that communities are under-represented so long as they are not present in proportion to their size in the population remains deeply problematic. Groups that are constructed for certain policy purposes cannot be taken as realistic entities that are natural and pre-existing. Nor can one ignore group histories and cultural orientations to ensure that each is, or must be, present in proportion to their numerical strength. Indeed, if we were to ensure proportionate presence in different spheres it is likely to undermine the commitment to diversity that the votaries of the under-representation argument often profess.

There are thus limitations to both the diversity defence and the under-representation argument when applied to the OBCs. Neither provides a satisfactory rationale for the new policy, and it is this that compels one to think beyond the expressed concerns of merit and to consider both the reasons for the current polarization and ways of going beyond the existing impasse.

Complex Equality

Over the past few decades, the demand for higher education in India, particularly for professional degrees, has been growing steadily. This demand has been propelled further by the opening up of the Indian economy and the growth in IT-enabled services. The Indian Government, however, has invested very little in this sector for a long time; it has set up very few professional colleges and institutions, and most of the demand is currently being filled by private institutions of varying quality. Hence, there is intense competition for entry into the few institutions that have been able to maintain high standards and guarantee employment to their graduates. This reality has made the demand for reservations more pressing and the opposition to them equally stiff.

It is now well-recognized that the denial of opportunities can exacerbate social tensions. A system that operates in a way such as to exclude some groups leads to the alienation of these groups. At the same time, a system that appears to favour some groups and add to the burdens of others can also create social divisions. Such conflict is neither beneficial for the effective functioning of democracy nor for sustaining the stability and peace that is necessary for economic growth. The political system, in other words, can neither be blind to the existing set of disadvantages nor pursue policies that seem to be unfair. This is the challenge that any democratic polity faces, and India is no exception.

Clearly, utilitarian arguments in support of reservations for the disadvantaged are insufficient and unhelpful, for they cut both ways. It could be said that the good of the society (or of the maximum number of people) lies in ensuring that all its members are given the opportunity to contribute their skills and talents. It is, therefore both necessary and desirable to extend the opportunities and overcome disadvantages that prevent some people from contributing to the larger pool of talent. It might also be argued that policies that polarize society and widen existing schisms are likely to create social conflict, and this cannot be in the interest of the society at large.

In the absence of utilitarian arguments, one has to rely on equality and a fairness-based defence of affirmative action. To put it in another way, it is the pursuit of equality that should be the guiding norm of affirmative action programmes. Policies involving special treatment should be designed so as to meet the requirements of fairness and concerns about equality. Such policies, instead of invoking the principle of general good or compensation, must be driven by the desire to treat all persons as 'equal'.

It is not easy, however, to determine, let alone spell out in detail, what it means to treat everyone as equal. Besides, as Walzer (1983) reminds us, equality is context specific: treating someone as an equal might not mean, or entail, the same thing in all circumstances. In each situation, therefore, one needs to ask what it means to be an 'equal', instead of simply extending existing policies to new spheres of social life. This is the vantage point from which one should approach and design strategies for minimizing existing disadvantages. The current problem is that existing policies are being extended and supported even though the issue of equal treatment is not being raised. In fact, the rhetoric of diversity and under-representation has erased even the need to ask this question.

We need to reconfigure the terms of the debate to make the question of fairness the optical lens through which we determine the appropriate policies for rectifying disadvantages. This is necessary because the same end results might be produced for different reasons, and we need to focus on those reasons while devising policies. To meet the conditions of fairness, in other words, we need to distinguish between various kinds of differences and sources of disadvantage: differences that arise from past choices and those that are the result of past social and legal practices; differences that are the end product of changes in economy and technology and those that are the product of environmental changes; differences with which people are born and differences that emerge due to their occupations; and so on. Each of these might yield existing differences in end results, but they do not justify the same treatment. Differences and disadvantages that accrue from certain situations are less acceptable than others and call for stronger measures. For instance, if one is disadvantaged through no fault of one's own then stronger corrective measures are warranted and justified. However, in the interest of fairness, relatively weaker measures (those that place a lesser burden on the individual or that call for a lower order of special treatment) might be supported to rectify other kinds of disadvantages.

To sum up, disadvantages among groups and individuals need to be minimized, but not all forms of prevailing disadvantages justify the same solution or policy prescription. The problem posed by the Indian Government's decision to extend reservations and quotas in higher education to OBCs is that it ignores this dimension and focuses only on existing differences of end results. This shortcoming is further accentuated by the government's decision to reserve seats in higher education without creating opportunities for disadvantaged groups at an early level, so that talents can be nurtured from a younger age and differences arising from background conditions minimized over the years. The merit of the capability approach is that, while it emphasizes the need to make basic social goods (such as primary schooling, health care) available to everyone, it also underlines the value of creating an environment in which individuals can develop their talents and capabilities and act as free agents. If we are to shift away from the politics of identity and patronage, then this is surely a better way of minimizing disadvantages and nurturing the democratic ethos.

References

Béteille, André (1991), 'Distributive Justice and Institutional Well-Being', *Economic and Political Weekly*, Vol. 26, Nos 11–12, pp. 591–600.

______ (2000), 'Universities as Institutions', in *Antinomies of Society: Essays on Ideologies and Institutions*, Oxford University Press, Delhi.

Bhambhri, C.P. (1997), 'Folly of Reservations', *Hindustan Times*, New Delhi, 23 May.

______ (2005), 'Reservations and Casteism', *Economic and Political Weekly*, Vol. 40, No. 9, pp. 806–7.

Chaudhury, Pradipta (2006), 'Doesn't Help to Typecast', *Indian Express*, New Delhi, 29 May.

______ (2007), 'Other Brahmanical Castes', *Indian Express*, 17 April.

de Zwart, Frank (2000), 'The Logic of Affirmative Action: Caste, Class and Quotas in India', *Acta Sociologica*, Vol. 43, No. 3, pp. 235–49.

Galanter, Marc (1984), *Competing Equalities: Law and the Backward Classes in India*, Oxford University Press, Delhi.

Guha, Ashok (2006), 'Beyond Sound and Fury: Reservations will Reverse the Growth Surge of India's Economy', *The Telegraph*, Calcutta, 23 May.

Gupta, Dipankar (2007a), 'Target Practice', *Hindustan Times*, 29 March.

______ (2007b), 'Towards Affirmative Action', in Ira Panday (ed.), *India 60*, Harper Collins, New Delhi.

GoI (1969), *Economic and Educational Development of the Scheduled Castes, Report*, Department of Social Welfare, Committee on Untouchability, Government of India Press, Delhi.

Irschick, E.F. (1969), *Political and Social Conflict in South India*, Oxford University Press, Delhi.

Jaffrelot, Christophe (2003), *India's Silent Revolution*, Permanent Black, Delhi.

Jogdan, Prahlad G. (1991), *Dalit Movement in Maharashtra*, Kanak Publications, New Delhi.

Quigley, John M. (1998), 'Urban Diversity and Economic Growth', *Journal of Economic Perspectives*, Vol. 12, No. 2, pp. 127–38.

Radhakrishnan, P. (1990), 'Two Steps Backward', *Frontline*, Vol. 7, No. 18, pp. 19–24.

______ (2006), 'Affirmative Action through Usurpation: OBC Reservations and the Tamil Nadu Model', *South Asian Journal*, Vol. 13, July–September.

Ramachandran, R. (2004), 'Warning Bells', *Frontline*, Vol. 21, No. 6.

Ramachandran, Sudha (2006), 'The Die is Caste for Corporate India', *Asia Times Online*, 29 April; available at *http://www.atimes.com/atimes/South_Asia/HD29Df04.html*

Recascino, Lois and Mary Tschirhart (2000), 'Examining Empirical Evidence on Diversity Effects: How Useful Is Diversity Research for Public-Sector Managers?', *Public Administration Review*, Vol. 60, No. 5, pp. 386–94.

Smelser, Neil J. and C.A. Alexander (eds) (1999), *Diversity and Its Discontents:*

Cultural Conflict and Common Ground in Contemporary American Society, Princeton University Press, Princeton, NJ.

Trzyna, Tes (2000), 'Convening Thinkers and Doers: Sweden's Dag Hammerskjöld Foundation', CIPA Publication 102, California Institute of Public Affairs, Sacramento, CA; available at *www.interenvironment.org/cipa/dhf.htm*, accessed 20 July 2007.

Walzer, Michael (1983), *Spheres of Justice: A Defense of Pluralism and Justice*, Basic Books, New York.

World Bank (2006), *World Development Indicators 2006*, World Bank, Washington, DC.

PART

III

Sustainability, Energy and Environment

8

Energy and High Growth in India
Sustainability Issues

YOGINDER K. ALAGH

The Issues

This chapter examines the sustainability of India's high growth from the angle of the energy sector both as an opportunity and a constraint. The relationship between energy and economic growth has, within a range, been a great constant in economic history; and the energy sector is an important infrastructure sector with growth linkages. The chapter begins with an analysis of India's growth strategies and projections and then presents the energy sector as a part of these scenarios. This is done from the demand and supply angles. India's fuel endowments are described, as are the augmentation possibilities, through interregional trade of energy and fuel imports.

The emerging policy issues are examined in the light of India's historical experience with the growth of the energy sector and its relationship with the economic growth process in the past. This analysis sets the backdrop for discussing policy initiatives and issues for the future. The refreshing experience in promoting energy efficiency is outlined and its relevance for the future is looked at. The role of renewables in meeting India's energy demand is discussed. Furthermore, generation from nuclear plants should be encouraged because it is relatively cost efficient when the entire supply chain is costed. India's not too successful experience with price reform, technological leapfrogging and operationalizing institutional designs is described and lessons are drawn for the future.

Energy and Economic Growth in India

A discussion of India's energy futures is handicapped because the Eleventh Plan, recently released by the Indian Planning Commission, is the first Plan in independent India's history which does not have a perspective chapter (Government of India, 2008). Some sections of the Eleventh Plan have a few 'Futures' figures, particularly for water and to an extent, energy, but the studies on which they are based are mutually inconsistent and are not a part of a growth projection or strategy. Our discussion is, therefore, based on independent studies and earlier Planning Commission reports.

Given the uncertainties regarding future policies, the projection scenarios we discuss are in terms of alternatives. The discussion is in the form of models, one set based on the Business As Usual (BAU) scenario and another on the Efficiency (EFF) scenario. This discussion is based on a number of studies conducted in the recent past on the future of the energy sector in India. The author along with Kirit Parikh produced an India 2020 model for the Rio Plus 10 Conference at Johannesburg which modelled energy and water constraints (UNU 2003; Alagh 2006). The Planning Commission had produced a Vision 2020 model, including energy in the analysis (Government of India, 2003), which is no longer used for operational purposes. The French Institute in India also produced a framework for strategic policy choices in the Indian energy sector with models up to 2020 and 2050 (see Audinet, Shukla and Grare 2000; also see Alagh 2000a). Kirit Parikh, as a member of the Indian Planning Commission, updated to 2003 the earlier United Nations University (UNU) work on energy (Government of India, 2006c).

Apart from differences originating due to the choice of structure—BAU or EFF—all these models use energy elasticities with respect to economic growth and end use methods to project demand. The EFF models set alternatives in terms of demand management, energy efficiency, improved distribution systems, use of renewables and technological choices. Despite the different growth profiles projected by these models, all of them, except the Planning Commission 2003 model (Government of India, 2003) (amended by the more recent

2006 work), highlight the central issue of the short supply of domestic fuel for power in India, particularly in light of the serious environment sustainability considerations. Apart from hydel options and renewables like photovoltaics and wind power in which India is already highly developed, a proper analysis of future choices needs to examine alternatives involving dramatic choices like thorium-based fast breeder reactors (FBRs), coal gasification, coal bed methane, ocean bed gas hydrates and interregional gas transportation.

The Economy

Unlike the earlier Brazil, Russia, India and China (BRIC) futures models where the supply logic of growth was not modelled (Wilson and Purushothaman 2003), all the Indian energy models use an economy level model for nesting the projections.

It is now globally accepted that India has been growing fast over the last two and a half decades and that, in fact, the 1980s were a period of equally good if not better performance. This change in the mindset of economists working outside India is belated; Indian economists have been writing for over a decade that India was growing fast and that its reform started in the 1980s (Alagh 1991). 'There are therefore two characteristics of growth in recent years. It is higher. It is more stable. The characterization of the economy as a gamble in the monsoons needs (to) change.' (Alagh 1996).

Panagariya (2005) is the most readable on Hindu vs reform-led growth. He has set at rest the *ad hoc* policy characterization of the 1980s (Desai 2004; Rodrik and Subramanian 2004) by asserting that 'in contrast to the isolated ad hoc policy measures taken to release immediate pressures prior to the 1980s, [the 1980s] taken as a whole, constituted significant change and an activist programme. For example, by 1990, approximately 20 per cent of the tariff lines and 30 per cent of imports had come under OGL. ... import licensing on many other products was eased up'. Therefore, the projection of a continued fast growth rate in this study is grounded in historical experience.

The earlier energy models postulated a 6 to 8 per cent annual growth rate over the first two decades in this century. Recent forecasts are now postulating an 8 to 9 per cent growth rate through 2031–32 although there are no long-run projections in the Eleventh Plan. To put the existing literature on growth prospects in a somewhat stylized manner:

India will grow annually between 6 to 8 per cent (possibly 9 per cent) and will become the third largest economy of the world during this period. The investment rate and productivity growth lead this growth. For example, around a third of India's GDP growth in 1997–2003 was technology driven in that it was accounted for by increases in total factor productivity (TFP). Trade will also matter—exports will become around 4 per cent of world exports. The drivers will be:

(a) Investment;
(b) Technology and Productivity: Knowledge; and
(c) Trade and Competition.

Productivity growth analysis: To sustain a high rate of growth of the economy of the order of 8 to 9 per cent, the optimistic so-called Scenario C, TFP has to grow by 5 per cent or more in the Alagh/Parikh UNU model (Table 8.1). Trade and competition will provide the environment for this TFP improvement. In the early years of this decade, it was projected that investment rates of 28 per cent annual would be needed to sustain the high growth; but, more recently, this threshold has been raised to 36 per cent; presumably since productivity growth assumptions have been lowered.

Table 8.1: Growth of Output, Factors of Production and TFP in India, 1970–2020

	Past Estimates			
Period	*GDP*	*Capital*	*Labour*	*TFP*
1970–80	2.60	3.59	1.98	0.49
1980–90	5.67	4.41	1.13	4.21
1990–2000	5.73	5.97	1.82	3.68
	Future Projections			
2000–10	7.54	4.79	2.69	4,62
2010–20	9.24	4.04	3.49	5.69

Source: Y.K.Alagh, UNU, 2000 based on one of the more careful TFP studies done in India; Mukherji, Chattopadhyay and Neogi (2001).

The target for the annual growth rate over the next five years has been raised to an upper bound of 9 per cent with an emphasis on higher savings and investment rather than on productivity increases. This has evoked some negative comments. The Planning Commission has been diplomatic in its response, saying that savings,

Table 8.2: Alternative Scenarios for the Eleventh Plan

Target GDP Growth Rate in 11th Plan	*7 per cent*	*8 per cent*	*9 per cent*	*9 per cent now*
Average investment rate	29.1	32.0	35.1	36.7
Average CAD as per cent of GDP	2.0	2.4	2.8	1.9
Domestic Savings Rate	27.1	29.6	32.3	34.8

Source: Government of India (2006a), p. 10. In the Eleventh Plan now the third alternative is preferred with minor changes in numbers (column 9 per cent now above); see Government of India (2008), Vol. 1, pp. 26–31.
Note: CAD is the deficit in the current account of the balance of payments.

investment and factor productivity must go up but it has spelt out only the savings and investment parameters. This is perhaps the reason it wants the savings rate to be higher than the projections of earlier models. The Planning Commission is probably more realistic, in a sense (see Table 8.2). With the framework of Indian policy and the cultural mindset, it is easier to postulate more frugality than more efficiency. In any case, the savings rate of 28 per cent postulated earlier has already been achieved and the implicit understanding of the Commission that the growth potential has only marginally improved and that the real task lies ahead is correct.

This discussion is of some relevance since most of the positive aspects of the growth in the last decade and a half have come from efficiency and not forcing investments. In fact, there are people who are sceptical about the growth projections. For example,

'An idea of the task ahead might be gauged from the following explicit calculations of Y.K. Alagh "...a one per cent increase in real inputs led to a 3.8 per cent increase in output in the 80s and a slightly lower increase in the 90s. This has now to go up to 5 per cent so that the dream of 8 per cent growth is achieved" (*The Financial Express*, 3 July 2006)' (Nachane 2006, p. 3141). Nachane, one of India's more serious macro-economists, sums up the prospects in the following words: 'The growth forecast for 2007–12 in the draft approach paper to the Eleventh Plan is based on unrealistic levels of private investment and productivity growth' (Nachane 2006, p. 3141).

These, however, are the growth and supply–demand projections in which energy forecasts are nested.

The Energy Projections

We now discuss the projections in the main studies regarding the energy sector. The United Nations had undertaken a major study on sustainable development as part of its millennium series (Van Ginkel and Thakur 2001).[1] Because large countries matter in this context, their impact and possibilities of strategic choices were discussed extensively.[2]

Some of the preliminary findings of the Indian study in this volume have been reported by Parikh et al. (2000) and Alagh (2000c). The main results are shown in Table 8.3.

Table 8.3: India: Projections for the Year 2020

Population	1330 million
Urban Population	Low: 465 million; High: 590 million
Slum Population	Low: 85 million; High: 130 million
Solid Waste Disposal	100 to 110 million tonnes
Demand For Coal For	Low: 817 million tonnes; High: 2016 million tonnes
Power Generation	Low:2200 billion kWh; High 3000 billion kWh
Cropping Intensity	More than 1.5
Net Area Sown	Constant at 141 million hectares since the 1990s
Irrigation Intensity	Around 1.75
Water Shortage	Around 10 per cent to 25 per cent between the years 2020–50
Noise Levels	Twice the norms in trend forecast
Air Pollution	Two to two and a half times the norms in trend forecast

Sources: Alagh (2000b, 2000c).

The UN country case studies on large countries brought out the severity of constraints that these countries face and the need to immediately try and move towards 'favourable' paths. The situation in China and India was used to illustrate the nature of the problem. Growth in these large countries underlined the quantum jumps

[1]This was part of the studies on 'A Sustainable Development Framework' initiated by the UNU in consultation with the Office of Strategic Management of the Secretary General of the United Nations.

[2]For a large country perspective in Van Ginkel and Thakur 2001, see chapter by Y.K. Alagh, pp. 73–84. Also see, *Towards A New Strategic Framework for Large Developing Countries: China, India and Indonesia,* UNU Press, Tokyo, 2002.

needed to tackle the severe emerging problems. The studies on India stressed that if bad coal of over a billion tonnes was not to be burnt for the power needs of around 3000 billion kWh, alternative energy management styles would have to be implemented and hydel and nuclear options considered, in addition to a major focus on renewables. The serious environmental implications of burning poor quality coal were apparent—underlining the critical energy situation in the country. The striking magnitudes brought into sharp focus the global and national hazards of following an unbridled consumerist path even as the studies emphasized the long-haul for improving living standards.

The need for a focused policy becomes clear because indigenous coal is the cheapest fuel option when market prices for alternative fuels are considered across different locations in India (see Table 8.4).

Table 8.4: Costs of Electricity Generation in Alternative Locations

(*in Rs/KWh*)

Fuel Type/ Location	*Delhi*	*Gandhar*	*Vizag*	*Cuddalore*	*IB Valley*
1	*2*	*3*	*4*	*5*	*6*
Domestic Coal	1.99	2.09	1.77	2.13	1.58
Imported Coal	2.48	2.16	2.15	2.16	2.26
Domestic Gas	1.82	1.90	1.75	–	–
Imported Gas	2.14	2.08	2.14	2.14	–
Imported LNG	2.47	2.21	2.21	2.21	–
Domestic Naphtha	2.44	2.66	2.61	2.60	2.66
Imported Naphtha	2.46	2.19	2.19	2.23	2.29
Domestic FO	2.47	2.48	2.41	2.49	2.55
Imported HSFO	2.45	2.17	2.17	2.21	2.27

Note: These figures were roughly with respect to 1994 fuel cost levels. With a naphtha price of Rs 7650/tonne, the levelized tariff works out to Rs 2.6/KWh; FO: fuel oil and HSFO: high sulphur fuel oil.
Source: Alagh (1997a).

However, it has to be recognized that indigenous coal reserves are available only in selected parts of the country and the availability of such coal all over the country for power generation is restricted due to financial constraints in mine development. Also, the above costs do not consider the social costs of transportation and the environment costs of mining and transportation.

A modelling experiment further illustrated the fact that lifestyle and development policy options outside the sector were important for the nature of development of the sector. South Asia is emerging as an energy hot spot in most global models; the two-way relationship between transport and energy is at the heart of the problem in India. In a BAU scenario, coal demand rises to 2 billion tonnes and puts considerable pressure on the transport system as power plants are often located away from the coal mines, and coal for power generation is already a significant part of bulk freight. Import of oil and gas and pithead versus demand-oriented locations of power stations determine the actual transport need. However, in an EFF scenario, Indian coal demand is significantly lower at 0.8 billion tonnes. Demand management, energy efficiency, optimal location of energy generation facilities and transport policies, lead to this rosier outcome. Indian power grade coal is plentiful, but of poor quality so that the environmental consequences of depending on it may be dire. Trade and globalization would help the economy to grapple with these questions. Regional arrangements could well be a part of the answer. In fact, good Indian modelling work shows that fuel development and international trade are possible options in an efficient pursuit of energy options.

The UNU built on earlier work by the late J.P. Maggo, who collaborated in the India 2020 study, which was close to the French–Swiss models. These studies brought out the stark dependence on

Table 8.5: French–Swiss Energy Models

S.No.	*Fuel Source*	*1996*	*2020*		*2050*	
		Actual	*BAU*	*EFF*	*BAU*	*EFF*
Percentage share of:						
1.	Coal	30	38	35	33	32
2.	Oil & Natural Gas	24	50	50	62	61
3.	Renewables	46	12	16	5	7
	[In (3) fuel wood falls and solar, wind, hydel and nuclear increases]					
Per cent growth over 1996 of:						
	Primary Energy		327	263	853	683

Notes: BAU is business as usual; EFF is energy efficiency.
Source: Schwank, von Stokar and North (2000), p. 135. Also in the same volume, 'Foreword' by Yoginder K. Alagh.

imported fuels, around two-thirds of the total by 2020 (see Schwank, Stokar and North 2000; also in the same volume, 'Foreword' by Alagh). Energy demand in 2020 is two and a half times higher in the EFF case and three and a quarter times in the BAU scenario (Table 8.5). Renewables such as photovoltaics and wind power are pushed to the maximum in the EFF scenario, but the overall share of renewable energy falls since forest-based non-commercial energy for households is substituted by nuclear, solar and hydel power. Two-thirds of a much larger energy base being fed by imported fuel is unsustainable from the trade viewpoint. The importance of hydel and nuclear power was obvious and was being neglected in the policy discussion then.

The Planning Commission has been extensively involved in analysing the prospects for the energy sector. The Report of the Committee on India Vision 2020 (23 January 2003, under the Chairmanship of Dr S.P. Gupta) stated that it was 'neither a prediction', 'nor simply a wish list', but 'what we believe it is possible for our nation to achieve...provided we make the requisite effort' (Government of India 2003, p. 1). A reference scenario of upper middle income (UMI) countries was created and India would meet this as a target, rather than the earlier tradition of a national projection model. In addition, the Commission had a sectoral vision of major sectors and sub-models on energy, water, agriculture and communications and transport.[3] The earlier tradition of detailed calibration of the sub-models with the Plan Model was not undertaken as it was necessary in a long-term vision statement. However, critics felt that some efforts towards maintaining consistencies in alternative approaches to genuinely long-haul issues like land, water, income growth and population could have been rewarding. This was particularly so if the Vision was to be a guide to action.

In this first study, the Planning Commission used very genteel energy forecasts. They were criticized as the 'energy importers' paradise'. Hydel shares fell in a big way by 2020 and the nuclear share, which was higher than the 1997 base level that they took, didn't rise much from the assumed base. This was both in the BAU scenario and the beyond coal scenario (BCS). Coal demand was kept at half a million tonnes, only through massive imports of oil and gas. In

[3]The tradition of sub-models for agriculture, energy, employment and demography was there in the Planning Commission models earlier (see Alagh 1987).

this it resembled the French Institute's analysis. As an afterthought to these projections, they added an even larger output from renewable sources; but earlier studies had shown that there was a limit to a strategy based on renewable sources, and even the 5 per cent renewables provision in the BCS would be difficult to achieve although it was worth aiming for.

The Planning Commission's 2003 study (Government of India 2003) has been revised to take into account the developments that have occurred till the middle of this decade.[4] The discussions about the policy options now only reinforce the earlier discussion. Table 8.6 brings out the revised framework.

The terminal year now 2031–32 is later than in the earlier projections. But the consumption level is the same as in the earlier projections despite the last year being later because consumption

Table 8.6: Alternative Energy Scenarios for 2031–32 as Visualized by the Planning Commission Expert Group in 2006

(*MtOE*)

S. No.	*Fuel Requirements*	*Scenario Coal Dominant BAU*	*Scenario EFF Nuclear, Hydel, Gas, Renewables Demand-side Management Coal/Transport/ Rail Transport*
1.	Crude Oil	486	350
2.	Natural Gas	104	150
3.	Coal	1022	632
4.	Hydro	13	35
5.	Nuclear	76	98
6.	Renewables	2	87
7.	Non-commercial	185	185
	Total	1887	1536

Note: The author has defined these scenarios as BAU and EFF; the original report does not use these terms.
Source: Government of India (2006a), p. 44.

[4]This study was directed by Kirit Parikh who also co-directed the UNU study, reported above.

grew very slowly between the initial year in the original projection and the later initial year in the later projection. Notice that the coal demand in the coal based scenario (the Expert Committee does not call it a BAU, we suspect since the Coal Ministry is a part of the exercise) ranges from a high of 1022 million tonnes of oil equivalent (MtOE) to 632 MtOE. This oil equivalent translates to over 2 billion tonnes of coal in the BAU and around 1.3 billion tonnes in the EFF. Around a quarter could be imported. Natural gas imports are higher in the EFF than in the BAU because of environmental considerations.

The EFF scenarios emphasize the maximum exploitation of renewables, which would be photovoltaics, human and vegetable waste recycling and biofuels here, since by that time the wind power potential would have been used up. However, there would still be considerable scope for demand side management. Nuclear energy, which in the Indian case would be working largely towards thorium-based nuclear power in FBRs, and hydel power alternatives would need to be exploited.

Thorium-based Nuclear Power and Sustainable Use of Coal

India's energy future depends immensely on thorium-based nuclear power as nuclear energy is the only way to reduce dependence on imported coal and natural gas; the only means of completing the nuclear energy cycle with domestic fuel and not importing nuclear fuel is through the development of thorium-based plants. India's energy requirements, we have argued, would go up around two and a half times by 2020 and even more later.[5] In the most optimistic sustainable energy variant, energy based on renewable fuels like wind power, photovoltaics and biomass can meet around five per cent of the estimated demand. India is already a super wind power and new sites are getting more difficult to find. Energy based on the sun has more scope. Both mini hydel, which minimizes environmental impact, and large scale hydel projects have potential, but they go only so far. Environmental impact limits the exploitation of hydel power. Bad projects with large environmental costs have to be stopped anyway. However, activists stop even the good projects. Some

[5]The numbers in the more recent Planning Commission projections are slightly different, but not so much as to affect the argument.

credit can also be taken for technological change and energy efficiency. But a situation where a younger, richer and growth charged population depends on fossil supplies for meeting its energy requirements presents a rather horrifying picture. India has plenty of power grade coal, but it is a nightmare from the environmental perspective. India's lungs will give up and of course the world won't let it do this. China is doing it, but India would be doing it incrementally to the current situation and will be stopped.

A way out is better technology for burning coal. India did have experimental technology for Integrated Gasification Combined Cycle (IGCC) Technology, based on fluidized bed boilers. But, as always, it is not sufficient to just have the technology. Ways of developing the management practices to bring it on board and integrating it within the existing systemic structures are also important. Since implementing this technology was an important priority for the Government of India it was suggested that the technology be made available experimentally in India. Furthermore, the development costs of the first boiler could be met through FDI and the implementation could be taken up by the S&T establishment (see Alagh 1996). A number of investments based on foreign investment were identified. However, no suitable arrangements could be worked out at that time so none of the investments came on stream. Given the importance of this matter, two groups were set up in February 1998 to pursue the IGCC.[6] They were:

(a) An Inter-Ministerial Steering Group (IMSG) for the commercialization of IGCC under the Chairmanship of the Secretary, Power, Government of India; and
(b) A Project Advisory Group (PAG) under the Chairmanship of the Chairman, Central Electricity Authority (CEA).

We recently checked on the progress of these for this paper. The IMSG never met, but the PAG unknown to the establishment went on working. It had representatives from the power para-statals, Bharat Heavy Electricals Limited (BHEL), National Thermal Power Corporation (NTPC), and the S&T Ministry, The Council of Scientific and Industrial Research and the Ministry of Forests and Environment. It submitted a report in 1999 stating that a 100 MW

[6]At that time, the author was remitting charge as Minister.

plant would cost around Rs 6000 million, but funds were not available for it. India's overarching S&T agreement with the US negotiated in the late 1990s by the present author had a High Technology sub-group where energy co-operation was on the radar and was intended to work on such projects (Indo-US S&T Forum 2002). An Indo-US agreement for co-operation in advanced power generation technologies was signed in September 2000 and a Protocol was signed between United States Agency for International Development, the US Department of Energy, Ministry of Power of India and the NTPC, which provided that the techno-economic feasibility study of the IGCC would be done, as also its implementation. This was not done. More recently it has been reported that the Technology Information and Forecasting Group of the Science and Technology Ministry (TIFACS) is working on the implementation of this project. But TIFACS is unlike the Technology Development Group which was set up to productionize Indian technology and since it is an information group outcomes are still uncertain.

Implementation of the IGCC is important but it only postpones the day of reckoning by getting more energy from coal. Ultimately, the limit of permissible coal based energy is set. Thorium-based nuclear power is, therefore, the only demonstrable method that India has of completing the fuel cycle. An experimental fast breeder on the thorium route, called Kamini, is already operating at Rameshwaram. But upgrading it to 500 MW will be costly. Placid Rodriguez, the man who developed the experimental plant, in a public lecture, placed the cost of the first-of-a-kind (FOAK) Prototype Fast Breeder Reactor PFBR in the context of learning-by-doing. He stated that the cost of an FBR becomes relevant as we travel up the learning curve through the production of a number of reactors. He (Rodriguez 2003) gave the example which the author had told him of the cost of the steam generator for the Pressurised Heavy Water Reactor PHWR manufactured by BHEL (where the cost was substantially brought down over a period of time). While BHEL took 1679 days to manufacture the first PHWR steam generator, the manufacturing time of the eighth steam generator came down to 258 days. This productivity improvement generated a controversy between BHEL and NPCIL, and was the basis for the cost reduction award. Rodriguez stressed on this aspect of cost reduction; this was discussed in his 1996 Brahm Prakash Memorial

Lecture. He said that if the capital cost of an FOAK PFBR is 100, building a replica will bring down the cost to 71.7. The cost comes down with series construction to 64 for a reactor with two plants on one site and 59.2 per reactor with four plants on one site and somewhat stabilizes at 57.7 per reactor for 12 plants on three sites. It is this stabilized cost of FBR that is relevant (and not the cost of the FOAK PFBR), when its cost is compared with other mature, stabilized technologies.

The economics of nuclear power in India depends on the cost of electricity generated by the nuclear power plant vis-à-vis the cost of electricity generated from a coal-fired thermal power plant. Coal deposits in India are concentrated in the eastern region in India. The setting up of a coal fired power plant in the west or the north west entails transporting coal over distances exceeding 1000 km. Thus the economics of nuclear power becomes favourable. There is a feeling in certain quarters that nuclear power is more capital intensive and requires a larger fraction of imported components. This does not seem to be true.

If one considers the total investment in a power plant, and all the associated facilities such as fuel cycle facilities including coal mine development and investment needed to transport coal, the difference between the two options may not be significant at all. Further, the method for comparison such as single station cost and system cost also influences the discussion of the relative costs of coal vs nuclear power plant. The comparison between coal and nuclear options on the basis of station cost method may give misleading results. The single station method fails to take an analytical account of system interactions. This could result in the plant being pushed lower down the operational merit order as it ages and as new and more advanced plants with lower marginal operating costs join the system.

In many regions in India, after the initial upfront costs are met, nuclear power would be a viable option economically and could be a part of business like co-operation options (Table 8.7 gives data estimates).

Past Experience

The growth of capacity and generation of electricity in the period of the reform process since 1991 was dismal. Thermal capacity which

Table 8.7: Long-run Marginal Cost of Supply per Unit of Energy at Consumer Point

(1999–2000 prices)

Base Load	*(Unit: Rs/kWh)*									
	Coal LC	*Coal PH*	*Imported Coal*	*Lignite*	*Nuclear 500 MWe*	*Gas LC*	*CC WH*	*Fuel oil OC*	*HYDRO Min.*	*HYDRO Max.*
NORTH	0.988	0.978	–	0.938	1.099	0.937	0.993 (0.927)	1.217	0.843	1.500
WEST	0.892	0.942	1.051	0.940	1.045	0.860	0.860	1.171 (0.927)	0.867	1.566
SOUTH	0.928	0.928	1.069	0.964	1.066	1.002	0.911	1.189 (0.898)	0.892	1.458
EAST	0.840	0.933	1.067	–	–	0.924	1.159	1.187 (0.895)	1.053	1.480
NORTH EAST	1.302	–	–	–	–	0.876	1.039	1.289 (0.988)	1.030	1.730

Notes: Cost of import of base load power from North East;
Gas CC = 0.962, Hydro Min. = 1.078, Hydro Max. = 1.473;
CC is Combined Cycle, OC is Open Cycle; LC is Load Centre;
Figures in brackets correspond to 1987–88 prices of petroleum products.
Source: Alagh (1997).

Table 8.8: Growth of Capacity and Generation of Electricity

(per cent growth in decade)

Period	*Generation Capacity*				*Electricity Generation*			
	Hydro+wd	*Thermal*	*Nuclear*	*Total*	*Hydro+wd*	*Thermal*	*Nuclear*	*Total*
	1	*2*	*3*	*4*	*5 6*	*7*	*8*	*9*
1980–81 to 1990/91	59.32	160.23	61.67	118.15	26.90	204.24	103.33	118.79
1990–91 to 2000/01	33.51	60.70	93.3	58.71	3.9	118.32	177.05	88.99
2000–01 to 2005/06	28.69	20.36	17.2	22.34	34.09	23.99	2.36	24.77

Source: GOI (2006b), p. S 26.
Note: wd is wind

grew by 160.23 per cent in the decade 1980–91 only went up by 60.70 per cent in the decade of reform (see Table 8.8). In other words, with a substantial increase in the growth rate of the economy, thermal capacity growth was only 38 per cent of the decade before privatization. Since thermal capacity was a large part of the total, the growth of total generation capacity in the 1990s was around half that of the previous decade. The situation in the first half of this decade was even worse.

How did India energize its growth with this dismal performance in electricity sector capacity growth. There were three factors at play which redeemed the failure. First, generating units were run better, not only in the Central public sector, but also in the states. The plant load factor in the electricity sector improved and generation grew faster than capacity. Second, 'efficiency-led economy level growth' was accompanied by substantial gains in energy efficiency in the power consuming sectors. For the manufacturing sector, this emerged partly as a matter of strategy since the second half of the 1980s of the last century and partly from the X-efficiency factor. Third, there was a substantial increase in the capacity in the non-utilities captive power sector as the grid failed to supply power. Growth of generation faster than that of capacity is shown in Figure 8.1

As Table 8.8 shows capacity growth which was around 120 per cent in the decade of the 1980s (top right hand side of Figure 8.1) went down to around 60 per cent in the decade of the 1990s and was only around 20 per cent during the period 2000–06. Generation

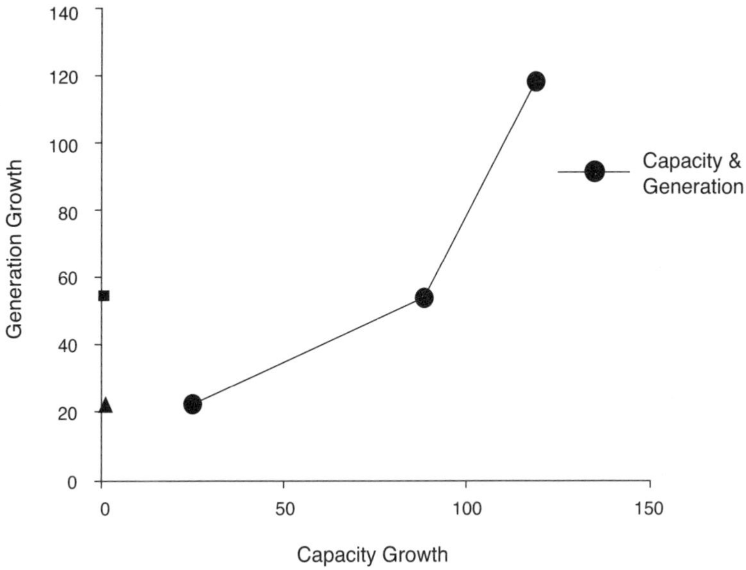

Figure 8.1: Capacity and Generation

Source: Table 8.8.

growth was also around 120 per cent in the 1980s and so capacity use was roughly constant (far right point in Figure 8.1). However, in the 1990s, at around 90 per cent it was much higher than the expansion of capacity at 60 per cent, showing a substantial increase in plant load factors (mid-point in Figure 8.1). But, in this decade the slack seems to have been used up and both capacity and generation growth are similar—at around 20 per cent (far left point in Figure 8.1). The plant load factor on an average is around 75 per cent for an average hydel year and this is high since planned shutdown for repair is also necessary. Generation growth is now low at less than 5 per cent annually as compared to around 9 per cent in the last decade and a near crisis situation is emerging.

Energy Efficiency

In the reform period and in fact, beginning with the mid-1980s the energy efficiency of Indian industry has gone up in a big way. The industrial reform of the Indian economy, as Panagariya (2005) brings out, started in the 1980s. As major industries were brought out of the quantitative control of output, import, prices and investment, tariffs, domestic taxes, dual prices (for the controlled and open market segments) were all used to give signals for technological change through scale economies and higher capacity use. There was clearly a huge energy saving potential in a single product continuous process industry, where technology mattered and start up costs of unplanned shutdowns were high. This actually happened in the great energy guzzlers such as cement, paper, steel, aluminium, petrochemicals and fertilizer. The first strategy of the Eighth Plan paper presented to Rajiv Gandhi in 1989 said that reform would mean higher factor productivity and lower capital cost per rupee of output. Energy use for cement would, on the basis of investments underway by the private sector, go down from 1.3 giga cal. per tonne to 1.0, for aluminium from 19,000 kWh/tonne to 17000, steel from 700 kWh to 415/tonne and so on (Alagh 1991, p. 215). The Bureau of Energy Efficiency (BEE) showed that this actually happened and more recent analysis shows that this decline in energy use has continued. For the decade 1995–2005 calculations show that specific energy consumption has gone down by 3.5 per cent annually in steel, 7.5 per cent in cement and1.8 per cent in aluminium. This has also happened in many other areas like public transportation, lighting and so on. In terms of kgoe/$2000 of GDP in purchasing power

Table 8.9: Global Comparisons

	Selected Energy Indicators for 2003	
Country	*TPES Per Capita (Kgoe)*	*TPES/GDP (Kgoe/$-2000 PPP)*
China	1090	0.23
Brazil	1094	0.15
Denmark	3852	0.13
India	439	0.16
UK	3906	0.14
US	7835	0.22
Japan	4052	0.15
World	1688	0.21
India 2031–32	1065–1279	–

Source: Key Energy Indicators—2005, IEA.

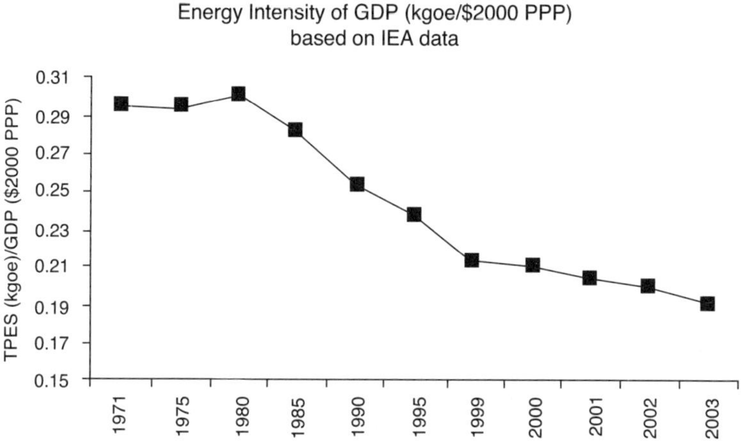

Figure 8.2: Decreasing Energy Intensity Behind India's Sustainable Development

parity terms, China, for example, has an energy consumption of 0.23 in 2003 as compared to a global average of 0.21 and India at 0.16 compares well with 0.14 in UK, 0.15 in Japan and 0.22 in the USA (Table 8.9).

The larger Indian reform, therefore turned adversity to advantage. For if energy reform is slow, energy demand can reform faster at the user end. Figure 8.2 shows this result for India. This was a case of so-called harmonization of reform, with developments outside the sector, in this case energy, determining outcomes within it.

Non-utilities power capacity also grew fast inceasing from 3500 MW in 1980–81 to 19,500 MW in 2005–06, leading to an incredible 15.69 per cent of power capacitey in the so-called captive sector. This, of course, was costly and inefficient.

Reasons for Poor Performance in Reform Period and Lessons Drawn

Reform of the traditional system was attempted from 1991. The evolution and main features of the process have been summarized well in a recent monograph by Kandula Subramaniam published by the Centre for the Advanced Study of India (CASI) of the University of Pennsylvania (Subramaniam 2004). Appropriately titled 'Thirteen Years of Power Sector Reform in India: Are We Still Groping in the Dark?', it highlights the reform process. The reform process for this sector was from the very beginning not very successful. On the generation side, the policy of allowing investment in the private sector through the independent power producer (IPP) route was unsuccessful. These were the so-called fast track projects. Subsequently, counter–guarantees on returns to the investors by introduced as a matter of State policy, but on account of reservations were not implemented. These guarantees ensured that fixed costs were met even if no power was produced. But it would be difficult for the government to make such payments as no power was being generated. The initial reform process was described as a failure by its authors. 'These protracted negotiations lasted through the tenure of the I.K. Gujaral government when Y.K. Alagh was the Minister of State for Power. However, during this period, the counter-guarantee issue did not involve a fight between the finance and power ministries. Prior to that,...the power ministry was always at loggerheads with the finance ministry on the issue of counter-guarantees' (Subramanian 2004). After the disillusionment with the fast track projects, the Finance Minister in 1996 came back with an offer from Germany for two large projects to be set up at less than the global competitive cost. An Eminent Persons Group was set up to negotiate these and later developed into a Mega Project policy.

The policy for large projects was introduced in 1997. It provided for either the bidding route or an Eminent Persons Group to negotiate projects with vendors with foreign government support, who offered them below global prices. Private investments in associated transmission projects were also allowed as the draft Transmission Bill had received support from a parliamentary committee. The Power Ministry had a dedicated monitor for each large project. This led to large-scale commitments of FDI in the power sector and also considerable investment during the period 1996–98, including the only private sector large transmission project under operation, namely the National Grid of UK's Transmission Project in the Mangalore STP. In 1997, FDI approvals reached Rs 25 billion (approximately US$ 675 million) from less than a tenth of that earlier and actual inflows reached around Rs 10 billion from nothing earlier. (In 1997–98, the exchange rate was US$1=Rs 37.17.)

With a change in government, the policy was renamed the Mega Project Policy, but lost its operating teeth. FDI dried up in the period 1999–2005 and by 2001 was close to zero. Approvals declined to less than a tenth by 1998 and reached close to nothing by 2004 and so did actuals. This aspect has recently been underlined again (2006) by setting up an Empowered Group of Ministers to review each scheme and by now ten mega projects are under consideration. Also there are associated transmission projects with private or public–private partnership (PPP) modes. The first large project has been sanctioned, although the original successful bidder for which a shell company was set up to obtain financial and technical clearance was disqualified by a group of ministers and the second lowest bidder was awarded the project. This led to some unease, but the sanctioned project is at low tariff rates and is successful in that sense. Ten more projects are under consideration. A number of large transmission projects have also been sanctioned in the PPP mode. Most investments promised are in the domestic private sector or in the PPP mode and the Mentors Group is now a shell company for each project which will wind up once it is implemented.

Transmission

Inter-state trade in power started on a large scale in 1997–98 and soon after merit order pricing also started. Agencies have now been mandated to back up interregional power trade and a retail market in power is underway.

The 1991 policy set up the structure of IPPs. These followed an American legislation which was meant to allow renewable energy producers to enter the power grid. According to Subramanian, 'To say that the 1991 Power Policy was not well conceived would be an understatement.' According to Alagh, former finance minister Manmohan Singh 'has been generous enough to admit that the power policy of the early 1990s was a mistake'. Dr Manmohan Singh spoke out against the reforms for the first time in 1996 at a seminar organized by the Tata Energy Research Institute in New Delhi. In an interview given later, he stated:

> I think we should have evolved a more coherent policy for economic reforms. Reforms were '...essentially a case by case liberalization. In the power sector, problems like Enron and now Cogentrix would have been avoided if we had evolved a more holistic approach' (quoted in Subrahmanian, 2004 p. 76).

The original Transmission Bill introduced in 1996 was seen through a Parliamentary Committee which was very cautious, particularly on private agents running an energy grid. The Opposition MP Jag Mohan chaired the Committee which patiently and laboriously saw through these objections, supported by the present author as Power Minister. Finally, the Bill was approved unanimously, which later led to support for reform-oriented provisions in legislation and practice and finally in the Electricity Act.

Regulators

The Central Energy Regulatory Commission (CERC) Bill setting up Central and state regulators in 1996 was not allowed to be introduced in Parliament. This was finally done by the author in August 1997. But the successor government instead of following through the patient political process of negotiating the legislation forced it through as an Ordinance. They had then to withdraw two of the original bills' main provisions; mandatory nature of the CERC orders and a minimum tariff rule. These infirmities continued in modified form in the subsequent legislation.

The regulators are almost all retired civil servants and the original intent in the legislation in 1996 was to avoid this and set up a transparent process for professionally qualified persons; this was later amended. There are unseemly wrangles in these processes and while this paper was being written, it was reported about appointment as Chairman, CERC, 'Power Minister Sushil Kumar Shinde is apparently unhappy with one of the two candidates selected by the selection (search) committee' (Ojha 2007, p. 15).

India's first and best professional electricity regulator has the following to say:

> as studied and reported by Joel Ruet, the Ministry and Executive control the electricity enterprises under the central and state governments, and the enterprises look for all direction, policy and procedures from them. The enterprises especially in the states function in an administrative and not an enterprise fashion. The Ministries do

> submit annual reports on performance to the legislature but they are little debated in the legislatures. Advisory committees to the departments are more window dressing than true consultative mechanisms...

and again,

> Search, selection and appointment of regulators have so far been left largely to government servants and have resulted in filling most appointments with former government servants. The relative lack of commercial and enterprise expertise is unfortunate since there is no understanding on what state electricity enterprises must do to develop such cultures. Members invariably are appointed at an age when they are nearing retirement or have retired (Rao 2006).

Financing and Administering Energy Efficiency

Turning adversity to an advantage was the metaphor in energy efficiency as the earlier analysis shows. If privatization and reform in electricity fail, the requirement seems to be to use it more efficiently every where else, while also making efforts to be efficient in electricity generation capacity use. As the slack in capacity use is taken up, these become more compelling and urgent systemic issues. In the present system the responsibility of energy efficiency is laid on the BEE, a subordinate office of the Ministry of Power.

The Government of India has designed a National Mission on Enhanced Energy Efficiency (NMEEE), as one out of eight missions planned under the National Action Plan on Climate Change. The BEE has produced a Draft National Mission on Enhanced Energy Efficiency for discussion. This provides the following initiatives:

(a) A Perform Achieve and Trade scheme as a market-based mechanism to enhance energy efficiency in the 'designated consumers' (large energy-intensive industries and facilities). The scheme includes, Goal setting: set a specific energy consumption (SEC) target for each plant; Reduction phase: within a three-year period (2009–2012) the designated consumers try to reduce their energy intensity according to their target; Trading phase: those consumers who exceed their target SEC will be credited tradable energy permits. These permits can be sold to designated consumers who failed to meet their target.

(b) Accelerated shift to energy efficient appliances in designated sectors will be enabled through innovative measures. These products would be made more affordable. This target would be achieved by DSM measures, supported with CDM financing wherever possible.

(c) Financing initiatives focusing on the creation of mechanisms that would help finance demand side management programmes in all sectors by capturing future energy savings. The initiative includes fiscal instruments like tax exemptions for the profits and gains made from energy efficiency projects by Electric Supply Companies (ESCos) and venture capital funds and reduction of value added tax (VAT) for energy efficient equipment (for example, CFLs), a revolving fund to promote carbon finance and a partial risk guarantee fund to provide commercial banks with partial coverage of risk exposure against loans made for energy efficiency projects.

(d) A power sector technology strategy aiming to enhance energy efficiency in power generation, including a roadmap for IGCC demonstration plants, development of know-how for advanced super-critical boilers and a road map for fuel shift.

(e) Supporting initiatives.

Decentralized Options

There is a large literature on decentralized energy options from renewables. India's achievements from wind power are commendable; much more can be done from photovoltaics, biofuels and waste. 7000 MW of projectized alternatives are potentially available from mini hydel by the Central Water Commission. There are exciting possibilities of shifting the about 20,000 MW produced by captive plants in factories, shops etc. to alternative renewable fuel sources. But if economic reform at the distribution end does not succeed, as shown below, particularly in bringing in local agents in energy trade systems, these opportunities will not materialize in action. If non-renewable energy is available cheaply there will be no built-in incentives to substitute it and exhortations have a limit. The cost of insensible subsidization has to be paid.

In the long run, however, the decentralized options can have consequences that we at present do not visualize. There is no unique way to success. In sectors which have large externalities and ripple effects, if the bottom line is always kept sight of—namely that the hard budget constraint has to be imposed at the lowest level—then mixtures of public and private initiatives will succeed. Co-operatives, NGOs with private or local body initiatives, contracted distribution systems, companies which originally grew for infrastructure for dedicated owners—but started selling to the larger economy—have all succeeded. Deliberate experimentation with alternative models can lead to results that 'Futures' do not envisage.

Conclusion

It is important for India's development to have a well worked out long-term strategy which the Eleventh Plan does not contain (for the first time in the country's planning history). As seen from a number of good independent studies and Planning Commission committees, the Indian energy outcomes will not only have to sustain faster and more widespread economic growth of its large population, but will to an extent intertwine with larger sustainability outcomes on a global plane.

The whole question of better performance of its energy sector on a PPP mode will involve international investments. Progress in India on this front is slow but is improving gradually. A study of India's policy strategies for the energy sector suggests that in the periods when there was a political commitment towards reform and there was agreement on legislation on transmission policies, separate policies for large generation projects and regulatory bodies, investment performance was good, but otherwise investment and generation growth have declined.

India's energy efficiency performance is good and there is scope for further improvement. Its capacity utilization in generation is high and there is no slack, thus emphasizing reform in capacity addition policies. There is considerable scope for distribution and transmission reform. The regulatory system is at present under considerable strain on account of politicization of appointments.

India's long-term energy scenarios are a matter of considerable concern. Studies show the importance of photovoltaics, vegetable matter as feedstock and reform of policies for renewables in general. On a larger plane, better utilization of coal through IGCC technology and thorium-based FBRs are important. India has considerable capability in these fields but a lot remains to be done especially in the more complex areas of cementing the reform that has taken place and expanding generation and transmission capacity. Reinforcing efficiency with users and building efficient distribution systems is well-known yet neglected. Decentralized options for renewable energy need greater emphasis. India has done well in wind power and mini hydel but its performance is poor in photovoltaics and vegetable waste. As always, the purchase of equipment is easy. Performing with it is the complex task. However, profitable opportunities for co-operation are almost limitless.

References

Alagh, Yoginder K. (1987), 'Modelling for Indian Plans', *International Journal of Development Planning Literature*, Vol. 2, No. 4, pp. 225–38.

_____ (1991), *Indian Development Planning and Policy*, *Wider Studies in Development Economics*, Helsinki and Vikas, Delhi.

_____ (1996), 'The Theory of Not Hastening Slowly', *Indian Journal of Labour Economics*, Vol. 39. No. 1.

_____ (1997a), 'Fuel for Power', Second Lov Raj Kumar Lecture, *Current Science*, Vol. 73, No. 1212, Indian National Science Association, 25 December, pp. 1051–6.

_____ (1997b), 'Economics of Nuclear Power in India', *Nu-Power*, Vol. 11, No. 1–3.

_____ (1998), 'Strategy for Power Generation', *Yojana*, Vol. 42, No. 1, January.

_____ (2000a), 'Foreword', in P. Audinet, P.R. Shukla, and F. Grare (eds), *India's Energy; Essays On Sustainable Development*, Manohar, Delhi.

_____ (2000b), 'Global Sustainable Future and Developing Countries', in Fu Chen Lo, H. Tokuda and N.S. Cooray, *The Sustainable Future of the Global System*, Tokyo, UNU-OECD, Ch.19.

_____ (2000c), 'Sustainable Development India, 2020', in H. Van Ginkel and R. Thakur (2001), *Embracing the New Millennium*.

_____ (2006), 'India 2020', *Journal of Quantitative Economics*, Vol. 4, No. 1, pp. 1–14.

Alagh, Yoginder K., J. Shah and V.K. Shah (1998), *Power Economics in Gujarat*, Har-Anand, Delhi.

Audinet, P., P.R. Shukla, and F. Grare (eds) (2000), *India's Energy; Essays On Sustainable Development*, Manohar, Delhi.

Desai, M. (2004), *Development and Nationhood*, Oxford University Press, Oxford.

Government of India (1999), 'Discussion Paper on Energy Pricing', CERC, Government of India, New Delhi.

_____ (2002), The Indo-US Science and Technology Forum, *First Annual Report*, Delhi.

_____ (2003), *Report of the Committee on India Vision 2020*, Planning Commission (23 January 2003, under the Chairmanship of Dr S.P. Gupta).

_____ (2006a), Approach to the Eleventh Five Year Plan, Planning Commisssion, New Delhi.

_____ (2006b), *Economic Survey:2006/07*, Finance Ministry, New Delhi.

_____ (2006c), *Integrated Energy Policy*, Planning Commission, New Delhi, August.

_____ (2008), *Eleventh Five Year Plan: 2007–2012*, Planning Commission, Oxford University Press, New Delhi,

Lo, Fu Chen, H. Tokuda and N.S. Cooray (2000), *The Sustainable Future of the Global System*, UNU-OECD, Tokyo.

MERC (2000), Order, Case No. 1 of 1999, MERC, Mumbai, 28 April.

Mukherji, R., M. Chattopadhyay and C. Neogi (2001), *Productivity, Human Development and Basic Needs in India*, Indian Statistical Institute, Calcutta.

Nachane, D.M. (2006), 'Approach Paper to the Eleventh Five-Year Plan, A Sceptical Note', *Economic and Political Weekly*, 22 July, p. 3141.

Ojha, O. (2007), 'CERC Appointment Delayed', *Financial Express*, Bombay, 24 September, p. 15

Panagariya, A. (2005), 'Hindu Growth vs. Reforms', *Financial Express Special*, 7 November, p. 2, based on his NBER working paper.

Parikh, K. et al. (2000), 'A Framework for Sustainable Development of India: An Overview' in Fu Chen Lo, H. Tokuda and N.S. Cooray, *The Sustainable Future of the Global System*, UNU-OECD, Tokyo, Ch. 19.

Rao, S.L. (2006), 'Evaluating and Building Capacity in Regulatory Commissions', New Delhi, TERI.

Ruet, J. (2005), *Privatising Power Cuts?: Ownership and Reform of State Electricity Boards in India*, Academic, Delhi.

Rodriguez, Placid (2003), 'PFBR—Atoms of a Power Dream', *Hindu Opinion Page*, 24 September.

Rodrik, D. and A. Subramaniam (2004), 'From 'Hindu' Growth to Productivity Surge: The Mystery of the Indian Growth Transition', NBER Working Paper 10376, National Bureau of Economic Research, Cambridge Mass.

Schwank, O., T. von Stokar and N. North (2000), 'Long Term Carbon Emmission Targets', in P. Audinet, P.R. Shukla, and F. Grare (eds), *India's Energy; Essays On Sustainable Development*, Manohar, Delhi.

Subramaniam, Kandula (2004), 'Thirteen Years of Power Sector Reform in India: Are We Still Groping in the Dark?', CASI Occasional Paper No. 15, Center for Advanced Study of India, University of Pennsylvania, Philadelphia.

Van Ginkel, H. and R. Thakur (2001), *Embracing the Millennium: Perspectives and Challenges for the United Nations and the International Community*, UNU Millennium Series; United Nations University, Tokyo

UNU (United Nations University) (2003), *A Sustainable Development Framework in Large Developing Countries in China, India and Indonesia*, UNU Press, Tokyo.

Wilson, Dominic and Roopa Purushothaman (2003), 'Dreaming with BRICs: The Path to 2050', Goldman Sachs, Global Economics Paper No. 99, New York.

9

Sustainability of India's Economic Growth

Aparna Sawhney

Introduction

India is an emerging economy which has experienced an impressive rate of economic growth in recent years. During the decade 1992–2002, the annual average growth rate of GDP per capita was 3.7 per cent, and it increased to 7.2 per cent per annum during 2003–07.[1] As India aspires to further accelerate its economic growth, or at least sustain the high rate of growth, the critical question today is whether sustained high growth is indeed possible? While institutional and structural constraints typically take the centre stage in such debates, this paper addresses the sustainability issues with respect to the underlying ecological system in which the economic system is embedded.

Sustainable development is broadly understood as development that meets the needs of the present without compromising the ability of the future generations to meet their own needs (WCED 1987). In the literature on economic growth, sustainability is interpreted as a condition where the present path of economic growth allows future generations to have economic opportunities at least as large as those

[1]Both measured at constant 1999–2000 prices. *Economic Survey 2007–08*, p. 1.

of the present generation in the form of capacity to produce and consume. The capacity to produce and consume goods and services depends on three kinds of producing capital assets of the economy, namely, natural, manufactured and intellectual capital; with the help of enabling institutions and social norms, which can also be considered as forms of capital.

Natural capital consists of natural assets of the biosphere that support all life forms, including air, water, energy, minerals, habitat and biological diversity. Manufactured capital consists of machines and infrastructures, while intellectual capital includes human skills, knowledge and technology—together these different forms of capital build on natural capital. The institutional capital, including markets, regulations and government policies, plays a critical role in determining the returns to capital and hence the rate of investment or disinvestment. Finally, social capital, including norms guiding the behaviour of people, determines the final demand and pattern of use of the different forms of capital.

During the process of economic growth, natural capital typically decreases while the other forms of capital increase. Accordingly, Pearce et al. (1989) define two sustainability criteria on the maintenance of the capital assets: *weak* and *strong* sustainability. Weak sustainability requires the aggregate wealth of the three heterogeneous capital assets be maintained for future generations; while strong sustainability requires that the stock of critical natural capital be maintained since certain natural resources are non-substitutable. For example, ecological services flowing from natural resources, including biodiversity, water cycle, climate change, etc. are irreplaceable, and cannot be substituted with other forms of anthropogenic capital.

To the extent that environmental aspects are ignored in the economic growth process, it is accompanied by environmental degradation and loss of ecological wealth. Industrialization and growing consumption leads to the depletion of natural resources and generation of waste resulting in a depletion of the quality of natural resources such as air, water, soil, etc. The adverse environmental fall-out of economic growth follows from underlying ill-defined property rights, inadequate pricing of environmental assets and distortionary government policies meant to promote growth. These factors institute a bias towards pollution-intensive industries; and encourage consumption substitution towards resource-intensive goods and services that results in a type of economic growth where the associated environmental costs are greater (with greater generation of waste per capita or resource-use per capita).

India's initial economic plan exercises, in the 1950s and early 1960s, focused on building economic self-reliance with a strong industrial structure biased towards heavy capital-intensive industries.[2] No attention was paid to the accompanying environmental costs of such a development approach. During this industrial incubation period (under protection), India witnessed phenomenal growth in traditional polluting industries like chemicals, fertilizers, iron and steel, distilleries, paper and pulp, among others.[3] The consequent environmental damage, in terms of contamination of freshwater, sub-soil, loss of pristine forests, etc. remains unaccounted for.[4] By the time India began an extensive and systematic liberalization of policies in 1991, the government was committed to promoting sustainable development as opposed to simply economic growth. Considering the ecological damage already caused by the growth process in the preceding four decades and the commitment to sustainable development, India substantially enhanced the environmental protection legislation and pollution-abatement policies—thereby increasing the enabling institutional capital required for sustainable development.[5]

[2]Especially in the second and third Five Year Plans.

[3]Over the years, the growth of small-scale industries including leather processing, chemical units etc., primarily to promote employment, added to the generation of untreated hazardous wastes. The pollution problem from small-scale units is compounded by the fact that subsequent environmental/pollution standards developed for different industries in India do not apply to small units. Recognizing the capital crunch of small units, the Central Pollution Control Board has adopted the instrument of common effluent treatment plants.

[4]This, of course, is not unique to India since industrialized countries too have journeyed through similar development processes, following which remedial environmental policies were adopted. A control mechanism for industrial pollution through environmental standards and regulations began in the 1970s.

[5]While preparing for the 1972 Stockholm Conference on Human Development, the Indian Government decided to establish a systematic set of environmental regulations and regulatory bodies. It began with the 1974 Water Act, 1977 Water Cess Act, and establishment of the Central Pollution Control Board and a few state pollution control boards. Indian environmental legislation prior to 1970 had been sporadic. Since the 1990s, the scope and depth of environmental regulations have continued to grow.

The sustainability of India's economic growth is significant in view of both the cumulative environmental damage since the initial industrializing phase, as well as the newer environmental challenges in the wake of rapid growth of a different nature in recent years. Economic growth has changed substantially during the last two decades in India with the services sector gaining significance. Our standard national account measures of gross domestic product (GDP) or net national product (NNP) are poor measures of the true welfare since they completely ignore the depreciation of the country's natural resources endowment and environmental quality. Thus, in order to gauge the sustainability of an economy, we need to use wealth measures that reflect the underlying environmental capital asset.

The second section in this chapter defines sustainable development and discusses its interpretation for measurement purposes in the literature; the third section reviews selected economic and environmental performance indicators for India; the fourth section reviews recent empirical work on India's environmental accounted growth. It also discusses some of the challenging dimensions of sustainability of economic growth in India, especially in light of the significant role of the service sector and the nature of consumption. The fifth section provides the concluding observations.

Sustainability Measures of Growth

Strong sustainability requires critical ecosystem measures like carrying capacity and resilience, while weak sustainability can be measured through aggregative indicators like genuine savings and wealth (Pearce et al. 1996). In economic models, the condition of weak sustainability has been more in vogue, concentrating on the management of a portfolio of capital assets including the physical, natural, and intellectual; as opposed to strong sustainability which would require the maintenance of some critical environmental resources.

Subsequently, the valuation of the portfolio of heterogeneous assets across time has gained importance in the measurement indicators of sustainability. The environmentally conditioned wealth and savings rate thus obtained have been used to judge the sustainability of economic growth experienced by a country. However, with the aggregation of different types of capital in the measure of wealth, one misses out on some 'critical bottlenecks that impose limits on substitution possibilities' (Arrow et al. 2004), which can be obtained with more direct ecological services estimation. While such complete scientific and ecological measures for nations are being developed, the physical measures of environmental pollution and degradation continue to serve as critical indicators of the environmental soundness of economic growth.

Indeed, economists have used the empirical association of income growth and environmental quality, popularly referred to as the Environmental Kuznets Curve (EKC), to characterize the ecological soundness of the growth process of an economy. Among the macro indicators to measure the cost to natural capital are *ecological footprint* and *ecological deficit*, which respectively measure the amount of bio-capacity used up by the anthropogenic economic system, and what is left over for the future generations based on the total productive capacity of the ecosystem. These different measures are briefly described in this section, and the corresponding estimates for the Indian economy are taken up in the fourth section.

Definition of Sustainability in Growth Models

The criterion for sustainability of an economy typically used in the growth models is that of *non-declining* total welfare path. This conditionality allows for appropriate intergenerational transfers over time—analogous to *potential* Pareto improvements—to achieve sustainability according to the definition. Defining sustainability as a non-declining welfare path, allows for exhaustible natural capital or resources to be transformed into man-made reproducible capital or productive capacity as an intergenerational transfer (Solow 1986).[6] This intergenerational equity aspect is intrinsically linked to efficiency since it involves transmitting productive capacity across time in the form of natural capital, manufactured capital or intellectual capital. Sustainability of economic growth is thus interpreted as encompassing both dynamic efficiency as well as intergenerational equity (assuming that intra-generational equity is taken care of within each time period), where the economy moves along a Pareto frontier consumption path such that the discounted stream of intergenerational welfare is non-decreasing over time (Stavins et al. 2003).

[6]The Hartwick rule requires the investment of all rents from exhaustible resources in reproducible capital for sustainability (Hartwick 1977).

The growth models thus inherently assume the substitutability between different forms of capital in the production function, as well as substitutability between natural resource services and anthropogenic goods and services in consumption. While the utility function in some growth models may differentiate between the consumption of anthropogenic goods and services and natural environmental services (as opposed to consumption of a homogeneous good), the underlying substitutability remains. Economists, however, do acknowledge that such consumption substitutability may not be feasible in the case of direct consumption of certain environmental resources like pristine forest, natural beauty, etc.

The distinction between consumption of economic goods and direct consumption of environmental amenities features in the Hamilton model (2000 and 2003) that has been used in recent measurement approaches to sustainability of economic growth.[7] In maximizing the discounted stream of intergenerational utility at every time period, subject to various constraints, the sustainability

[7]Utility of consumers is considered to be a function of consumption of the produced composite good (C), and environmental services (B), in a model with constant population. Based on the Solow model, the economy is assumed to produce a homogeneous good that may be either consumed (C) or invested as capital (K). The economic goal is to maximize the discounted stream of intergenerational utility (U) subject to the various constraints including production, capital accumulation, natural resource stock and environmental pollution. Utility of consumers is considered to be a function of consumption of the produced composite good (C), and environmental services (B). Using the sustainability criterion of non-declining intergenerational welfare at any point in time, it reduces to an intertemporal optimization problem, where the discounted stream of welfare is maximized at every point in time:

$$Max\,Vt = \int_t^{\infty} U[C(\tau), B(\tau)]e^{-r(\tau-t)}d\tau$$

s.t.

$$K = F - C - a - m;$$
$$X = e(F, a) - d;$$
$$S = -R + g;$$
$$N = q(m)$$

where the first constraint shows that the production of the composite good (*F*) at any point in time is invested in manufactured capital (*K*), consumed (*C*), used in pollution abatement (*a*) and invested in education (*m*). Pollution, which is determined by production and abatement at every period, accumulates as a stock to the extent that it is not naturally dissipated. Thus the second constraint gives the change in pollution condition in the Hamilton model is reduced to non-negative *genuine saving* or investment at every time period.[8] In other words, a non-declining welfare path across time periods requires non-declining wealth and hence non-negative genuine savings.

Indicators of Sustainability and Environmental Costs of Growth

Genuine Savings Rate and Genuine Wealth

Following the principle of sustainable growth, the sustainability of an economy is measured in terms of savings and capital bequeathed each period for future consumption. The measure of capital encompasses all forms of productive capital—natural and anthropogenic. Genuine saving is estimated from traditional net savings minus the value of resource depletion and environmental degradation plus the value of investment in human capital. In order to estimate the genuine savings rate of various countries, the standard approach currently followed by the World Bank (Hamilton model) has been to obtain the traditional savings from the national accounts, which are then adjusted for manufactured capital disinvestment, intellectual investment and natural capital use and depreciation. Four types of adjustments are made: deduction of capital consumption to obtain net national savings rate; addition of current education

---

stock (X) as equal to total emissions (e) less the natural dissipation (d). The flow of environmental services (B in the utility function), is negatively related to this stock of pollution. The third constraint indicates that growth in natural resource (S) is equal to its natural growth rate (g) less the extraction (R). The last constraint represents the change in human capital (N) as an increasing function (q) of education expenditure (m).

[8]Considering b to be the marginal cost of pollution abatement and thus the marginal benefit of abatement (or marginal damage of pollution) at the optimum, the optimum Pigovian pollution tax on production is be_F. The genuine saving G is equal to investment in manufactured capital K, plus change in real value of environmental resources (change in stock $R - g$, valued at resource rental rate F_R net of the effective pollution tax be_F), plus change in pollution accumulation e-d valued at the marginal damage of pollution b, plus change in human capital q times the marginal cost of creating a unit of human capital $1/q'$.

$$G = K - (l - be_F)\, F_R\, (R - g) - b(e - d) + \frac{q}{q}, \text{ and}$$

$$V = U_C\, G = rV - U$$

The static first-order condition for the maximum (of non-declining V over time) is equivalent to genuine saving being non-negative in any period.

expenditure in lieu of human capital investment; deduction of natural resource depletion (imputed values of selected minerals, based on estimated resource rents); and pollution damage from atmospheric particulate matter and global warming.

The genuine savings would be non-negative so long as investment in produced assets and human capital is greater than the value of natural resources' depletion and of pollution accumulation. The environmental components of genuine savings capture the impact on productivity in the economy. Also since economic development and improvement in lifestyles or welfare are associated with higher consumption of environmental amenities like clean air, water, nature parks, etc., environmental pollution and depletion of natural resources are accounted for within a more genuine measure of national savings and wealth.

The genuine wealth is measured through the valuation of the different asset components of manufactured capital, natural resources and human capital. While valuation of physical capital is relatively easy through market prices, natural resource valuation is challenging since natural assets are often under-priced in the market, so Hotelling rent imputations have typically been used. Human capital has typically been measured through education expenditure (or adjustments thereof), and knowledge/technological improvements have often been proxied through factor productivity improvements.

Genuine wealth per capita

Sustainability requires that the productive capacity available in the future be enough for a growing population. While a non-negative genuine savings rate is necessary for sustainability, it is not sufficient, since real capital wealth per capita may be declining in case the population growth rate is relatively high. Genuine savings indicate the change in total productive assets or wealth at each time period; however, to measure the availability of such capital per capita in the future, one would look at the change in wealth per capita.[9] Thus wealth per capita

[9]In an economy with a growing population, it is not enough to have non-negative genuine savings in the Hamilton model. In case of population growth, the Hamilton rule for sustainability is non-declining wealth per capita.

$\frac{d}{dt}\left(\frac{W}{P}\right)=\frac{W}{P}\left(\frac{\dot{W}}{W}-\frac{\dot{P}}{P}\right)>0$. Where P is the population and W is the total wealth equal to manufactured capital, natural capital and intellectual capital, (as well as institutional capital in some cases).

needs to be non-declining in order for the future generation to have the capacity to be at least as well off as the present generation.

Environmental Kuznets Curve

The relationship between economic development versus environmental pollution/emissions has been investigated empirically since the 1990s; however the relationship is not unique. In some cases, the environmental quality improves with higher income per capita (like inadequate sanitation, indoor air pollution); while in some other cases pollution actually increases with income (for municipal waste generation, carbon emissions). Interestingly, for several local or regional environmental problems, pollution increases with increase in per capita income but beyond a critical level of income, environmental pollution starts to decline (like atmospheric particulate matter, sulphur oxides, organic water pollution). The last phenomenon, depicting an inverted U-shaped relationship between GDP per capita and pollution, is popularly called the EKC. Largely, the EKC captures three kinds of growth–environment relationships: as income per capita increases, there is an increase in the demand for environmental quality (termed as the *income effect of growth*) and more stringent environmental regulation and enforcement (termed *regulatory effect*), both of which offset the pollution with economic growth—at least for certain pollutants. Moreover, with economic growth as the relative significance of the underlying production structure shifts away from heavy industries towards the service sector (termed *composition effect*) the traditional air and water pollution reduces.[10]

It is pertinent to remember, however, that to the extent pollutants have a cumulative impact (say, heavy metals in land or water), the degradation of environmental quality can continue even after the income grows beyond the critical level, that is, the EKC cannot reflect the irreversible nature of some environmental damage when the level of pollution goes beyond the ecosystem's buffering capacity, since it typically shows the trade-off between emissions and income per capita. In order to gauge the sustainability of growth, in such cases one would need to fall back on ecological parameters which depict the health of the natural resource stock (say aquatic life in a lake or river) or flow of ecological services.

[10]Grossman and Krueger (1995).

Ecological Footprint

The ecological footprint measures the environmental stress of consumption of a community. It estimates the pressure on the biosphere in terms of productive land area required to support the consumption in different sectors. Biologically productive areas include cropland (for cultivation of food, fibre, rubber, etc.), grazing land (for meat, milk, hides, etc.), forests (for timber, fuel, wood, fibre, sequester carbon dioxide), fisheries and built-up areas (infrastructure for housing, transportation, industrial production, etc.). The ecological footprint measure of a country is based on the consumption, production and trade data. Most countries run a national ecological deficit since the ecological footprint of an average consumer is greater than the available national biological capacity per capita. The ecological deficit that exists when ecological demand exceeds supply can be financed by importing bio-capacity, liquidating existing stocks of ecological capital, or allowing wastes to accumulate and ecosystems to degrade

India's Economic and Environmental Performance Indicators

In examining the sustainability of India's growth experience, we first discern a relationship between the anthropogenic economic system and the natural environment, by reviewing the pattern of growth in the country and the current state of the environment. Since both the stock as well as the quality of resources determine the productive capacity of natural capital, economists continue to rely on physical environmental indicators (as evident from growth of the EKC literature).

Economic Growth and the Structure of the GDP

In the first three decades following the initiation of planned growth in India in 1951, economic performance was lacklustre. Income per capita grew on an average of only around 1 per cent per annum during 1950–80; although, given the stagnation experienced prior to independence the low output and income growth during 1950s through the 1970s was not surprising.[11] Growth analysts place the

[11]Before independence in 1947, the per capita income was stagnant or declining over a long period (Mohan 2006).

take-off period for the Indian economy in the early to mid-1980s, during the first set of liberalization reforms (de Long 2001). The growth of income per capita in the 1980s accelerated to about 3–4 per cent per annum, and is considered as 'a major departure in our recorded history' (Mohan 2006). The growth of income per capita further accelerated during 1992–2006 to rise to 6–7 per cent per annum.

The income growth in India was led by the industrial and services sectors, with the latter taking over in subsequent years (see Table 9.1). In the last 15 years, the contribution of agricultural growth to real GDP growth in some years has even been negative (1995–96, 1997–98, 2002–03), and industrial growth has sometimes dipped low, but the services sector has emerged as the principal driver of real output growth. For example, 57 per cent of the real GDP growth in 2003–04 was due to the services sector (RBI 2004). The remarkable growth since 1993 has followed the 'rapid expansion of service-producing industries', rather than the more traditional development path of low wage manufacturing expected of a labour-abundant developing country (Bosworth and Collins 2008). The share of the value-added from the services sector to GDP was only 40 per cent in 1980 and it had increased to 55 per cent by 2006 (WDI 2008).

An important source of high growth in India is found in the output growth per worker: during 1993–2004 output per worker grew at about 4.6 per cent per annum compared to 2.4 per cent

Table 9.1: Average Annual Growth Rate of GDP and Income Per Capita in India, 1950–2005

Period	*Agriculture*	*Industry*	*Services*	*GDP*	*Income Per Capita*
1951–52 to 1960–61	3.1	6.1	4.6	3.9	1.9
1961–62 to 1970–71	2.5	5.4	4.9	3.7	1.3
1971–72 to 1980–81	1.8	4.4	4.2	3.2	0.8
1981–82 to 1990–91	3.1	7.6	6.7	5.6	3.2
1991–92	*–1.5*	*–1.2*	4.5	*1.3*	-1.5
1992–93 to 2001–02*	*3.4*	*6.1*	*7.7*	*6.1*	*4.1*
2002–03 to 2005–06*	*1.9*	*8.3*	*8.7*	*7.0*	*5.6*

Note: * Data up to 1999–2000 are at the base year 1993–94 and data from 2000–01onwards are at the base year 1999–2000.
Source: Mohan (2006).

during 1978–93 (Bosworth and Collins 2008). Labour productivity increased remarkably in the industrial and services sectors, compared to the agricultural sector. The growth in output per worker is estimated to have been driven by higher physical and education capital per worker, and more significantly, higher total factor productivity (the residual productivity of the Solow growth model, after taking into account physical capital's contribution to productivity increase); that is, while both manufactured and intellectual capital per worker increased, their contribution to growth of output per worker was less than that attributable to sheer increase in factor productivity.

The growth of the services sector is typically associated with a more mature state of development, and is considered to be relatively less pollution-intensive in terms of traditional pollutants (from the manufacturing sector). In India, the service sector has prematurely become the driver of economic growth since the 1990s, as illustrated in Table 9.1. Given the underlying shifts in the output structure in India, one is tempted to ask whether the higher growth of the recent years, led by services, has been relatively clean and environmentally sustainable.

We discuss here three aspects of the structural change in output in India: first, the energy resource use per unit of output; second, the nature of industrial growth in recent years; and third, the pollution risks from the unbridled growth of certain modern segments.

Declining energy intensity of output but higher energy use and GHG emissions

With structural changes in output and the development of energy-saving technology over time, countries across the globe have seen a decline in the energy-intensity of GDP. This is true of India too for the period 1980–2006. Declining energy intensity of output reflects greater efficiency in energy use, as well as change in output structure (growth of less energy-intensive sectors). Since energy is one of the most critical resources in production and consumption, reduction in energy-intensity over time is an important factor for sustainable growth. However, more significant is the total consumption of energy and residual energy reserves (of non-renewable) left for the future generations. For instance, greater use of non-renewable fossil-fuels has accompanying pollution, and hence environmental damage costs.

Figure 9.1 illustrates the energy-intensity of output of selected advanced countries including the United States, United Kingdom and Japan, vis-à-vis China and India. The energy intensity is given in terms of total primary energy use (in Btu) per unit of GDP in constant US$ (year 2000), that is, total primary energy consumption per dollar of GDP at purchasing power parities for the different countries.[12] Although countries like China and United States have experienced a more dramatic decline in energy intensity than India, it is notable that India has by far the lowest energy intensity per unit of output among this group of countries.

However, it is important to observe that the total consumption of primary energy has more than quadrupled over 25 years from 4 quadrillion Btu in 1980 to 16.2 quadrillion Btu in 2005 (EIA 2008). Since domestic production continues to fall short of India's energy consumption, energy imports have increased from 0.9 quadrillion

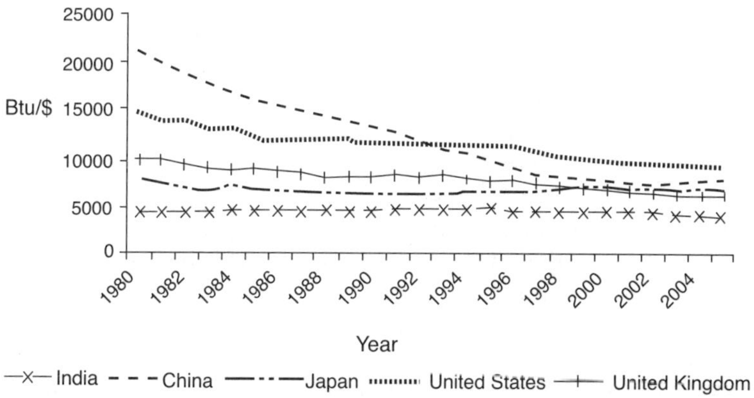

Figure 9.1: Energy Intensity of Output of India Compared to Selected Countries, 1980–2006

Source: Energy Information Administration (EIA),US, available at *http://tonto.eia.doe.gov/country/country_time_series.cfm?fips=IN# prim*, last accessed 1 November 2008.

[12]Energy consumption covers petroleum, dry natural gas, coal, and net hydroelectric, nuclear, and geo-thermal, solar, wind, and wood and waste electricity (including net electricity imports).

Btu to 4.5 quadrillion Btu over the same period. The fall-out of higher consumption of fossil fuel based energy is higher greenhouse gas emissions—the EIA estimated that carbon dioxide emissions in India have increased from 288.7 million metric tonnes in 1980 to 1165.7 million metric tonnes in 2005. Not surprisingly, the estimates of genuine wealth and savings incorporate the damage costs from carbon emissions, though the impact of economic growth on energy resources bequeathed to future generations is not included.

Nature of Industrial Growth and Service Driven Polluting Industries

As indicated earlier, the initial industrial growth in India (during 1950–80) was programmed towards heavy capital-intensive industries (like iron and steel, electrical, chemical, cement), which are also pollution-intensive. The enhanced industrial growth during 1980–2006, while more market-driven, was dominated by the performance of selected industries such as electronics and information technology, textiles, pharmaceuticals and basic chemicals—industries which are recognized as highly polluting, imposing significant environmental damage through atmospheric emissions, water effluents and hazardous solid waste (World Bank 2007).[13] Thus the impetus to growth from the industrial sector in the past three decades has continued to come from segments which are highly polluting and whose environmental costs are not reflected in our growth accounts.

Also the growth of the services sector created an impetus for the growth of its support industries that are used in providing the services. The growth in the Indian services sector has been primarily driven by transport and communications services, and construction services[14]—which have grown in tandem with production of vehicles, cell phones, cement, steel—allied industries that are pollution-intensive (wastes generated during the production process or after consumption). Thus, the main service segments associated with higher growth in India are polluting in terms of allied industrial production and end-of-life disposal of the equipment integrated with

[13]The Central Pollution Control Board (CPCB) classifies these industries among others (metals, fertilizer, pesticide, petrochemicals, etc.) under the 'red category' of pollution-intensive activities.

[14]In the last five years (2002–06), the annual growth of transport and communications services ranged between 14–16 per cent and that of construction services between 8–16 per cent (*Economic Survey* 2007–08).

the service provision. Some of the pollutants are also extremely toxic and pose more serious hazards than the traditional atmospheric or water pollutants associated with industrial growth.

Hazards from the Electronics and Information Technology Sector

Among the fastest growing service-oriented sectors in India is the electronics and information technology hardware industry, which has grown annually in the range of 21–29 per cent during 2002–07 (production in rupees, MOCIT 2008). The remarkable growth of this industry has been driven by software services, communication services, entertainment services, household consumer appliances, etc. While the software, communications and entertainment service sectors are seemingly 'clean' in terms of conventional pollutants, they are intrinsically related with the manufacture and consumption of electronics which are responsible for the fastest stream of hazardous e-waste, including personal computers, mobile handsets, audio video devices, printers, scanners and the like.

Electronic waste consists of heavy metals and toxins such as lead, cadmium, beryllium, brominated flame retardants, which are generated both at the production stage (when components are defective) and at the end of the life of the equipments. The waste from electrical and electronic waste in India is estimated to be about 0.15 million tonnes per year (Toxics Link 2007). The hazardous e-waste is largely handled by the informal sector in India and remains unmonitored.[15] It is known that the improper disposal of e-waste in landfills or incineration leads to extensive dispersion of toxins in land (and groundwater through leaching) and air, but in India there is neither data nor account of the extent of damage imposed by the growth of the modern service and manufacturing sectors.

State of the Environment in India

The worth of the natural capital assets of an economy is determined by their quality, apart from their quantity. Thus the quality of air,

[15]The recycling of e-wastes for the extraction of valuable metals (such as copper, gold, lead, mercury, etc.) is also hazardous when done in improper facilities, as is mostly the case in the informal sector in India. The low cost of recycling in the country has also led to illegal importing of e-waste into India, particularly after the implementation of stringent regulations on producer responsibility of e-waste in the Europe Union and United States (Toxics Link 2007).

water, forests, soil, etc, is important in determining the value of the natural resource stock. The estimation of *genuine saving* does incorporate the damage costs from selected pollutants, as does the measure of *ecological footprint*, but not completely. If one considers air and water among the critical resources (required for survival) that the present Indian generation is bequeathing to the future generations, it is instructive to review the state of these resources in the period of high growth in India, especially since environmental legislation on standards has been enhanced since the 1990s.

The environmental degradation currently being witnessed in the country has resulted from urbanization, industrialization, population growth and the erosion of customs and norms that had previously helped traditional Indian communities conserve the natural environment. This section reviews selected local pollution measures of air and water during the last twelve years to gauge the quality of these critical resources.

Air Quality

Ambient air pollution problems are widespread in rural and urban India, although they are better documented in urban areas due to mandatory regular monitoring of certain pollutants. Urban atmospheric pollution has been severe—primarily due to emissions from vehicular and industrial sources and depletion of tree cover. The conventional indicators of air quality are measured in terms of concentration of suspended particular matter (SPM), sulphur dioxide, nitrogen dioxide, respirable particulate matter, lead, ammonia and carbon monoxide (latter in selected cities). In India, air quality standards are differentiated by area (industrial, residential and sensitive) in the prescription of the National Ambient Air Quality Standards (NAAQS), and monitored under the National Ambient Air Quality Monitoring Programme.

The atmospheric pollution in the residential areas of Indian cities since the mid-1990s indicates that it has improved somewhat for a few pollutants, but not for others. As depicted in Table 9.2, the ambient concentrations of sulphur and nitrogen oxides have been within the standard in most cities (residential areas) in recent years, following the implementation of stricter emission norms for vehicles (Bharat III) and the use of cleaner natural gas as domestic fuel (and for commercial vehicles in major cities). However, violations of the standards

Table 9.2: Annual Average Air Quality in Urban Residential Areas, 1995–2007

Pollutant parameter	*Attainment of NAAQS prescription in residential areas*	*Annual Trend*
SO_2	Within prescribed limits for most cities	Decreasing trend
NO_2	Within prescribed limits for most cities	No trend; fluctuating
SPM	Exceeds standards in most cities	No trend; fluctuating
RSPM	Exceeds standards in most cities	No trend; fluctuating

Source: Central Pollution Control Board, CPCB (2008a).

for SPM and respirable suspended particulate matter (RSPM) have been widespread. In most cities, the annual average concentrations of both suspended and respirable particulate matter have exceeded the national standard. The main sources of particulate air pollution are vehicular exhausts, road and construction dust, incomplete combustion of fuel, industry emissions and burning of garbage.

Since air is a directly consumed good, poor ambient quality reduces welfare through adverse health impact as well as depreciates natural and physical capital (including heritage capital like the Taj Mahal). Although estimations of *genuine savings* have attempted to value the cost of local air pollution, so far the adverse health and material effects have not been valued completely.

Water Quality of Surface and Ground Water

India has a large network of rivers that provide freshwater, and vast alluvial basins to hold groundwater—and the stocks of both are being depleted and water quality is deteriorating. Water pollution has been acute, stemming from three main sources: untreated domestic sewage, industrial effluents and chemical run-off from agriculture.[16]

[16]During the 1990s, municipal wastewater accounted for three-quarters of the total wastewater generated by volume and almost half the total pollution load (CPCB 1999).

The untreated waters have polluted freshwater bodies, coastal waters, contaminated the groundwater and also caused land pollution. Today water quality monitoring stations cover 200 rivers, 60 lakes, 5 tanks, 3 ponds, 3 creeks, 13 canals, 17 drains and 321 wells.[17] The water quality monitoring data, analysed with respect to measures of oxygen consuming substances (bio-chemical demand, BOD) and of pathogenic bacteria (total coliform and faecal coliform), indicate that organic and bacterial contamination is a critical problem in India.

The discharge of untreated sewage is the single most important cause of pollution of surface and ground water; approximately 80 per cent of water pollution in India is due to untreated domestic sewage. There is a large gap between the generation and treatment of domestic wastewater in India, and most Indian cities do not even have sewage treatment and municipal solid waste processing facilities. As the municipal corporations continue to discharge untreated sewage into the rivers and the receiving water bodies do not have adequate water for dilution of these wastes, the oxygen demand and bacterial pollution have increased (as well as risk for water borne diseases). The number of observations having BOD and coliform density has increased during 1995–2007.[18]

The freshwater available in India often does not even meet the standard for 'bathing', let alone drinking. Table 9.3 shows the extent of violation across the monitoring stations for the period 1995–2007, in terms of percentage observations violating the stipulated standard for bathing. Poor water quality imposes health costs on the present generation as well as future generations, and also imposes greater clean up costs on the future generation which our standard growth measures fail to incorporate.

Learning from Empirical Analyses of the Indian Growth Story

Estimates of Genuine Saving and Wealth for the Indian Economy

Several studies have estimated the genuine savings rate and the wealth per capita in India as criteria of sustainability. Based on the principle of maintaining a portfolio of capital assets, the studies

[17]By 2005, the water quality monitoring network in India had expanded to include 1019 stations in 27 states and 6 union territories (CPCB 2007).

[18]CPCB, New Delhi, available at *http://cpcb.nic.in/highlights.php.*

Table 9.3: Extent of Violation of Water Quality Measures in Indian Freshwater, 1995–2007

(percentage observations violating stipulated standard for bathing in surface and groundwater)

Year	*BOD > 3 mg/l*	*Total Coliform > 500/100ml*	*Faecal Coliform > 500/100ml*
1995	43	54	45
1996	41	53	40
1997	40	55	41
1998	43	50	33
1999	43	37	52
2000	41	53	44
2001	40	54	35
2002	36	56	37
2003	33	55	42
2004	34	56	41
2005	32	54	40
2006	36	55	47
2007	31	50	34

Note: Since the total number of readings have been increasing over the years with the extension of the monitoring network stations, the percentage of violations across the years has been considered here.
Source: Based on data in CPCB (2008b).

differ in their specific valuation (monetization) of the components of intellectual, natural and institutional capital. This section highlights the different estimates of genuine investment and per capita wealth made for India.

Following the Hamilton Model, the WB has generated a time series on genuine savings as well as point wealth estimates for most countries. Starting with the national accounts data, adjustments are made to the national savings rate for deforestation, energy depletion, damage from particulate pollution, global warming and enhancement in human capital (public expenditure on education). The genuine savings or investment rate as a proportion of gross national income was estimated to be steadily increasing in the period 1970–2006. During the 1970s and 1980s, the rate was a little under 9 per cent, it rose to 11 per cent in the 1990s and since has rapidly increased to 20.6 per cent in 2006 (see Table 9.4).

Arrow et al. (2004), following a similar methodology, estimated the annual average genuine investment rate of 9.47 per cent for India during the period of 1970–2001, which was close to the WB estimate. However, as the authors observed, these estimates of genuine savings tend to overstate the savings and investment in productive capacity since several natural resources cannot be included due to the absence of environmental data on carbon sequestration, pollution, biodiversity etc; and the valuation of natural assets through market prices. The estimate of 9.5 per cent of genuine investment for India over the 30-year period is also misleading since it does not reflect the change in per capita terms, especially since population increased significantly during the period. When Arrow et al. (2004) made adjustments for population growth, the wealth per capita in India was found to have *declined* during the period 1970–2001 at an annual average rate of 0.57 per cent, that is, growth was not sustainable during these three decades.[19] Since factor productivity is considered to have increased in India during the same time, Arrow et al. made another adjustment in terms of technological improvement or enhanced factor productivity which changed the estimate further. The rate of dissavings per capita due to population growth was found to be more than offset by the projected increase in factor productivity such that per capita wealth was estimated to have grown at 0.54 per cent in India during 1970–2001. Thus India's growth is considered weakly sustainable, in view of the technological and productivity enhancement (subject to the data and measurement constraints).

In a more recent estimate of genuine savings, Dasgupta and Gupta (2008) augmented the human capital valuation by including both public and private spending on education and weighing it with the social return to schooling. Moreover, valuing natural capital depletion (wood, five minerals and two fossil fuels) with marginal Hotelling rents (instead of average rents), their genuine investment estimates for India are higher than those of the WB as well as Arrow et al. (2004), due to the enhanced estimates of intellectual investment.

[19]Arrow et al. (2004) observe that since developing countries suffer from low levels of consumption, greater investment could cause misery by reducing consumption per capita in the present. Since poverty alleviation of the present generation is a foremost goal, there arises a conflict between saving for tomorrow versus consuming more today, given the abysmally low consumption in some of the poorer developing countries.

Table 9.4: Genuine Savings Rate (per cent of GDP) and Growth Rate of Per Capita Genuine Wealth Estimates for India, 1970–2006

Year	*World Bank**	*Arrow et al. (2004)*	*Dasgupta et al. (2008)*	*Kumar (2008)*
Genuine Savings/Investment Rate				
1970–80	8.68		–	2.15
1981–90	8.99		11.77	4.77
1991–2000	11.13		13.16	6.12
2001	13.54	9.47 (1970–2001)	13.38	7.84
2002	15.59	–	–	9.61
2003	18.25	–	16.55	11.65
2004	19.46	–	19.80	14.60
2005	20.28	–		15.40
2006	20.57	–		15.58
Growth Rate of Genuine Wealth Per Capita				
1970–80			1.54 (1977–78)	–2.32
1981–90			1.73 (1980–81)	0.44
1991–2000	–0.6 (1997)	–0.57 and 0.54**	2.52 (1990–91)	0.81
2001		(1970–2001)	2.26 (2000–01)	2.02
2002		–		1.98
2003		–		2.95
2004		–		3.73
2005		–		4.06
2006		–		4.08

Note: *Based on time series data in World Bank (2008). Note that from 1990 onwards, damages from particulate matter are also incorporated;
**Adjusted for population growth only, and adjusted for population and technological change (productivity growth).

Another recent work by Kumar (2008), adopts a more comprehensive approach to estimating genuine savings by incorporating certain damages from environmental degradation of soil and water (besides air, as done in the other studies). The cost of soil degradation is strong enough to reverse the genuine wealth estimates obtained in the other studies. The results in Kumar (2008) indicate that the growth rate of genuine wealth per capita was negative during the period 1970–83, and has been positive since the mid-

1980s. In recent years, the true growth rate of the Indian economy has been in the range of 3–4 per cent only. Kumar concludes that growth in the last one and a half decades can be considered to be 'barely sustainable', and observes that biodiversity losses (among several other natural resources and services) have not been accounted for in the study.

It is evident that the empirics of genuine savings and wealth per capita are less optimistic when economists incorporate environmental damage costs in the estimation of natural capital valuation. Considering the lack of data coverage on the status of several environmental resources, the estimated genuine savings are obviously overstated. For instance, if due to an increase in acid rain, the cars in the country are subjected to more corrosion and need to be replaced more rapidly, this is also depreciation which should be included but is currently not included (World Bank 1997).

The aggregate estimates of genuine wealth and savings also do not reflect the skewed economic development taking place across India. A study by Mukherjee and Kathuria (2006) illustrates the regional disparity in growth and environmental degradation in India. Testing for the EKC at the state-level, Mukherjee and Kathuria (2006) found that the trade-off between economic growth and environmental quality has been markedly different across the different states during the 1990s. In order to accommodate different types of environmental problems, they used a composite Environmental Quality Index (enumerated for two time points, pre- and post-liberalization years) for 14 major Indian states to test the EKC hypothesis. Their result did not support the EKC hypothesis that environmental quality improves with economic growth, and instead suggests that economic growth has mostly been at the cost of environmental quality in the high growth states across India.

Pressure on Bio-capacity

The genuine wealth and investment of a nation are estimated in constant dollar terms by economists, while ecologists in the Global Footprint Network (GFN) have gauged the cost of economic growth termed *ecological footprint* estimated in global land area. Water being a critical natural resource for human existence, a measure of *water footprint* has also been developed recently by the GFN. By both counts, the ecological pressure of India's growth seems unsustainable. The pressure on the regional ecosystem has been mounting over

Table 9.5: Per Capita Ecological Footprint in 2005 and Annual Per Capita Water Footprint, 1997–2001

Country	*Ecological footprint (hectares/ person)*	*Bio-capacity (hectares/ person)*	*Ecological reserve (hectares/ person)*	*Annual water footprint (m^3/person)*
China	2.1	0.9	*–1.2*	702
India	0.9	0.4	*–0.5*	980
United States	9.4	5.0	*–4.4*	2,483

Source: GFN–WWF (2008).

the years, and the availability of natural ecosystem services per capita has been steadily declining.

The total ecological footprint of India, which indicates the anthropogenic demand on the biosphere in terms of the land and sea area (required to provide the resources used and to absorb the waste generated) has more than doubled since 1961, contributing to the degradation of its natural capital. India has the third largest total footprint in the world today, exceeded only by the United States and China. Taking into account the steep growth in population in India in the past 50 years, the demand on bio-capacity per capita, that is, ecological footprint per capita, seems rather small (see Table 9.5 showing the per capita measures for the three nations). In water use, India is estimated to be the highest consumer in the world today, although its per capita water use remains lower than that in many nations with similar or higher per capita incomes (though not China as evident from Table 9.5).

The eco-footprint per capita in India declined from 0.85 global hectares in 1961 to 0.9 global hectares in 2005 (GFN–CII 2008; GFN–WWF 2008). At the same time, the supply of bio-capacity per person has also declined from 0.72 global hectares per capita in 1961 to 0.4 global hectares per capita in 2005 (ibid.). Consequently, the present Indian generation is running an ecological deficit of 0.5 global hectares per capita—more than 100 per cent of its available per capita bio-capacity. Thus, although the cropland productivity has increased due to technological innovations, the population growth pressure has more than offset that increase. Essentially limited resources are now spread over a larger number of persons today than before, technological innovation notwithstanding, and the growing ecological deficit puts India's economic improvement at risk.

Role of Consumption in Sustainable Development

While resource and pollution intensities in production are critical in determining sustainability, it is the consumption demand of a society that drives the production systems of the economy (and that of other nations for open economies). With the development of resource-saving technology, the resource intensity of output decreases, but such efficiency gains can well be offset by *rebound effects* where improvement in efficiency become a stimulus for increased consumption. For example, UNEP (2002) observed that while vehicle fuel efficiency increased significantly in the 1990s so did the passenger miles travelled, as income saved on motor fuel was spent on travelling more miles or on other forms of transport. In effect, as the total GDP has grown faster than the improvement in energy efficiency, there has been a net increase in total resource use. Indeed the problem of unsustainability can arise from extravagant and wasteful consumption of goods and services, no matter how efficiently they are produced, since it imposes a negative externality on others by limiting the resources left for them.[20]

The average Indian lifestyle is frugal by current average standards in developed countries, not merely due to widespread poverty but also due to traditional consumption habits. In the past decade, the consumption pattern has been changing with increase in average income, urbanization and globalization—where the latter has pushed the Indian urban society towards similar consumption aspirations as those in the industrialized countries.

For instance, in the national capital Delhi, the single largest sector contributing to atmospheric pollution today is vehicular transport. While in 1970 vehicles contributed to barely 23 per cent of the total atmospheric pollution, it steadily increased to contribute 72 per cent in 2000 (see Table 9.6). Since the time of independence in 1947 until 2002 when a partial metro rail system was started, Delhi continued with a single mode of public transport by road, even as the urban population grew at an unprecedented rate. The lack of

[20]Remarkably, the Agenda 21 observes that industrializing countries should seek to achieve sustainable consumption patterns during their development process, 'avoiding those unsustainable patterns, particularly in industrialized countries, generally recognized as unduly hazardous to the environment, inefficient and wasteful' (Agenda 21, Chapter 4, paragraph 8).

Table 9.6: Sectoral Contribution of Air Pollutants in Delhi

Source	*Year*			
	1970–71	*1980–81*	*1990–91*	*2000–01*
Vehicle	23 per cent	42 per cent	63 per cent	72 per cent
Industry	56 per cent	40 per cent	29 per cent	20 per cent
Domestic	21 per cent	18 per cent	8 per cent	8 per cent

Source: CPCB (2003).

Table 9.7: Vehicular Growth in Delhi, 1995–2005

Category	*Number of vehicles (in millions)*		*Decennial growth rate (1995–2005) (per cent)*	*Annual compound growth rate (per cent)*
	1995–96	*2005–06*		
Private Vehicles				
Four wheelers	0.6	1.5	132	8.6
Two wheelers	1.7	3.1	77	5.4
Subtotal	*2.3*	*4.6*	*91.6*	*6.8*
Commercial Vehicles				
Auto Rickshaw	0.08	0.07	–6.3	–1.4
Taxis	0.01	0.02	50	1.9
Buses	0.03	0.04	57	3.6
Goods Vehicles & Tractors	0.1	0.1	–0.7	–1.7
Sub-total	*0.25*	*0.27*	*6.7*	*0.06*
Total	2.6	4.8	83.6	5.8

Source: *Economic Survey of Delhi 2005–06*, Ch. 12.

public transportation and increasing incomes led to an explosion of privately-owned vehicles on the road.

The vehicular fleet is dominated by privately owned passenger cars and during the last decade, passenger car ownership has been further bolstered with a booming domestic auto industry and easy imports. Table 9.7 illustrates the composition of the vehicular fleet in Delhi in 1995 and 2005, and their corresponding growth rates. While the commercial vehicles experienced a growth of barely 6.6

per cent over the ten years, private vehicles registered a growth of 91.6 per cent. Within privately owned vehicles, it is the four-wheeler segment that experienced the highest decennial growth of 132 per cent. Although the fuel efficiency and tail-pipe emissions of the newer fleet of vehicles, especially passenger cars have improved substantially, the *rebound* effect has more than offset the environmental efficiency gains, such that the atmospheric pollution load from vehicles have increased.

Consider another rapidly growing sector with highly toxic pollution risk, namely the electronics and electrical industry. Although the household sector is not the largest generator of electronic waste, the continuous design upgradation and lower cost of electronic products is beginning to move Indian consumption away from extended usage towards a high waste society. With programmed obsolescence in electronic and electrical equipment, the new pattern of consumption today poses the risk of higher waste per capita.

The redeeming feature, however, is the Indian tendency for extended use of commodities including electronic equipment, through repair and second-hand informal markets. The propensity to prolong use of equipment rather than discarding them, not only helps to minimize waste but also extracts the maximum use-value out of them. While industrialized nations have now begun to promote attitudes and policies of 'reduce, reuse, recycle and recover'—these have constituted the traditional way of life of an average Indian.

Conclusion

The economic development path of India may at best be considered weakly sustainable in view of the productivity enhancing technology, innovation and education; but with a large part of the natural capital depreciation remaining inestimable. More ecological-capacity oriented measures however, indicate the current growth pattern in India to be unsustainable, since the direct and indirect demand for environmental resources and services far exceeds those available. Since the economic growth in India over the last 40 years has been running on an environmental deficit (not offset by enhanced physical and intellectual capital), high rates of growth cannot be sustained unless quality of the critical natural resources (like air, water, etc.) is maintained and resource cost of growth reduced.

The challenge facing India is two-fold: to raise the per capita consumption (given poverty and consumption below subsistence for many), and to reduce the real resource cost of growth. To maintain a robust economy and a decent standard of living, there is need for not only positive *genuine* saving and investment, but also declining resource cost of consumption. Greater investment in resource-saving technology, intellectual capital, renewable clean energy and a resource-efficient urban structure would help to reduce resource costs on the supply side. It is equally important, however, to uphold and reinforce the traditional Indian culture (that several developed nations are now trying to inculcate) of extended use, repair and recycle, in order to minimize waste from consumption. Indeed, true welfare enhancement does not require runaway material consumption, since true happiness as Scitovsky (1986) observed is driven by satisfaction from family life, work and leisure to develop talents and friendships.

References

Arrow, K., P. Dasgupta, L. Goulder, G. Daily, P. Ehrlich. G. Heal, S. Levin, K. Maler, S. Schneider, D. Starrett and B. Walker (2004), 'Are We Consuming Too Much?', *Journal of Economic Perspectives*, Vol. 18, No. 3, pp. 147–72.

Bosworth, Barry, and Susan M. Collins (2008), 'Accounting for Growth: Comparing China and India', *Journal of Economic Perspectives*, Vol. 22, No. 1, pp. 45–66.

CPCB (1999), *Status of Water Supply, and Wastewater Generation, Collection, Treatment and Disposal (in Class I and Class II Cities)*, Central Pollution Control Board, New Delhi.

——— (2003), *Parivesh Newsletter* (November), Central Pollution Control Board, Ministry of Environment and Forest, New Delhi.

——— (2007), *Annual Report*, Central Pollution Control Board, Ministry of Environment and Forest, New Delhi.

——— (2008a), *National Ambient Air Quality Status 2007*, National Ambient Air Quality Monitoring Series: NAAQMS//2008–09, Central Pollution Control Board, New Delhi.

——— (2008b), *Status of Water Quality in India 2007*, Monitoring of Indian Aquatic Resources Series: MINARS/29/2008–2009, Central Pollution Control Board, New Delhi.

Dasgupta, Purnamita and Shikha Gupta (2008), 'Measuring Sustainability with Macroeconomic Data for India', Working Paper 214, Indian Council for Research in International Economic Relations, New Delhi.

DeLong, J. Bradford (2001), 'India since Independence: An Analytic Growth Narrative', *http://www.economics.pomona.edu/Andrabi/Economic per cent20Development/India per cent20(DeLong).pdf*

Energy Information Administration (EIA), US, available at *http://tonto.eia.doe.gov/country/country_time_series.cfm?fips=IN#prim*, last accessed 1 November 2008.

FSI (2008), *Forest Survey of India Report 2005,* Forest Survey of India, Dehradun, India.

GFN–CII (2008), *India's Ecological Footprint: A Business Perspective*, Global Footprint Network and Confederation of Indian Industries.

GFN–WWF (2008), *Living Planet Report 2008*, Global Footprint Network and World Wildlife Fund.

Grossman, G. and A.B. Krueger (1995), 'Economic Growth and the Environment', *Quarterly Journal of Economics*, Vol. 110, pp. 353–77.

Hamilton, Kirk (2000), 'Sustaining Economic Welfare: Estimating Changes in Wealth per Capita', prepared for the 26th General Conference of The International Association for Research on Income and Wealth, Cracow, Poland.

______ (2003), 'Sustaining Economic Welfare: Estimating Changes in Total and Per Capita Wealth', *Environment, Development and Sustainability*, Vol. 5, pp. 419–36.

Hartwick, John (1977), 'Intergenerational Equity and the Investing of Rents from Exhaustible Resources', *American Economic Review*, Vol. 67, No. 5, pp. 972–4.

Kumar, Surender (2008), *Is India on a Sustainable Development Path?*, MPRA Paper 10086, University Library of Munich, Germany.

Mohan, Rakesh (2006), 'Economic Reforms in India: Where are We and Where do We Go?', *RBI Bulletin*, 14 December.

Moffatt, Ian (2000), 'Ecological Footprints and Sustainable Development', *Ecological Economics*, Vol. 32, pp. 359–62.

MOCIT (2008), *Annual Report 2007–08*, Department of Information Technology, Ministry of Communications and Information Technology, Government of India.

Mukherji, Sacchidananda and Vinish Kathuria (2006), 'Is Economic Growth Sustainable? Environmental Quality of Indian States after 1991', *International Journal of Sustainable Development*, Vol. 9, No. 1, pp. 38–60.

Pearce, D., A. Markandya and E. Barbier (1989), *Blueprint for a Green Economy*, Earthscan, London.

Pearce, D., K. Hamilton and G. Atkinson (1996), 'Measuring Sustainable Development: Progress on Indicators', *Environment and Development Economics*, Cambridge University Press, Vol. 1, pp. 85–101.

RBI (2004), 'Growth, Savings and Investment', *RBI Bulletin*, 14 June.

Scitovsky, Tibor (1986), *Human Desire and Economic Satisfaction*, Wheatsheaf Books, New York and London.

Stavins, R.N., Alexander F. Wagner and Gernot Wagner (2003), 'Interpreting Sustainability in Economic Terms: Dynamic Efficiency plus Intergenerational Equity,' *Economic Letters*, Vol. 79, pp. 339–43.

Solow, Robert (1986), 'On the Intergenerational Allocation of Natural Resources', *Scandinavian Journal of Economics*, Vol. 88, No. 1, pp. 141–9.

Sterner, Thomas (2003), *Growth and the Environment*, SIDA Environment Policy Division, Swedish International Development Corporation Agency, Sweden.

Toxics Link (2007), 'WEEE: Other Side of the Digital Revolution', *Toxics Link Factsheet*, Number 31, November, *www.toxicslink.org*.

UNEP (2002), *Sustainable Consumption: A Global Status Report*, United Nations Environmental Programme, DTIE, Production and Consumption Branch.

World Bank (1997), *Expanding the Measure of Wealth: Indicators of Environmentally Sustainable Development*, Environment Department, World Bank, Washington, DC.

_____ (2006), *Where is the Wealth of Nations: Measuring Capital for the XXI Century*, World Bank, Washington, DC.

_____ (2007), 'Keeping up with Environmental Challenges of Rapid Growth', World Bank. Washington D.C.

_____ (2008), *Adjusted Net Savings Time Series by Country 1970–2006, http://siteresources.worldbank.org/INTEEI/1105643-1115814965717/21683424/ANS_time_series_by_country_1970to2006.xls*

WCED (1987), *Our Common Future*, World Commission on Environment and Development, Oxford University Press, Oxford.

WDI (2008), *World Development Indicators 2008*, World Bank, Washington, DC.